WIND STAR

WIND STAR

THE BUILDING OF A SAILSHIP

Joseph Novitski

MACMILLAN PUBLISHING COMPANY
NEW YORK

Macmillan Publishing Company
866 Third Avenue, New York, N.Y. 10022
Collier Macmillan Canada, Inc.

Library of Congress Cataloging-in-Publication Data
Novitski, Joseph.
Wind Star : the building of a sailship / Joseph Novitski.
p. cm.
Bibliography: p.
Includes index.
ISBN 0-02-590830-8
1. Wind Star (Ship) 2. Andren, Karl G. I. Title.
VM383.W56N68 1987
387.2'24—dc19 87-14036
CIP

Macmillan books are available at special discounts for bulk purchases for sales promotions, premiums, fund-raising, or educational use.
For details, contact:

Special Sales Director
Macmillan Publishing Company
866 Third Avenue
New York, N.Y. 10022

10 9 8 7 6 5 4 3 2 1

Printed in the United States of America

For F. J. and Mary D.,
who made it all possible

Contents

Acknowledgments

I do not build my own boats. I did once and we all called that rowboat the *Titanic* because it leaked visibly for every moment it was afloat. Therefore I am very grateful to the people who made it possible for me to watch shipbuilders at work and who trusted me with portions of their lives.

Karl Andren was the first who said, "Sure," when I asked if I could watch them build his windship and write about it. I had been following the attempts to design and build modern sailing ships for ten years when I heard about Andren's project, on a windy New Year's Eve, 1984. I am grateful to Andren and Daniel Kavanaugh, who first told me what Andren had decided to do. Jean-Claude Potier showed me how real the project was and introduced me to Gilbert Fournier. I am very grateful to Monsieur Fournier and to François Faury for their initial and continuing trust.

I met the shipowner and his shipbuilders in April 1985 and followed their joint adventure until November of the next year. I must thank them all for their patience and add thanks here to Alain Adam, my unfailing host at the shipyards in Le Havre. Hugh Lawrence, of Ocean Carriers Corp. on the West Coast, Lloyd Bergeson, a founder of Windship Development Corp. in the East, and Kathy Hill at Sail Assist International Liaison Associates kept me abreast of developments in modern commercial sail from their first-hand perspectives. Diana Hernandez, at the Miami-Dade Public Library, introduced me to the marvels of interlibrary loans. In the publishing world, first Wendy Lipkind, agent, then Robert Stewart, editor, and finally Hillel Black at Macmillan Publishing Company deserve my gratitude for their confidence in this story.

The story of the building of this ship told itself, thanks to the people you will meet in this book. I am grateful to them, too, and grateful besides to Sten Sundman, the editor of the *Ålands Maritime Gazette,* who introduced me to the Åland Islands and to the people who showed me the history of those islands: Göte Sundberg, Captain Karl Kåhre, as well as Stig Dreijer, Karl Weber, and all the research staff at the Ålands Museum.

My thanks go to all the officers and men of *Wind Star*, sailors and engineers, for their patience with a nonworking observer, and to Marc Held for explaining the obvious to me when I was slow. René L'Heryénat, Jean-Eric Enault, René Turquetille, and Gérard Jouan were all very good at that also, each in his own field. Captain Jean-Marie Guillou and his tail-gunner, Yvan Martin, seemed to have almost universal competence. I have translated their French, conversational and technical, as it flowed, with an eye to maintaining the same sense and style in an English context as it had in French. I am grateful to Professor Heinrich von Staden, friend of the curious, for quick counsel in the classics.

Paul Allen Cassady and his daughter Paula encouraged me without stint. They liked everything they read. And I liked everyone I met while I watched *Wind Star* grow. In fact, I have only one regret at the end of my year and a half among shipbuilders and seamen. I never met Elis Karlsson, chief mate of the *Herzogin Cecilie*. Wherever he is now, I wish him fair winds and following seas.

Introduction

I first started clamoring to go to sea when I was nine. My family lived at the time in Capetown, at the confluence of many ocean trading routes, and the whaling fleets of Norway and England then stopped in Capetown each spring on their way south to their Antarctic hunting grounds. A Norwegian skipper suggested that I could come along for the six-month season as a cabin boy, once I turned twelve. The wait seemed wholly unfair.

By the time I was twelve I had got to sea as a deckboy on fishing boats and I was thoroughly identified with seamen. I had even learned to affect the scorn that sailors show seagoing engineers, the black gang down below. We lived then on the coast of Peru, and between the school vacations during which I was allowed to ship out, I went with my father to the naval shipyard in Callao as often as he had weekend business there. It was principally a repair yard, and there I saw ships at their most vulnerable: stranded in dry holes that smelled like the dead wrack at a high tide mark, balanced, all ungainly, on greasy blocks of wood and displaying every wound and blemish.

The small, old refrigerator ship that my father's company sent to the Callao yard always shared the dry dock. Once she was in with a freighter that had grounded briefly in the Straits of Magellan and I picked rocks from the end of the continent out of the gash in that ship's side and took them home for souvenirs. Once she shared the dock with a Peruvian navy cruiser bought from Italy after World War I, and the draining of the dry dock showed that the lean, gray hull of that warship, so dashing above the waterline, rested on a rusty barrel of armor plate under water. The cruiser looked like an aging but elegant cavalry officer, suddenly uncorseted.

Shipyards, from that time on, were like hospitals for me: necessary, but only *in extremis*. And shipbuilders, yardworkers, naval architects, and engineers were as arcane, remote, and difficult to trust as doctors and overbearing floor nurses. Yet they had to be trusted if one went to sea and I continued to do that: fishing, serving in the U.S. Navy, and racing and cruising oceangoing sailboats. It was enough for years to read Joseph Conrad and feel, without examining it, his seaman's faith in a ship's spirit. But it has become clear to me that the deep confidence any sailor feels in a good ship is not faith in her spirit alone but also in the honesty, truthfulness, and patient skill of her builders. And so I have come, late perhaps, to the recognition that shipbuilders are brother seamen.

Now I believe we are all brother seamen, because sailing ships and the sea run so deep in our blood that it takes very little listening to hear them there. If you do not believe me, try this. Stand someday on a seawall or a rock, a dock, a pier, or a sheltered ocean beach, anywhere that the waves do not roar but where you can hear salt water move and feel a breeze on one cheek or the other. Listen, with your eyes closed, and feel the wind. In time you will begin to sense inside a long and gentle motion. I first felt it as a boy and never recognized that internal sense of movement until, years later, I went to sea, deep sea, under sail. The shift and balance, the pause and run, that you can sense on the shore is the internal echo of the motion of a sailing ship at sea.

1

PART

ANCESTRY

1

CHAPTER

The Country of the Sea

Navigare necesse est, vivere non est necesse.

—Roman proverb, attributed to Plutarch

Sailing is an ancient art. Shipbuilding, the craft that must have come before it, is even more ancient. It carries traditions that endure unbidden and skills that have survived for centuries.

It would be hard today to step a wooden mast in a wooden hull and forget to put a silver coin under the mast, where its wood stump presses onto the boat's keel. Anywhere that Europeans have sailed, some bystander would be sure to call out that the mast needs a coin under it, because that is the way it is done. For luck. Because it has always been done that way. The wreck of a barge raised not thirty years ago from the Thames, after eighteen hundred years on the bottom, had a silver coin franked with the image of the Emperor Domitian still wedged beneath its mast.

Shipbuilders have passed on their craft through generations and across oceans. Until at least 1972, native Brazilian shipwrights still searched what was left of the coastal rain forests between Salvador and Camamu for wood formed by nature to the exact shape needed in their small wooden schooners.[1] For masts, a shipwright in those forests looked for straight trees and cut them on the waxing moon, when the sap is full up the tree! For deckbeams and hull frames, he looked for trees that had grown into bends that echoed the curves of the boat he saw in his mind's eye. He ordered the bent trees cut on the waning moon, when the sap is down and the wood at its driest.

Shipwrights in Europe did the same thing for centuries, until there were no more forests. Then they built ships out of iron, then of steel. Always the shipwrights who raised hulls and launched them were doing the opposite of settling down. They built for voyaging. Their hulls floated free from impermanent sheds and disordered piles of lumber and scraps at the shore, ready to set sail, cross the bar, run free. All of these are phrases that have been taken into everyday use from the working language of seamen.

When men build houses they break ground, take root, settle in, cover, and enclose. Building a house means that you have decided to stay. Building a ship means that you are longing to be gone. Pride goes with both, but the pride in building a ship is split between owner and builder and the owner must eventually take his new ship away from her builder. A ship always sails; a new house stays.

For at least fifty centuries, sailing ships were as common as houses. They were built on sloping riverbanks, at the flat edges of backwaters, and on beaches all over the world. Sailing ships were everywhere for so long that we, who live in a world whose populations were planted by those ships, all seem to know what a sailing ship should look like. We must know them from ancestral memory, since true sailing ships, large, working ships without engines, have not been built for sixty years.

We recognize the sailing ships that remain, although most are scaled-down copies of working ships, and we gather wherever these go. Seven million people went to the water's edge to watch in New York, when the tall ships came in 1976. Six hundred thousand saw them that same year in Boston. Ten years later, more millions watched them return to New York. The memories rose in all of the watchers like the sap drawn up a mast tree by the moon. Our ancestors came to North and South America, to Australia and to all the Pacific islands and archipelagos, by sea, under sail. They migrated over seas, worked at sea, fought at sea, and made money at sea, all under sail. We, their descendants, are sure we know what sailing ships look like. We know what they mean. We know it so well that building a new sailing ship would be an undertaking filled with the risk of disappointing centuries of human memories. In a world shaped by windships, everyone seems to know their true shape and purpose by heart.

A man might be moved to build a modern sailing ship by that human memory. He would build a monument, in the likeness of the ships that have gone, and so many men do, who build the curves, the rigs and deck lines, and whole historic plans into cruising replicas. Other men, as oil has grown scarce and expensive, have felt driven by a dream of technical purity to build modern sailing ships, with the technology of the space age. They have engineering visions of wholly new windships that will sail someday on unpolluted seas in winds unfouled by burning oil, but few of these visions have been built. A curious embarrassment has risen around sailing ships. They have become wholly romantic.

Sailing ships now mean adventure, although they were once as commercial as beans and hides, and commercial men have shied away from building them. They have commercial reasons to hesitate. True sailing ships were slow, in average speed three times slower at their fastest than modern, diesel-driven cargo liners, and speed is the unitary standard by which all means of transportation are measured in our world. And sailing ships were dangerous. Their crews were expendable and their hulls were lost on every ocean shore and in every deep. Who can tell now whether any of the new sailing ship designs that promise some speed from the wind, with aluminum rigs built like airplane wings and hydraulic motors instead of sailors to handle canvas, will work in safety?

Finding out would be costly and venturesome, and modern businessmen do not like to be thought of as adventurers, nor to be considered romantics. The bulk of shipowning businessmen now are landbound and set in the traditions of their trade. They own hulls and rent them out, the way other people own warehouses or apartments and lease them. Still, it has often been true that what many men dismiss as a romantic dream can become one man's realistic plan.

In mid-December of 1984, a man named Karl Gösta Andren announced in New York that he would build a new sailing ship, 440 feet long, with 150-foot-tall roller-furling sails on four taller masts, as well as auxiliary engines. His purpose was wholly commercial. The ship would carry 150 passengers on luxury cruises in the Caribbean, beginning exactly two years later. He did not call attention to the fact that the hull of his windship had been designed on the same scale as the largest ships that had ever sailed, or that it would be the first large ship, using sail for her principal propulsion, to be built from the keel up for commercial purposes since 1926. Those things were apparent only to well-informed enthusiasts. He did not say that he intended, with his ship, to relaunch the age of commercial sail. Sail enthusiasts might have hoped that he wanted to, but none of them knew Andren, or who he was or why he, of all those who had dreamed of doing so, had resolved to build the first full-scale modern commercial sailing ship.

All that the world knew about Karl G. Andren was contained in a press release for that December announcement. He was a thirty-eight-year-old immigrant from Finland who had gone to a small college and then graduate school in the United States; he was an entrepreneur on the rise, whose holdings included barges, tugs, real estate, and the Circle Line of New York, which claims to be one of the largest waterborne passenger operations in the world on the basis of the three million people it carries every year on tours around the island of Manhattan; his father was a sea captain. The release did not say that he and all his ancestors before him had been born and raised on islands in an archipelago called Åland.

The Åland islands lie along the northern rim of the Baltic Sea, scattered between two arms of the Northern European mainland where the glaciers left them at the end of the last Ice Age. They are low islands, of granite that weathers to the color of ancient brick inland but is gray at the water's edge. The name is pronounced "*AW*-land," and, depending on one's interpretation of ancient Nordic vowels, it might mean either "Land of Islands," or "Country of the Sea." Both names fit the place.

Baltic seawater, clear, very slightly salty, and so faintly blue it looks like fresh ice, closely surrounds all the dry land in Åland. The meadows end in salt marshes. The bays twist inland for miles and the sounds run such narrow and sinuous courses through the main islands that seagoing ferries steaming through them, on their way from Sweden to Finland and back, must sometimes stop to let each other pass.

There are 6,654 islands[2] in the archipelago called Åland, about two-thirds of them on the cold, northern side of sixty degrees north latitude, the same parallel that runs through Leningrad, Oslo, Cape Farewell at the southern tip of Greenland, and Seward, Alaska. To a seaman or mapmaker, the scattered islands look like stepping-stones between Sweden and Finland and so they have served for more than a thousand years. The oldest living Ålanders can remember Russian troops marching across the frozen sea from Finland to garrison the islands during World War I.

More than a century earlier, czarist Russian soldiers had trooped across the Baltic ice to conquer Åland and separate it from Sweden, after six and one-half centuries under Swedish kings. Culturally, then, the Ålanders consider Sweden their mother country. The succession of events and sovereignties after the Russian conquest and occupation in 1809 can be confusing to outsiders. To Ålanders, the results are clear: they speak Swedish, carry Finnish passports, pay Finnish taxes, elect their own local government, and consider themselves Ålanders. By virtue of a League of Nations decision in 1921, Finland holds sovereignty over the archipelago but Åland is as autonomous in law as it has proven itself to be in fact for centuries.

Since before recorded history, native Ålanders have been what New Englanders used to call salt-farmers; farmers who fish, working both their land and the sea in front of it, and men of the soil who build their own ships and go to sea as traders. Salt-farming is a calling that runs in the blood in certain parts of the world: Cornwall or Brittany, for example, as well as Maine, Nantucket, and the Chesapeake Bay. At home or at sea, the salt-farmers from all those places have needed to be independent and self-reliant to a high degree. They are not given to the combination of grand gesture and careful recordkeeping that claims a place in the big books of Western history. It seems that in their code deeds speak for themselves. Formal history is something that others keep.

The Vikings, who were salt-farmers at home, did not keep written records of their voyages and raids from what was then the northern edge of the world and now includes the Åland archipelago. The most a Viking might do for history was set up a stone with runic signs to state: "They left bravely to seek gold far off and became prey for the eagles."[3]

In the long and largely unrecorded history of Åland, the landbound Russian invaders came and went over the course of 107 years that ended with the czarist regime. Before the Russians, the ancestors of today's Swedes and Finns had fought across the islands that lay in the sea between them for centuries. Before them, the Vikings are known to have landed and traded in the knobby bays and inlets of Åland, on their way to and from trading markets established on the banks of the great Russian rivers. Before the Vikings, the people who came and went have no surviving proper names. They were all Scandinavians. Archaeologists digging in the brown clay soil of the islands find evidence that vocations were constant from the seventh century through the nineteenth century. The Ålanders were farmers, fishermen, and traders. History passed. The island way endured.

Some of the islands in Åland are little more than stepping-stones, granite humps so round and low in the water that they look like the backs of breathing whales. Pressure ridges in the Baltic pack ice can sweep these clean in a hard winter. Other islands have a juniper or two, or perhaps a fir and a landing place among the rocks. Still, an energetic fisherman can walk around these in half an hour or so, casting for the pike that wait like mottled logs in their underwater hollows.

On the eight large islands, however, pine, spruce, and fir grow on the granite ridges, and the short, irregular valleys scoured out by glaciers are full of soil squared into fields by farm tractors. Solid wooden houses with small windows back up to these ridges and tree lines, as if seeking shelter, and the cultivated fields, wherever the rocks permit, run to the edge of the sea. Long, flat arms of the Baltic reach in and through the islands. Ålanders grow up with the sea at their feet everywhere and not many things higher than their heads except trees, the roof ridges of their houses, and the severe stone steeples of their medieval country churches, each one capped with black slate.

These islands, like so many others where the glaciers have been, in New England, Canada, Sweden, and the Pacific Northwest, are nearly featureless for any stranger coming on them from the sea. Without the local knowledge of the shape of each headland and the size and coloring of the trees on the highest inland ridge behind it, they all look the same from the water: lump after rolling lump of land covered with evergreen trees.

The most prominent landmarks for a seaman bound up the Baltic to the main harbor at Mariehamn, the archipelago's capital and the only city in Åland, are the three tallest masts of the square-rigged sailing ship *Pommern*. The ship, a 294-foot steel bark with four masts, has been moored like a monument in a place of honor halfway up the harbor since 1953.

Mariehamn has been *Pommern*'s home port since 1922. As a working freighter, the ship sailed from this small town near the edge of the Arctic for seventeen years. Her yearly trading route went around the world, north of Scotland and east around the Cape of Good Hope on the way out, and west past Cape Horn then north to England on the way home. Between each of these grand drives out of the Baltic to Australia for wheat, the ship rested at Mariehamn and refitted for a month or two during the northern summer. In those years, between the two world wars, there were eleven other tall square-riggers that came home to Mariehamn in each short, green summer and lay quietly at anchor there like images from the memories of old sailors.

Pommern is a museum ship now. Her sheer steel sides are painted black and her riveted bottom plates white. Her towering rig is kept in running order, and the long springing curve of her bow faces seaward, as though she were only awaiting sails and a crew to get underway. On her last trip to a dry dock, under tow, a westerly gale began to blow behind her as she was hauled downwind to Finland. One of the helmsmen on that trip claims that *Pommern* sailed so fast under bare poles that the tug had to get out of the way.

Where *Pommern* lies, just beyond the concrete and glass terminal where five-story car ferries to Sweden or Finland dock every day, the tapered steel tips of her topmasts catch the inbound eye, above all the ridgetop pines, from several miles at sea. Her fore, main, and mizzen masts all rise 185 feet off the water, as high as the roof of a fifteen-story office building. On all but the murkiest days, they are the first man-made marks that show above the island ridges smudged with dark green conifers.

Pommern's masts seem to measure Mariehamn and even to overreach the small city, the way Gothic cathedral spires still overreach French towns. One sees cathedrals first from far off, too, and they signal what sort of people once lived in their towns. As that kind of man-made symbol, the tall ship fits Åland well. Natives of these islands owned, manned, and managed the last commercial fleet of deep-water sailing ships in the world and kept them sailing for profit until almost halfway into this century. *Pommern,* with *Pamir,* and *Passat, Viking, Lawhill, Olivebank, Moshulu, Melbourne, Hougomont, Archibald Russell,* and the lovely *Herzogin Cecilie,* big square-riggers 300 feet or more in length, all sailed around the world each year from Mariehamn, without engines or radios, for twenty, thirty, and forty years after their nineteenth-century owners and builders had given up on sail and gone to steam for power. *Pamir* and *Passat* came home to Mariehamn from Australia for the last time in 1949.

The Åland square-riggers were the last of their kind. Between the world wars, it was obvious that pure sailing cargo ships would not survive competition from steam- and motor-driven ships. Åland then enjoyed a flash of fame as the home of the seamen and shipowners who were keeping the last of the truly tall ships alive and working. The British popular press made the annual voyage of the square-riggers to England from Australia into "The Great Grain Race," and dubbed Gustaf Erikson, the Åland sea captain who owned most of the ships in the Australian trade, the King of the Square-Riggers.

When Erikson's *Herzogin Cecilie,* the prettiest and best known of all the big steel barks hauling wheat from Australia, went ashore in a Channel fog at the foot of a cliff in southwest England, the dying ship became a tourist attraction. Extra police and Royal Automobile Club volunteers came to direct traffic and control parking in the Devonshire fields behind the promontory where the four-masted ship struck. It was the spring of 1936, and steam- and motor-driven war was coming fast in Europe, but for six weeks Britons contributed to a fund to save that stranded sailing ship.[4]

Then a gale from the East, an unexpected direction, killed the *Herzogin Cecilie.* Seas surging ashore broke her back over a rock ledge.

Her crew could hear rivets popping like gunshots in the hold as her steel hull plates buckled and tore. Gustaf Erikson sent for all her sails, rope, and rigging. He ordered home to Mariehamn the deep-red mahogany paneling of her salon, and all its furniture, then sold the pride of his fleet for 225 pounds. Everyone in Åland knows that shipping is a business.

Shipping has remained the principal business in Åland, where Karl Andren grew up. The ships are all motor-driven, but commercial sail is a sharper and more recent memory there than anywhere else in the world. I reached the islands in November of 1985, looking for the roots of Andren's ambition. The autumn had closed down into winter. The most sheltered bays and inlets had their first solid cover of creaking ice. Boats were laid up ashore. Even the seagulls had flown south. The land had taken on the dark gray and dun colors of the European crow, the only bird left in the islands in November. But the mark of the sea was everywhere. There were ship pictures in hotels and on menus, ship models in the banks, and sailing smacks on the postage stamps. There were world maps in almost every business office, including the telephone company's. There was, in Mariehamn, a higher concentration of living men who had rounded Cape Horn under sail than in any other town on earth.

The cold stilled outdoor noises and cut through masonry walls. Trees, fields, ridges, and roads were bare and even the sky was most often gray. Only the open sea moved and changed color in the watery daylight that came from somewhere far away in the south. Children and the people who walked or bicycled had already pinned plastic reflectors to their clothing for the long dark season. And yet the place felt almost snug, like a well-worn and trusted winter coat.

The scale was well suited to humans. No building was so big as to require a backward tilt of the head to take it all in. No distance in Mariehamn was so long it could not be walked, allowing for the cold. The country began, with plowed fields and well-tended woodlots, at the edge of town. The countryside of the main island, Fasta Åland, is divided into six administrative districts called parishes, which are just what the name implies: the areas surrounding each village church. The district attached to each parish is not large. The church villages lie so close together that, in the time when questions of doctrine divided Lutherans, a stubborn man might have walked or sledded to church in the next parish, if he disagreed with his pastor at home.

Many village churches on the main island have stood since the eleventh century, at the end of the Dark Ages, when Christianity first rooted in the north. They were built, and rebuilt, out of irregular blocks of the red island granite with a grout so gray that a church wall looks like a sunrise seen through fog at sea. Each Åland church, old or new, has a ship model hung from a wire pinned into the gloom under the church's wooden rafters, so a ship sails above the nave where each congregation gathers.

Outside the churches, all of the bottomlands, flats, and hollows, and many of the hillsides had been plowed for the winter. The light brown soil, limestone-sweet from its years on the bottom of a brackish sea, had been turned that fall to soak up winter moisture and furrowed for spring seedings of cabbage and cucumber, onions and sugar beets, wheat and rye. There were houses with hip roofs banked against every low ridge in groups of two or three or five, many of them painted a shade of red that was for years reserved for barns in American farming country. In Åland, that shade comes from the earth itself. Red paint pigment was once made from iron oxides separated from crushed island rock. The loose groupings of houses count as villages, and have place names so timeworn that the connection between place and meaning is not always clear to modern Ålanders.

There are villages of twelve houses and villages of five, and hamlets of two or one, each with its proper name. Karl Andren's ancestral home, where his seafaring father Wikar grew up, is a one-farmstead hamlet called Karholm, where the highest knoll of land rises 18 or 20 feet above the Baltic which has crept inland there along a 20-mile sound. It is on the map. It has a sign at the edge of the road.

Karholm means "peasant's island," and the Baltic teems with those: places where there is just enough soil to sustain a crop, which must, however, be taken off in boats. The Andren farmstead is all dry land now, and that fact sets up a rough scale by which to measure the age of its place name. Sea level in the Baltic has been dropping slowly for centuries at the rate of about three feet every hundred years, because the dry land in and around the northern Baltic is still rebounding from the weight of ice sheets that vanished ten thousand years ago. Calculating by the slow retreat of Baltic waters, the family farm at Karholm, now about 20 feet above the sea, was last an island between six and seven hundred years ago.

Without signposts in Åland, one would think oneself in coastal Washington, Massachusetts, or Maine, all places where the glaciers walked, grinding the granite clean and leaving irregular sweeps of moraine to be gentled into soil by rain and sun and grass. In all those places, human occupation follows the glacier-made contour and people build houses on the high, dry, hard ground that they cannot farm. The shape of the countryside is set by nature. And people live their long seasons by nature's rules, much the way they always have. In places like these, people still mark the passage of time, the way farmers and fishermen do, by seasonal changes. In Åland conversations, I heard time measured by the blooming of trees and the spawning runs of Baltic cod.

In the last two generations, however, Ålanders have begun to abstract their formal history from the repeating round of seasons and lives lived the way they have always been. There are two museums in Mariehamn, which ought to be enough for a town of twelve thousand. One is wholly maritime and the other is principally archaeological, since the record at home in Åland is largely in the ground. Both are well-endowed and maintained for what seems to be a popularly felt purpose. In the space of ten days, four different Ålanders described the benefits of a well-preserved past for me in very similar words.

"It is good to know the past," they said, "because if you know whence you came you have a better idea of who you are."

It sounded like an old saying in the making.

Formal Åland history is unavoidably maritime. Invasions and seafaring brought the islands out of obscurity and into the world. And, long before the big, famous square-riggers went to Åland at the end of their lives, the tall masts of sailing ships were established as the standard for aspirations that reached beyond the low island horizon. Ships built there began to trade under sail throughout the Baltic in the ninth century. Sometimes trading was closed off for centuries by politics or wars. Sometimes it was permitted, and the islands thrived. Living in any of the times of opportunity, a young Ålander knew what he had to do to excel, to adventure, or just to get off the farm. The masts of sailing ships stood all winter like signposts at the edge of the bays and harbors. An ambitious boy could learn sailing and seamanship from his father, his uncles, brothers, or cousins. The rewards for going to sea were clear. The largest houses in town belonged to sea captains. The best were built by shipowners.

After the Napoleonic Wars ended, the nineteenth century became an unparalleled time of opportunity. In Åland, subsistence farmers who knew how to build became shipwrights and their sons became captains and shipowners. From 1850 to 1920, Ålanders built 290 ships that were registered for trading off the islands. These ships were so widely owned, in shares put up by sailing landowners and farmer captains, that by 1875 there were 2 or 3 net registered tons afloat for every one of the fifteen thousand Ålanders living on the main islands.[5]

Wooden shipbuilding in Åland was a neighborhood business. A shipwright set up on a farmer's sloping seafront that was too rocky to plow. He slapped together a sawmill, a bunkhouse, a toolshed, a carpenter's shed, a boiler box to steam-bend planks, and a forge. He saved his care for the slipway and the ship he would erect on it. Then he gathered men, with a preference for those who could walk to work. Sailors between ships helped out for wages; farmers threw in their labor in return for shares in the ship.

As late as 1920, there was such a neighborhood yard at Skunholm, north of Mariehamn, where a shipwright named Johan August Henriksson built his last ship as though the Industrial Revolution had just begun. For the tightest curves in his ship, at the bow and where the cambered deck met the swell of the side, Henriksson used the shapes he had found in his wood. A sawmill with a steam engine made rough-cut planks. His men shaped and fit those planks and the ship's frames with adzes. They smoothed and finished with big, wooden box planes. There were no factory-made iron fittings; the builders forged them. There was no imported coke for the forge. They fired it with charcoal, which they made the Iron Age way by covering a smoldering fire of green sticks with a mound of sod blocks cut from between the rocks, where red-tinged moss and summer grass grew thick enough to hold the sandy soil together.

The charcoal mound is where a boy might have begun, watching the sod and clambering over it quickly to stuff moss into any little vent where the white smoke worked its way to the air. Later, he could pump the bellows, his face smarting when he dared to watch the iron turn red, then yellow, then nearly white, when it could be shaped. He would learn how to tell by eye when the iron was hot.

Apprenticeship was, as it had been for centuries, a matter of watching and being occasionally useful. The artisan's talents that a boy might follow grew from the ground in that place, after so many centuries of boatbuilding. Henriksson pulled together a steady crew of six men. Four bunked with him at the yard. Two walked in each day from Svartsmara, just east over the rise. The shipwright sailed home singlehanded in an open boat every weekend to Appelö, an island at the western mouth of Skunholm's sound, 12 winding miles away.

Skunholm had been in use as a shipyard, off and on, since 1849, long enough for use to lend names to the place. When Henriksson launched his last ship she floated across the inlet to a high granite bluff called Mast Rock, where the water was deep close under a cliff. He rigged tackles on Mast Rock to haul her two masts upright. She was christened *Fred,* which means peace. The shipwright had laid the keel for another like her, a brig of about 100 feet to be called *Fred II* for good measure after the carnage of World War I and the civil war in Finland that followed the Russian Revolution. But the shipyards of the world had caught up with the loss of shipping tonnage in the war. *Fred II* was never finished.[6]

Henriksson told his daughter before he died that he had laid sixteen keels but built only fifteen ships in his life, as if his epitaph might be somehow flawed. The Industrial Revolution had finally reached Åland, and there was no need for him again. His ships, and others built by island shipwrights, lived on for a while. They were strong and some of them were pretty. In their oldest age, many of them sailed with windmills erected on deck to constantly drive the pumps that kept them afloat.

Ships were the only way out of the unchanging round of farming and fishing the short summers through, then hunkering down in October for a winter of smoked fish, salt meat, cheese, potatoes, and dried peas; each winter spent hoping that the food, the fodder, and the firewood would all last through May when the seabirds returned, bringing the first hope of regular fresh meat. Certainly for as far back as living memories go, boys growing up in Åland knew that central fact about ships. The girls, who farmed for life until recently and only traveled if their fathers or husbands became ship captains, must have known it too. From their mothers, hurrying back to the house from the evening milking on nights when the wind buffeted the firs or hooted in the barn eaves, they learned a quick prayer to say for absent men: "God bless the ships at sea."

Men now over sixty remember growing up in Åland as a roughly comfortable chore. The boyhoods they recall were cupped in farm routine. There was food enough, always plenty of hard work, and, at the water's edge, or in the next bay, ships that held the hint of escape and a promise of adventure. None of their early lives were easy, and the oldest Åland seafarers now alive speak very sparingly about childhood. It is clear, when they do, that the nineteenth century lasted much longer in those islands than in the rest of Europe.

Choices were limited not by tradition but by reality. As late as 1939, an Åland adolescent could consider himself lucky to get a job at sea as a mess boy. Dishwashing at sea beat hauling a gill net by hand into a heavy rowboat on every ice-free day but Sunday, in order to catch enough fish for one or two family meals a day. And eight months at sea on a salary then brought in the equivalent of two years of salt-farming effort ashore.

Earlier, the choices had been even more stark. Karl Andren's father left the family farm at Karholm twenty-four years before World War II began. When he went to sea, he followed the patterns of an earlier century.

"You must remember that life was just plain hard then," Captain Wikar Andren says when he thinks back to the Åland where he grew up. I met Captain Andren before I went to his native islands and he was at polite pains to prepare me for a place that had, until recently, been very different from the modern world. He was born in 1915, went to sea as soon as he was considered able, rounded Cape Horn under sail twice before he was eighteen, then went to Åland's Maritime Academy, became a ship's officer, a captain, and, finally, a director of shipping operations.

The whole sweep of Åland's change from a frugal, traditional society constrained by climate and the real limits of islands to a consumer society linked to the world by ocean trade was encompassed in Captain Andren's lifetime. Age-old necessities framed his early life, but never those of his two sons, his only children. Wikar was born in a farming village called Morby. His father, Uno, was a farmer who had gone adventuring to the Klondike and to Puget Sound and come back with enough money to buy the family farm at Karholm when Wikar was six. There he built a house and took a ship carpenter's hand in building a sailing ship called *Esperanza*. He held a one-fifth share in *Esperanza*'s ownership, and owned shares in other sailing cargo ships, but he was not a seaman.

Seafarers, in Uno's time and for generations before it, led lives that were compressed into one Åland saying: "A seaman comes home once a year to kill a pig and make a baby."

A fattened spring pig died on Åland farms for the Christmas table, when the ice had closed the Baltic and the ships were laid up like frozen black islands in the bays. That was the only time Åland seamen were at home. Uno did not think much of the life described in the saying, so he urged his sons not to follow the sea.

"Better they should stay at home, my father said, or emigrate to America," Captain Andren remembers. "There were only those three choices then; only three: you could farm, or go to sea, or emigrate to America."

An island can keep only as many people as it can provide food for, by farming, foraging, and fishing. The rest must leave. So far as Åland's historians can judge, the population of their islands held steady for centuries. The resident population had never risen above twenty thousand before 1960. Since then it has grown to almost thirty thousand inhabitants because tourists, an off-island transient population, have brought job opportunities to Åland that never existed before. Before tourism, freight and seafarers' wages supplemented the islanders' farm earnings and emigration took away what the islands could not support. The descendants of Ålanders live in large numbers in Sweden, in Australia, and all over the United States and Canada.

When Captain Andren's father sickened and the Great Depression closed in on the family, his elder brother stayed on the farm and the boy, Wikar, went to sea. He signed on first as a mess boy on a leaking lumber schooner at the age of fourteen. On his first trip, the schooner foundered in a gale blowing her down onto the Finnish coast, but her cargo of wood kept her barely afloat until she grounded and the crew could pump her out. For the ensuing season of Baltic trading, Andren signed onto the *Shakespeare,* a cut-down clipper ship.

"One night late in October—it was dark and blowing—she went ashore in East Bothnia and there she is still," Andren said. "The next year I went in the deep-water ships."

That year, at sixteen, he was an able-bodied seaman, rated and recognized. He remains able-bodied, built tall, as many Ålanders are, with a high, broad forehead and shoulders as solid and square as a ceiling joist. There cannot be many like him in the Maryland suburb where he retired, but there were in the crew of the *Lawhill* in the European summer of 1931. There had to be. She was a huge, slab-sided bark 317 feet long, built by Scots in 1892 to carry 4,600 tons of bulk cargo.

Lawhill had four masts, with five square sails, on spars that swung across the ship's axis, on each of the three forward masts. There were two bigger sails set along the ship's axis on the mast at her stern; staysails between the masts; and three jibs set from bowsprit and jibboom, ahead of her looming bow. She set twenty-six sails, and it could take a morning to get them all unfurled and drawing, starting from bare poles. Hull and masts, *Lawhill* was all steel and the Ålanders sailed her with a crew of, at most, twenty-four men, boys, and officers. The British at their most frugal had shipped more than thirty in the crew. Any sailor on modern oceangoing sailboats who has felt the strength of the wind in sails a fraction of the size of *Lawhill*'s can only ask: how did they do it?

"We were all young and it never occurred to us that we couldn't," Captain Andren says. "You know how it is when you are young. You can do anything."

Wikar Andren shipped on two trips to Australia and back, for the sea experience under sail that was then required of merchant marine officer candidates in several countries. He studied mathematics in his off watches in the soft trade winds, but not in the North Atlantic or the rolling, lonely waters at the southern end of the world that are called the Southern Ocean. The winds there—south of Australia and New Zealand; beyond the Cape of Good Hope and below Cape Horn—have a strength, and sound, all their own. A sailing ship's path south around the world went through the Roaring Forties, between forty and fifty degrees south latitude, and dipped into the Howling Fifties, at least to pass Cape Horn. Further south were the Screaming Sixties.

It was a very hard life. Work and wet were constants, outside the tropics. Fresh water was rationed and salt water turned every cut into an open sore. Climbing 100 feet or more into the air on writhing wire ropes to handle thrashing sails was a true terror for most men in the square-riggers. It was the work of the ship and had to be done, day in and day out. The food was harsh and monotonous. Even Ålanders deserted ships for bad food. The foreign apprentices who paid to learn deep-water sailing in Gustaf Erikson's ships, like the *Lawhill,* sometimes could not eat Åland rations of potatoes, salt beef, and pea soup every Thursday.

"But only at first," said Wikar Andren. "By the end of a week, they ate it all. You had to, or starve."

After his two years of Cape Horn sailing, Wikar stayed ashore at the Mariehamn navigation training school, successfully took his mate's examination, and with his papers went back to sea in steam. There was a difference. Life aboard steamers and, later, motor vessels, was drier, calmer, more comfortable. But the exhilaration was gone.

"Under sail we went to sea God's way, the way God made the oceans and the winds; we were part of it," the retired captain recalled, fifty-four years later. His large, blunt hands in a V pushed the air between us, where we talked, and chopped downward together as he searched for the right words. "A steamer, a motor vessel; they all fight the sea and the wind."

"I am very glad I went to sea under sail," he said then, and it was his final judgment on that life. "But I would not want to do it again and I would not send my grandsons to do it."

As it turned out, even his sons did not have to. Anders, the firstborn, and Karl Gösta grew up in a new apartment, one of twelve in a three-story building owned by their successful sea-captain father and eleven other seafarers. The brown stucco building with small rectangular windows stood at the intersection of Captain's Street and Skipper Street, but the captain, their father, was not often at home. In the nonunion years after the war, Captain Andren stayed at sea year round to hold onto his job. The family joined him aboard his commands for parts of school vacations.

The Mariehamn where the New York shipowner Karl G. Andren grew up was a small town, where he was known as Gösta. The Swedish name is pronounced "Yeuh-stuh," and the young Andren dropped it after his first full year at an American school. When Gösta was a boy, Mariehamn had a population of about six thousand. Life in the little city of shipowners and seafarers had a calm, ordered quality in which boys could thrive on limited mischief, well-tolerated by tradition. There were no notable luxuries and not many distractions. After a week of listening to the recollections of men born there in 1946, the year Karl Andren was born, I was reminded of Tom Sawyer and Huckleberry Finn.

Anders Fagerlund, one of Andren's classmates for nine years in the straitlaced Mariehamn schools, went abroad to train as a pediatrician but came home after trying adult life in the United States and Finland. I found him in a broad, southwest-facing office, as white as the inside of an ice cave, at the new Mariehamn hospital. The china-white walls were splashed by the bright colors of children's paintings, pinned up in clusters. One of them showed a girl with stiff brown pigtails wearing a blue smock dress and sitting in a swing. Above her head there was a legend in blue block letters. "Tak, Anders," it said. "Thanks, Anders."

The doctor remembers that the twenty-six children who began first grade together in 1953 split up into neighborhood groups after school each day. The northern group, which included Fagerlund and the Andren brothers, played on the way home in the no-man's-land of Mariehamn's adjoining backyards. In the older sections of the city, around the complex of granite-faced school buildings, tall wooden houses still stand at the street edge of large lots with apple trees at their backs. The deep, continuous backyards make it seem that a strip of orchard runs down the inside of each block.

"We went from one garden to another, playing hide-and-seek," the doctor said. "The people didn't like it, especially when we took apples. Mariehamn was a very small town, then. We could play soccer in the main street. We had bicycles, later, and I can't remember ever being afraid of cars or traffic.

"It was such a small society that everyone took care of you. And watched you. If you took an apple someone saw you and knew right away who you were. You heard about it quickly."

AT LEFT: Three Cape Horn barks near the end of their days: Viking *(*left*),* Passat *(*center*), and* Pommern *(*nearest shore*), laid up in the West Harbor at Mariehamn during World War II. (*Ålands Maritime Museum*)*

BELOW: The Southern Ocean, 1909. This picture of four men struggling to secure the foresail of the British bark Garthsnaid, *running before a storm under topsails south of forty degrees south latitude, was taken by the second mate from the end of her jibboom, thrown skyward by the comber seen rolling away from her starboard side amidships. The next breaking wave is building high over her port quarter. Sir Basil Greenhill, former curator of the National Maritime Museum at Greenwich, England, considered this the most revealing photograph in his collection of a big merchant sailing ship in a storm at the southern end of the earth. (*National Maritime Museum*)*

Ålands shipbuilding. The schooner Lyckan *with her heavy frames showing and her planking just begun in 902 on a neighborhood slipway at Kvarnbo, near Saltvik. (*Ålands Maritime Museum*)*

ABOVE: Ålands shipbuilders. Seventeen local men—farming sailors or sailing farmers—and two boys built the schooner Ingrid *in 1906. Their labor was repaid by shares in the completed vessel when she started voyaging. (*Ålands Maritime Museum*)*

*AT LEFT: Johan August Henriksson, Ålands shipwright. The builder of one of the last wooden sailing ships launched in the Åland Islands sat for this portrait when he was about seventy-eight years old. (*Ålands Maritime Museum*)*

*The crew of an Åland Islands Cape Horner. Wikar Andren, father of the shipowner Karl G. Andren (*second row, seventh from the left*), stands directly behind Captain Arthur Soderlund. He was seventeen and had been made sailmaker and bosun, one of the ship's leading petty officers, on his second sailing voyage around the world to Australia for wheat. (*Captain Wikar Andren*)*

The five-masted, full-rigged Preussen, *1902. With at least 50,000 square feet of area in forty-seven separate sails to drive a hull 434 feet long,* Preussen *captures the imagination as probably the most powerful pure sailing ship ever built. The German full-rigged ship was not the largest sailing ship ever built; the biggest was the five-masted bark* France II, *launched in Bordeaux in November 1911, but she had two auxiliary engines to assist her 68,350 square feet of sail. They were later removed. (*National Maritime Museum*)*

Preussen, *1911. The wreck of the only five-masted, full-rigged ship ever built, ashore beneath the South Foreland of the Thames estuary, is a stark sign of the end of fifty or sixty centuries of the age of sail. A steamship tried to cross* Preussen's *bow in the English Channel and the huge sailing ship ran the steamer down. She lost her bowsprit in the collision, her fore topmast toppled over the side, and the sailing ship became unmanageable. The steamer sank. (*National Maritime Museum*)*

AT LEFT: The Duchess. The four-masted steel bark Herzogin Cecilie, *the flagship of Gustaf Erikson's sailing fleet, under full sail in a bare breeze. This picture was taken from a yardarm of the* Archibald Russell, *another Erikson ship, when the two captains brought their ships to near touching so that they could talk—and show off their maneuvering skills—leaving the Baltic in ballast, outbound to load wheat from Australia for Great Britain. (*National Maritime Museum*)*

*BELOW: Gustaf Erikson, "King of the Square-Riggers." There were men who had owned larger fleets in the last days of sail, but Erikson owned the last fleet of working square-rigged ships. He bought his steel-hulled Cape Horn barks at scrap prices when no one else would have them and sent them to sea uninsured but with confidence since his captains, officers, and many of his seamen were Ålanders bred to seagoing under sail. He stands at the center of a portrait taken in the summer of 1931 of shipowning captains, partners in the first ship Erikson bought after retiring from the sea, a square-rigger captain himself. He was forty-one, and the force of his will seems to have drawn the lens so that even though he is the shortest man in the group, he is the focal point of the picture. (*Ålands Maritime Museum*)*

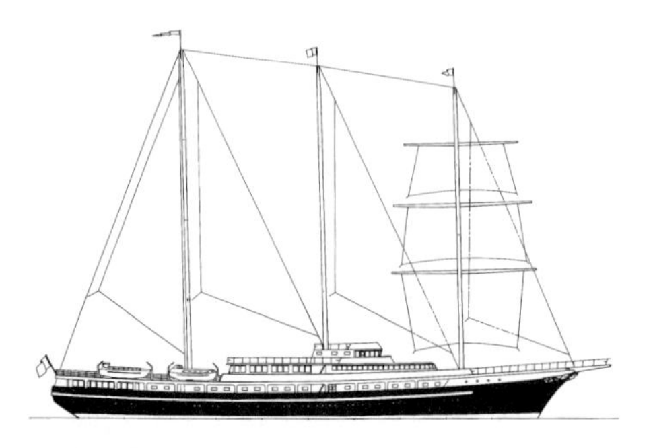

*Dream Ship I. A classical design for a 320-foot barkentine with square sails on her foremast, finished by Frank MacLear of New York in 1983. This was Karl Andren's first attempt to have his dream of a sailing cruise ship drawn by a naval architect. (*Frank MacLear/ MacLear and Harris, Inc.*)*

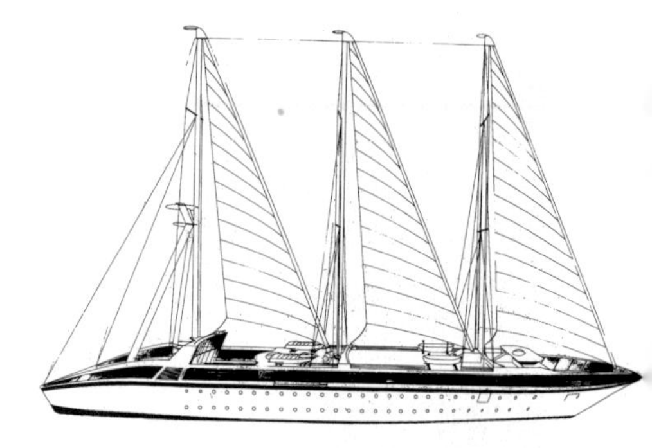

*Dream Ship II. The first design for a modern sailing cruise ship made at the Wärtsila Helsinki Shipyard followed the simplifying and streamlining principles of modern Scandinavian design. But this project was too modern even for Scandinavian clients and it was set aside. (*AB Wärtsila Oy, Helsinki Shipyard*)*

ABOVE: *Dream Ship III. A hull model drawn from Wärtsila's second sailing cruise ship design undergoes tank testing in Helsinki in March 1983 during development for a Swedish shipping line. One broad bilge keel is visible just underwater toward the model's stern. (*AB Wärtsila Oy, Helsinki Shipyard*)*

AT LEFT: *Dream Ship IV. The Wärtsila Windcruiser goes sailing as a scale model. The operator's head is just visible under the aftermost staysail. In the summer of 1983, the Finnish sailing cruise ship design had four roller furling staysails set on crane booms, but Karl Andren did not think the design looked enough like a ship. (*AB Wärtsila Oy, Helsinki Shipyard*)*

Dream Ship V. The French transformation of the Finnish design had been completed by April 1985 when Jean-Claude Potier, president of Windstar Sail Cruises, posed with a model of Wind Star *in the design offices of the Graville shipyard of the Société Nouvelle des Ateliers et Chantiers du Havre (ACH). Sven Hansen added the jib forward; Karl Andren added the boomed sail aft and the flying bridge beneath it, where passengers would be able to steer the ship standing at a wooden wheel. Potier added the solarium-style discotheque below the third staysail as well as more extensive passenger spaces and crew accommodations. The French shipyard added fin stabilizers, which folded out of the hull in the blank space between two reduced lengths of a thinner bilge keel, visible below the waterline at the discotheque. (*Copyright © 1985 Jean Guichard/GAMMA*)*

*The Owner and the Yard (*from left to right*): Jean-Claude Potier, François Faury, Karl G. Andren, and Thomas F. Heinan looking at shipfitters' work in the Graville shipyard of the Société Nouvelle des Ateliers et Chantiers du Havre. (*Christophe Rioult/ACH*)*

*Gilbert Fournier, president of the shipyard. (*Joseph Novitski*)*

*René L'Heryénat, chief of the Graville design office. (*Joseph Novitski*)*

*Alain Adam, engineer in charge of hull production. (*Joseph Novitski*)*

*René Turquetille, master shipwright. (*Joseph Novitski*)*

Kell Guldborg Andersen, naval architect and owner's supervisor of construction and outfitting at the shipyard. (Joseph Novitski)

Michel Lesage, the self-taught boss of the outfitters at the Harfleur dockyard. (Joseph Novitski)

Yvan Martin, the Harfleur master foreman. (Joseph Novitski)

Marc Held, architect and industrial designer, with his assistant. (Joseph Novitski)

BELOW: Keel-laying. On March 27, 1985, the windship's keel was laid by settling the first two bottom blocks (F8 and F9) onto the building ways and aligning them with the ship's imaginary backbone, which passes here in the air over the white pine keel blocks. (Christophe Rioult/ACH)

Assembly. The hull was put together starting near the middle and building out toward the ends and up; therefore, it grew highest amidships first. (Christophe Rioult/ACH)

Construction. The first curve of the bow, the stem below the waterline, put together in the West Shop at Graville. (Christophe Rioult/ACH)

ABOVE: Mast-making. Three welding machines, three welders, and a foreman ready to begin welding one mast section. (Christophe Rioult/ACH)

AT LEFT: The hull completed. It stands ready on launching morning, with bilge shores still in place along the sides. (Christophe Rioult/ACH)

ABOVE: Sail-training. A radio-controlled model of Wind Star *sailed on a pond near Harfleur to try out sail control procedures. The model could not always be made to bring its bow through the wind and often refused to bring its stern through the wind.* (Christophe Rioult/ACH)

AT RIGHT: Mast-stepping. Two cranes hoisted Wind Star's *first mast upright on July 5, 1985. The mast bore the unforeseeable lifting strains without damage and was swung on board. The same technique was then used for all masts.* (Christophe Rioult/ACH)

She takes the water well. Wind Star *slipped down the building ways and into the sea at Le Havre on November 13, 1985.* (Christophe Rioult/ACH)

That close support and control might have been very necessary in a society where so many fathers were away at sea for months at a time. Dr. Fagerlund's father was not one of those, but Nils-Erik Eklund's was, as was his classmate Gösta Andren's.

"Being sons of men who were at sea, we were the only men at home," Eklund said, when he thought back to his school days. "You had to do your own growing up; you had to do your own research, finding out what to do with that boat, how to use that tool. In a way, you had to be very grown up, even when you were a small kid."

Eklund, whose seagoing father became a shipowner on a borrowed shoestring and introduced the first tourist-carrying car ferry on the route from Mariehamn to Sweden, remembers growing up as a responsibility. For him, that responsibility expressed itself daily in terms of food. He remembers that he had to come home at noon every day to prepare porridge for his younger brothers and sisters, because his mother and father were busy working as office and reservations staff, accountants, and ticket takers for their nascent ferry line.

Food, too, illustrates the difference between Åland then and Åland now for Eklund. Breakfast in his youth was a fat slice of farm cheese between two rye crackers and a glass of hot water. No tea or coffee; coffee was for formal, and slightly festive, occasions. For dinner there were always potatoes, and meat or fish. His children now have fresh fruits all through the winter, and what seems to him a blindingly wide selection of food. Nils-Erik's lunch, as a boy, was always porridge, every day including Saturday. It was a school day.

"Up to the beginning of the nineteen sixties we were living in a fairly poor community, you see," Eklund said by way of explanation. He is a formal man, tall and carefully considered in manner and speech, and now a shipowner like his former classmate. He received me one afternoon in the carpeted and paneled offices of the family ferry line, listened to the reasons for my impolite curiosity, then deliberated for a long moment in silence. "Gösta was always wearing a very happy face," he said. "It was very difficult to keep Gösta down. He was very positive-thinking and when he wanted to do something, he went ahead. He set his own priorities. Which were not necessarily those of the school here."

The current superintendent of Åland schools, Borje Karlsson, agreed later, quite politely. Karlsson looked up K. Gösta Andren's school record, through the tenth grade when he left for the United States, and found it just above average. Andren stood above the middle of his class as he worked through elementary and middle school. Karlsson taught

English then, in the time he called "the good old days," and ran the middle school.

"I remember him as a round-faced boy who was pleasant," Karlsson said. "He must have been good at mathematics because his English was not good. I don't know how he's done it with that English."

Gösta Andren's success as an emigrant has been widely reported in Åland, and Johan Dahlman, a classmate, claimed that he found nothing surprising in it. He remembered Gösta as the joker in the back row.

"He always sat toward the back of the class," Dahlman remembered. "We were forty by middle school, half from town and half from the country, either boarders or boys who rode the bus up every day to town. And there was always something going on around Gösta's seat. . . . Not bad, not naughty. You must remember it was a different time. Students were much more formal with their teachers than they are now. Our teachers came from a world apart, it seemed. And this was a different place."

It was 1960 when Andren reached middle school and the Western world was learning the Twist. There were three dances a year at the school in Mariehamn. The girls were more interested than the boys. In the winter the boys played *bandy,* a terrifically speedy version of ice hockey played with a hard round ball, and in the summer there was the water. The sailors, like Nils-Erik Eklund and Anders Fagerlund, joined the Åland Sailing Society to get their hands on a sailboat. But every family had a boat of some utilitarian sort. Fish was not considered fresh in Mariehamn then unless one had caught it oneself.

The Andren boys put blankets in the family's aluminum skiff and, if they could not borrow an outboard motor, rowed off late in the summer into the maze of islands south of Mariehamn, exploring alone and living on the fish they caught. Their mother still remembers wildflowers the boys brought her one Mother's Day, from a favorite, sheltered islet. They had rowed out and back before dawn to gather them.

The two were town boys, but not very far removed from the country or the past. On long winter evenings, over coffee and cake, their fathers talked with friends who had also gone to sea on the deep-water sailing ships. They talked of ports and people, mates, good and bad, and ships, dry and safe or wet and cranky. They argued over the best way to handle the hair-raising task of furling a flailing sail to a yardarm, rolling 80 feet off breaking deep-sea combers in a Southern Ocean gale at the other end of the earth. Their voices rose, in the close warm kitchens, with the wind they remembered. And fell, when the crisis of the tale had passed, leaving the boys with the feeling that they had caught a sideways glimpse of something immensely thrilling, one of the secret pinnacles of life.

The veteran sailors also recalled the shipmates who had died on those three-month-long trips to Australia—gone off the yardarm in the shrieking dark, or crushed when one piece in the miles of wire and rope tethering tons of force aloft and moaning in the wind let go at the wrong time. Nonetheless, the square-rigger men sometimes talked of putting sails on the old *Pommern* and dreamed aloud of ways to take her to sea in God's way again, before it was too late.

It was too late by 1960, when the modern world, impatient and seductive, came to Mariehamn on the tourist ferries. Life there changed, and all of Andren's schoolmates mark the turning point by the first winter there were television sets on the island, straining to catch programming from the Swedish mainland. The second set was brought home by Johan Dahlman's father, and his classmates all trooped in to see it. They stood at the edges of the living room and applauded each time the signals on the gray screen stabilized enough to form an intelligible picture.

"It was once a very simple place," Nils-Erik Eklund told me gravely. "I would say the change came for good just after Gösta left the Åland islands."

The Andren family left in 1962 to join Captain Andren in New York, where he had become the port captain for Sweden's Wallenius Line. In the two summers before they emigrated, both boys signed on with many friends for two successive summers as diggers in excavations of the islands' buried history. They worked for the government-appointed archaeologist for the Province of Åland. His budget was limited and his projects were not then considered men's work. He used boys to dig out the early Christian burials in front of the altar of an eleventh-century country church and to explore ancient, abandoned villages.

The team dug in the mounds of a meadow above a long and sheltered bay near Saltvik, the oldest continuous settlement on Fasta Åland. They were working, they found, in a Viking village that had once died violently. The men who touched their own past that summer have not forgotten it. Anders Fagerlund remembered:

"It was very fascinating. You could find things people had tried to hide, their little treasures, including Arabian coins from Constantinople. There were bones, broken bones, the evidence of fire, and tools and beads."

Every Friday afternoon, the archaeologist drove out to the dig and wove tales of their forebears around the objects the boys had found.

They were fascinated, but not overawed. Anders Andren remembers the afternoon they lined up skulls on the altar of a church where they were working unsupervised. They sorted the skulls by size and, therefore, by resonance. With sticks and femurs they were tapping out the second chorus of "When the Saints Go Marching In" on the bones of their ancestors when the parish priest stalked through the door.

"That summer was great," Karl Andren recalled later. "We lived at my mother's aunt's house and we learned history by picking it up in our own hands. I loved it. I came over here the next summer, dreaming of being an archaeologist."

In New York, however, an older, almost racial, ambition prevailed. Karl Andren, the emigrant, found he wanted to be a shipowner as intensely as though he had stayed at home.

"Where I grew up, the biggest people in town were the shipowners," he said. "In Åland, you were either a shipowner or you worked for a shipowner. I decided to become a shipowner when I was ten or eleven."

2

CHAPTER

The Last Days of Sail

Navigare utile est.

—motto of the Åland Shipowners Association

The walls of the Åland Maritime Museum look back at the visitor from high, bright spots and odd corners. Between glass cases full of stained charts and handworn sextants, by the brave oil paintings of square-rigged ships under full sail, hang black-and-white photographs of the last generation of pure, wind-working sailors, their shipowners and the native shipwrights who first made the islands a maritime nation. All of those photographed, in their dark Sunday going-ashore best, look straight into the camera and thus out at the museum full of memories of their trade.

The shipwrights were photographed with their wives, and their pictures, black-framed and unmatted, are gathered into a gallery above a side door to the museum's library. These portraits are strongly reminiscent of the stiffly posed pictures of Great Plains farmers, made by traveling American photographers late in the last century. The men are seated; the women often standing. Both face the camera squarely. The men look slightly up from under their brows. Their shoulders are hunched, as if their powerful bodies were tensed in preparation for some unknown calamity. Their hands, large and not quite white, are joined in front of them, touching but unclasped on a plain table, or laid like downed tools over both knees. Most of them were photographed in middle age or later and, of course, the hands of a man who has worked with maul, adze, planes, and chisels all his life become so stiff with calluses and bound by scars that they will neither clasp nor fold easily.

The Åland sea captains, by contrast, were often photographed young, in their ambitious prime. They favored poses in three-quarters profile, their eyes leveled at the camera. In the pictures on display the captains almost always jut their jaws at a slight upward angle, like a tautly braced yardarm. That upward thrust and their uniformly large, clear eyes make it appear, although they may have been on the same level with the black-draped photographer, that they are looking down at his camera.

The photographs of the island shipowners, well matted in thick white cardboard, are arranged in four rows by date of death on their own uncluttered wall. The pictures are of equal size and there is no ambiguity about the point of view. All the owners are looking down at the camera. Even after the middle of this century the photographers summoned to preserve an Åland shipowner's likeness made all their portraits into two-dimensional equivalents of sculpted busts.

Gustaf Erikson, the grandest of all the Åland shipowners, left behind a three-quarter-length portrait in realistic and well-lit oils for the museum that he endowed. That portrait of a bald old man with wide-set eyes, long nose, large ears, and an immensely strong jaw over a wing collar, hangs above eye level in the central hall of the museum, directly opposite the main entrance. Gustaf Erikson's portrait looks down on all who enter.

Wherever you walk on the varnished wooden floor that creaks like a ship in a cross sea, that portrait's black eyes follow. Whenever you look over your shoulder in the high-ceilinged museum hall filled with the clean odor of pine tar, the old smell of men at sea, the king of the square-riggers is watching. Wherever they went that is undoubtedly how his captains all felt.

A sailing ship captain for years himself, Erikson in retirement built up a fleet of thirty windships that he bought from just before World War I to the beginning of World War II, when no one else would have them. His ships were a historical spectacle abroad, but frugally normal at home. He ran his fleet for thirty-four years out of an office stiff with leather seats and straightback chairs, arranged in a front corner room of his home in Mariehamn. For at least half of that time, he was the whole office staff. He wrote letters full of orders, queries, congratulations, and counsel in his own hand and copied them for his files with a patent duplicating press. There was no typewriter and no typist in his office until Erikson's twenty-second year as a shipowner. His letters of instructions, advice, and admonishment followed his sailing ship captains to England, the United States, Africa, Australia, and the west coast of South America.

The shipowner told his captains how to handle anchors and stevedores, and what to buy for stores and provisions. He instructed them on the holding ground in certain harbors and on the best way to stir their paint. He sent them detailed directions, halfway around the world, on how to load and stow unfamiliar cargoes. The captains were strong and independent men. They cannot have liked being treated as apprentices, but Erikson had been one of them. Then he became the largest employer in the islands and finally the first Åland tycoon.

In the outwardly egalitarian island society, Erikson liked to be called Gustaf. When he became preemininent in the islands' native business, his younger officers called him "Papa Gusta'." Later, after the Finnish government had awarded him an honorary office, with title, as maritime counselor, younger Ålanders knew him only as *Sjöfartsradet,* the maritime counselor.

For boys born in the islands after World War II, like Karl Andren, Erikson was the only native example of success on a heroic scale. The boys had other heroes, of course; war heroes and sports heroes, and, closer to home, the sailing captains who had been able to make 6,000 tons of square-rigger hover in a running tide or back away from a dock under sail, unassisted. Erikson, however, was the only Ålander who had both succeeded in and been recognized by the modern, commercial world outside the Åland Islands. His business style, solitary and intuitive, the style of a gambler who was willing to buy out less assured shareholders in a ship headed straight into the 1918 German U-boat blockade, so that he alone might collect her war-premium freights, was the one that had triumphed in the world at large.

Erikson was tightfisted, tough-minded, and competitive. His son Edgar, who inherited the Gustaf Erikson Line and presided over its conversion to diesel-powered ships until his death early in 1986, remembered that it was always easier to talk to the old man about a million marks than about 150. Gustaf bought sailing ships at scrap prices and sent them to sea uninsured. He watched over every detail of his business himself and knew all his ships from keel to masthead. He worked every day from eight in the morning until dinner.

He became a rich man, and every Ålander knew it, but not through any Erikson ostentation. He rode a bicycle to the harbor, because he never learned to drive. His family walked to worship on Sundays. In the church the ship model sailing over their heads was that of the *Tjerimai,* Gustaf Erikson's first ship and his most profitable venture.

Although he was a singleminded businessman, Erikson had a sailor's deep and lasting affection for sailing ships. His thirty years at sea had marked him. After the crash of 1929, Erikson found himself resisting urgent advice from his agents in England to get out of sail as every other serious shipowner had. He wrote back: ". . . as I have been brought up with these sailers since the age of ten, I cannot help loving them. Malicious tongues will even allege that these vessels are closer to me than my wife and child."[1]

What boys like Karl Andren knew about the nature of sailing ships, when they were growing up in Åland, they learned from their fathers and uncles. What they knew about the final period in the long history of commercial sail, they learned from the career of the maritime counselor.

Erikson's life precisely spanned the last days of sail. He was born three years after the Suez Canal opened for ship traffic, and broke the 280-year-old sailing ship monopoly on trade around Africa to the Far East. He died in 1947, two years before two of his big square-riggers became the last commercial sailing ships to pass Cape Horn homeward bound with paying cargoes. He made himself a modern success by aggressively taking an anachronism to market.

When Gustaf Erikson was born on a farm late in October 1872 at the bleak leading edge of an Åland winter, steamships had been crossing the Atlantic for just over thirty years. In fact, steamships and sailing ships were both such common sights at sea in that year and held such nearly equal shares of the world's cargoes that they were colloquially known, in English, as steamers and sailers. That usage, reflecting the side-by-side normality of wind power and engine power, lasted well into this century. There were steamers, when Erikson was born, and they were good for short runs calling at lots of ports where they had to find coal, but these smokey new ships were not yet entirely proven. And there were the familiar sailers, good for the long blue-ocean runs because the winds would always bring them to port somehow, no matter what broke down.

Still, the time a sailer might take to cover any given route was as unpredictable as the winds. Predictability was the key to the new Industrial Age, which had the sense of progress and the presumption of human ascendancy over nature in its name. Predictability was wanted, and regularity, and progress measured by human standards, not by the will of the winds.

Maritime historians tend to identify the opening of the Suez Canal in 1869 as the turning point in competition between sailers and steamers. From that date forward, the expansions in world cargoes went to steamers. Sailers slowly disappeared, for purely business reasons. Layer upon layer of individual business decisions, laid down by thousands of shippers, insurers, and shipowners, favored first coal, then oil, over wind power for ocean shipping. The shippers were first to see what reliability meant for them. On route after route, from the middle of the century forward, trade after trade went to steam, not sail, but sailing ship owners held on. Then, in 1897, the shipping underwriters at Lloyds of London decreed a general insurance rate increase for sailing ships only. The cost of insuring steamers held, and the British sailing fleet, with the exception of a few ships, had been sold by the time the new century began.[2] In England first, then in the rest of the world, shipowners finally saw that sailing ships did not fit the central formula of the industrial age: Time is money.

A sailing ship at sea moves on a fluid balance between air and water, two of the ancient, ungovernable elements. The ship moves with the elements and therefore carries with herself an elemental sense of time, time that cannot be controlled and counted closely enough to fit in the same equation with money. If one is determined to measure time as precisely as money, a sailing ship will not serve. Ships driven by sail alone can rush through the water for twenty-four hours or a week, then fall into a calm and sit in the heaving swells with blocks clattering and sails flapping heavily, like wet wash on a dull day, for another week. Cargo ships using wind power alone regularly ran into headwinds on their long trade routes and sometimes had to turn the other way around the world to get home. Sailing ships just do not move with the kind of timed precision that men can count in money. Steamships and motor vessels carry time that precise inside them. The mechanical measurement of time that gives us our modern idea of speed as distance covered while a clock ticks, as miles per hour or feet per second, is always in the fiber of any engine-driven ship underway. Vessels driven by engines vibrate constantly, as do the elements in a cesium clock or inside the electronic movement of a digital wristwatch.

Any modern ship's vibration spreads from her propeller, which cuts slices from the sea and thrusts them backward in a rhythm that is measured in propeller shaft rpm (revolutions per minute). Each of those revolutions thrums along the shaft and through the ship's fabric and she vibrates. That vibration, which is exactly like the constant marking of modern time, only stops when the ship does.

For an age determined to measure time minutely enough to allow the illusion that men control it, any ship driven by engines is the vessel of preference. It does not wait to catch the elements that move outside human control. It imposes human control on those elements, pushes over them and appears to shove them aside. The sailing ship sailors of the nineteenth century saw that about steamships straight away. So did shippers.

Once steamships proved they could reliably cross the Atlantic, in

1838, they became financially faster than sailing ships because their times at sea were predictable, and could therefore be measured in a shipping businessman's calculations of cost. Eventually steamship crossings, particularly westbound to America against the prevailing North Atlantic winds, became truly quicker, but reliability was enough for a businessman. If a shipper bought his cargo with borrowed money, he could calculate how much it would cost him in interest to ship by steamer and gamble at small stakes with a higher freight. If the same shipper chose a sailer, he gambled on time at sea and thus with his interest due, and that made his total investment unpredictable. By 1842, not thirty years after regularly scheduled sailing ship service was first introduced between New York and Europe, transatlantic sailing packets westbound against the wind had lost their first class passengers and ten-dollar-per-ton fine freight to steamers.

Decades passed before shipowners were all convinced that the days of sail had gone—in part, perhaps, because for many years sailing ships, under the right conditions, could outrun powered vessels at sea (for a few glorious hours, at least). Gustaf Erikson's son Edgar remembered ripping through the Kattegat, homeward bound to Mariehamn from England as a young passenger on his father's flagship, *Herzogin Cecilie.* The white bark sailed so fast that the motorboat sent out to deliver her mail as she passed through that narrow throat between the North Sea and the Baltic could not catch her. It is likely that the great number of collisions recorded after the turn of the century between sailers and steamers in close, crowded waters like the Kattegat and the English Channel were the result of miscalculation by steamer skippers who had forgotten, or had never known, how fast a big windship could move.

Sailing ship owners also resisted the logic of the new, industrial age out of a conservatism that was traditional, and came naturally to men who had the certainty of centuries of practice behind them. A leading British innovator in iron shipbuilding, trying to sell the newfangled steel wire to rig sailing ships in 1843, lamented what he called "the opposition of seamen, who view innovations with an extraordinary degree of abhorrence."[3]

Fifty years after that remark an extraordinary amount of commercial logic had accumulated in favor of steamships. Any shipowner who hires out his hull space works under unvarying financial conditions: he has a fixed capital investment in each vessel and pays out constant costs to operate her, no matter what drives the ship. The owner's income is a product of the amount he charges to move 1 ton a contracted number of ocean miles. His profit is the difference between each ship's costs and her freight fees. The longer a cargo stays at sea, the more that ocean move costs the shipowner and the smaller his profit will be. The faster—or more regularly—cargoes move, the more often the shipowner can profit by moving them. It was their regularity that first recommended steamships to shipowners. Speed and fuel efficiency came later, but the initial advantage was plain: steamships did not wait for the wind, they sailed and arrived on man's time, not nature's, and therefore made more voyages in a useful lifetime.

For love, like Gustaf Erikson, or money, like Erikson, the owners of sailing ships tried for fifty more years to find ways around the economic arguments which had already concluded that the age of sail was over. First, owners reduced the number of men in each crew while building bigger ships. At the peak of the age of sail, aboard a British East Indiaman in 1815, there were 138 in the crew, 1 man for every foot of length. The pace for sailing passengers and freight was so leisurely then that the East India Company masters regularly took in over half their sail area at nightfall.

With steam competition declared in 1852, the clipper ship *Sovereign of the Seas* sailed with 106 men, or 1 for every 2 feet of length. Twenty-three years later, with steamships chuffing across every ocean, the big, iron-hulled, full-rigged ship *British Ambassador* signed on a crew of only 41, or about 1 for each 9 feet, on a ship one-third longer than the clipper.

Iron used in shipbuilding helped to keep sail competitive, because iron proved to be about one-quarter lighter, for a given length of hull, than wood. Iron hulls could be built longer and deeper than wooden hulls. Steel hulls were lighter still, for a given length, and they had become the rule for new deep-water sailing ships before the turn of the century. Long, deep, steel hulls were born faster, because speed through the water is a direct function of waterline length. The longer a ship is built, the faster she will go.

The steel hulls of the 1890s and early 1900s were 300 feet long, or more. With 4,000 to 5,000 tons of cargo aboard 2,000 tons of ship in the right winds they could sail at 12 knots or better, faster than most steamers, but bursts of speed were not enough for the last tall ships.[4]

Pure speed under sail had already been tried in the brief glory days of the clippers, the most famous sailing ships of all. Some of the large clippers were capable of sustaining 16 knots for twenty-four hours, in the right wind, and at least two of these ocean flyers recorded bursts of 20, and as much as 22, knots in one furious hour. The clippers were first built by shipyards on the east coast of the United States to carry men in a rush to get rich around Cape Horn to California and to bring back gold and those who had found it. Beginning in 1850, they served the California gold rush, and the Australian gold rush two years later, and their usefulness lasted not much longer than easily found gold.

These ships, with hulls as graceful as a lifting flight of geese, the clippers we have read so much about, were queens of all the oceans for only twenty years. After 1870, those that were left afloat struggled on in different trades, their tall rigs that had looked like towers of cloud at sea cut down for crews that followed fishing fleets or hauled lumber from port to backwater port.

Huge steel barks, with four steel masts reaching as high as 185 feet above the water, and miles of steel cables, chain, and rope leading aloft to tether their sails and move their spars, represented the last widespread attempt by the owners of deep-water sailing ships to compete hard with steamers. British and Scottish shipyards built the big steel hulls first. By the turn of the century, French yards, responding to government subsidies for sailing ships, had developed beautiful examples. German shipyards went on building them longest.

The steel barks were floating adaptations of new technology to the old, sailing way of carrying freight at sea. Their hulls embodied modern engineering methods, and they carried labor-saving machines like mechanical winches, cranked by deckhands, and steam engines fed by head-high boilers built on their decks to lift steel spars and heavy rolls of furled sails aloft and to hoist and lower cargo. These ships, with deep, flat bottoms and straight sides, looked like steamers below the waterline; above it, their hull lines spoke more of power than of beauty. Because of their high-sided, blocky hulls, they were impossible to sail without substantial weight in the continuous open, hollow space below the main deck; but well-loaded and in their stormy element at the southern end of the earth, they inspired awe.

These last big deep-water sailing ships were called Cape Horners, because they were designed to ride the Southern Ocean gales around the world in the Roaring Forties, where the cape called "the Horn" at the tip of South America is at once the hardest place to pass and the finish line, a turning point toward better weather either homeward or outward bound. The steel barks were meant to search out and sail before winds other ships could not stand up in. It was their speed in the ocean waste south of forty degrees south latitude that made the last sailers competitive. Days on end sailing inside a gale on purpose made up for days of slow rolling in equatorial calms. Some maritime historians have judged the steel barks, which were the true tall ships —the biggest and tallest ever built—to be the most thorough technical achievement in the history of sail power. The men who sailed them called them mankillers.

They were too big for small crews of mortal men to handle in reliable safety. Hand-cranked winches and steam-driven capstans gave their crews a small mechanical advantage over nature. But, in competing with steamships, it was impossible for the steel barks and their shrunken crews to beat the mechanical advantage of carrying a ship's energy source on board in little black lumps, as the coal-fueled steamships did. Steamships did not have to search out energy for propulsion, chasing the wind across the oceans, nor did their crews have to wrestle that energy out of the moving air by main force.

The best marine engineers of the time took their new careers to steamships, where the clearest mechanical advantage had already been established, and their inventions quickly and steadily made engine-powered ships bigger, faster, and more fuel-efficient. Sailing ships just got bigger, and, at their biggest, nearly unmanageable. It was said of the five-masted, full-rigged *Preussen,* the largest engineless sailing ship ever built, 433 feet long with well over an acre of sail area, that no deckhand would ship for two successive voyages on board. She was too hard on her crew. And the *Thomas W. Lawson,* the largest American-built sailer, a 395-foot-long steel schooner with seven masts, rolled over at anchor, waiting for a fair wind in the Scilly Isles, and killed fifteen of the seventeen men on board.

All but one of the large, square-rigged sailing ships that parade as tall ships today are purposely scaled-down versions of the last big sailing ships, rigged much shorter than their ancestors for safety's sake.[5] The original steel barks required intense and unblinking seamanship. They were too big, too powerful to be forgiving. Sailing them safely meant years of training at sea, and constant vigilance, and youth, and stamina, and, in their officers, a weather sense that could read clouds and currents and foretell winds along 25,000 miles of ocean routes. Lacking any of these, or luck, at the wrong moment a ship could be quickly lost. The unlucky sailed into the Southern Ocean and were gone forever.

Denmark gave up full-size sailing barks for sail training after the five-masted *København,* with a full complement of cadets aboard, left Buenos Aires for Melbourne in 1928 and disappeared. Germany did the same after the four-masted *Pamir,* which sailed for Gustaf Erikson with thirty-two men aboard, sank in an Atlantic storm in 1957 and took eighty of her eighty-six crew members, including many cadets, with her.

Beginning in 1917, Gustaf Erikson defied the shipping trend. He bought every one of the last and biggest steel sailing ships he could find at the right price, and sent them to sea with confidence, because he and his countrymen understood them, because his Åland crews were small, very knowledgeable, and inexpensive, and because these ships and no others under sail alone still had an ocean trade that offered a promise of profit. To understand why, one has to know something of the Southern Ocean, the wide ring of salt water between the southern tips of all the earth's inhabited continents and Antarctica.

The ocean rolls unchecked around the world there. Normal waves are as high as a house and storm swells can be as high as three. The west wind blows, and blows and blows. It has a dry fierceness about it, south of forty degrees south latitude, that makes the skin on one's neck and shoulders move and curl as though ancient hackles were lifting there. The summers are as cold as uncertain New England Octobers and in winter the air is always taut with frost. In southern Chile and Argentine Patagonia, in Tasmania and on the southern tip of New Zealand, landsmen hunch before the winds of the Southern Ocean, and their houses huddle. It is not a place where a working seaman goes lightheartedly.

The last square-riggers, however, made their living in the Southern Ocean. On their way to Australia, they sailed a long, looping route down the South Atlantic nearly reaching Brazil then standing southeast to forty south, well below Capetown. They turned east near the gray volcanic cone of Tristan da Cunha island, and ran downwind with the west winds roaring at their backs. Homeward bound they steered east again, running before the Roaring Forties and dipping into the Howling Fifties to round Cape Horn. The big steel barks were made to do this, and, in trades where the cargo was imperishable and slow to load from difficult ports, steamship owners left it to them. Wheat from the hinterland of southern Australia, waiting by the shallow shore of the Spencer Gulf, filled all these conditions, and after 1932 carrying it around the world to England was the only trade left for deep-water windships.

A modern sailor, used to exercising a comfortable mechanical advantage over every scrap of his efficient sail plan, can visit a four-masted steel bark. Four survivors from Gustaf Erikson's fleet are museum ships, one each at Mariehamn, at Göteborg, Sweden, at Philadelphia, and at Travemunde, near Hamburg. The modern sailing yachtsman can go aboard, and feel his toes curl and his breath begin to come short, when he looks up into the rigging that the tall ship crews climbed, watch in and watch out, for three months at sea. He can feel his fingertips ache as he thinks his way through the effort of furling a sail to one of the lower yards, slung quiet and bare across the mast above him. Those tapered steel spars are as long as the hulls of the largest ocean racing yachts now allowed by the International Offshore Rule. The masts of a steel bark are taller than two America's Cup yachts are long.

I have been aboard two Cape Horners, cold and still at their museum berths, and felt my seagoing courage wilt when I looked aloft. It was reassuring for me to discover that their working crews could be just as overawed as I was at the prospect of handling something that big under sail. Some did not confess it; others did.

Elis Karlsson was one of Gustaf Erikson's Åland-born sailors, with a gift for writing English that he displayed decades after he had left the sea and was settled on a Rhodesian farm. Karlsson was born in 1905 and served his seagoing apprenticeship in the Baltic, then started a career as a ship's officer under sail, just as his father and elder brother had done before him. He first caught sight of *Herzogin Cecilie,* the four-masted steel bark known as "the Duchess" to all who sailed in her, in a corner of the harbor at Dunkirk. Forty years afterward, in 1964, Karlsson wrote: "Her spars and cordage reached upward until they were swallowed by the December murk, her mighty yard-arms across the sky over our heads. And we, puny humans, were supposed to handle all that, I thought. At that moment, it did not seem credible."[6]

In our time, with only a few fleets of working sailboats left in isolated corners of the world, most of us necessarily see sailing ships as a part of history, a part so far removed from our experience as to require as much of an effort to understand as a thirteenth-century donjon. One can look at the sailing ship, in the abstract, as a tool and reflect intellectually that it was the most influential vehicle in human history. Sailing ships rediscovered the continents and islands over which men had scattered themselves for millennia, and made the human world one again. Sailing ships carried human commercial impulses around the globe and fed the concentrations of capital that, in turn, fed cities and civilizations, and they did it—from discovery, to trade, to conquest, to empire—in what was almost a flash at the tag-end of their days. The wind-driven ships did all that in the last five of the fifty centuries during which boats with sails carried all the world's maritime freight. With a technical eye, one can look at the sailing ship as a machine, always potentially dangerous to the men who worked it, but more beautiful than other machines. Or one can look on the sailing ship as a kindred spirit, and begin to understand how those who sailed in them felt about their windships.

Sailors learned their way around sailing ships as tools. They used them as machines, but they thought of them and treated them as companions in the life-or-death business of going to sea. Sailing seamen knew their ships as individuals, and knew what each could be expected to do best and what some could not be forced to do. They learned, too, that occasionally a ship might exceed herself, as any man or woman could.

For his last three years aboard "the Duchess," Elis Karlsson sailed as first mate. On her last trip home, Karlsson was thirty-one, his captain not much older. The crew were probably all in their teens. Between Australia and the Horn, with 4,295 tons of wheat aboard, the captain went hunting for wind in the Howling Fifties and found it. One night, running before a gale under sail, with a following sea so big the 315-foot-long bark pitched up onto her bows at what seemed an impossible angle as each great, gray wave roared up under her high, rounded stern, captain and mate, on deck together, tacitly resolved to let the canvas stand for one last squall, perhaps to see what their ship could do. Karlsson wrote:

> I was watching spellbound the most awe-inspiring, and at the same time the most magnificent sight I shall ever see. I knew then that nothing would carry away; nothing would stop this marvellous ship in this her hour; she was part of the elements; as she was carried eastward in the heart of the gale, ship and elements were one. The spectacle was so overwhelming in its display of power that ordinary awareness, stark fear, or even apprehension, vanished and were replaced by an exultant feeling of one-ness with the elements and the ship.[7]

The canvas held. The ship practically steered herself, as sailing craft hurtling downwind on the face of an ocean swell sometimes will. After forty-five minutes, the squall passed. Karlsson checked the patent log streaming astern. *Herzogin Cecilie* had averaged 19 knots for that three-quarters of an hour.

The mate's description of his ship at the height of her power has a loving, almost religious tone and Karlsson is not ashamed to let it ring. Writing about his spiritual attachment to the Southern Ocean, he recalled:

> Out here everything was simple and familiar. Effort held its reward in itself. Sham, pretense and bogus feelings, the all-too-common by-products of life ashore, had no place here. Out here,

> in the loneliness of the great oceans, assuredly dwelt God, not Jahveh with his jealousies and petty favouritism, but someone infinitely greater, impersonal but ever present. This was an instinctive feeling, rather than a conscious faith. . . .[8]

It was never a self-conscious faith, for any of the men or occasional women who sailed in the last tall ships out of love for them and for the sea; but it touched them all. Theirs was a spartan religion, requiring discipline, strength, courage, skill, and the kind of self-denial that allowed hard-worked adolescents to go without enough food and men not much older to forgo all the normal pleasures of life ashore. The seaman's calling, in the age of sail, was as much a vocation as a monk's, and required similar kinds of self-discipline.

The elements of the sailor's faith were harmony with the large and living forces of nature, independence from conflicting human codes, and skill sufficient to the task at hand. The liturgy consisted of courting speed at sea under sail, and all of the square-rigger sailors I have met or read about speak of the exhilaration that came with the sheer, natural speed of a windship, hurtling down a moving mountain with the wind caught, leaping, in its sails and moaning through its rigging. Like all religions, deep-water sail had its inarticulate faithful who followed the sea out of necessity, because it was the way things had always been done; it had its devotees, like Karlsson, or Wikar Andren, who spoke of going to sea in God's way; and it had its lip-servants and fellow-travelers, like the apprentices who put in their time and dreamed of dry motorships or the seamen who jumped ship in Australia, fed up with bad food and hard work for low pay.

Gustaf Erikson was one of the faithful, in his own profit-making way. After his apprenticeship and study, he had a seven-year career as a blue-water sailing ship captain and boasted about both his ships in letters home. In his second career, he became a shipowner and boasted about all his ships. He came up through the hawsepipe, in the seaman's expression that evokes an image of a dripping boy whose ambition is so desperate as to drive him up the anchor chain, through its pipe, and onto a ship's deck for a chance at a job, an opening for success.

In the summer of 1963, two generations after Gustaf Erikson had gone ashore to begin his shipowning career, Karl Andren decided that his way to become a shipowner would not lead through the hawsepipe. One day that summer, Andren was in the dusty, black hold of the motor vessel *Fidelio*, a Swedish car carrier that had hauled coal from Norfolk, Virginia, on its way back to Europe for another load of Volkswagens. The ship offloaded the coal in Aviles, a small port on the northern coast of Spain, and shoved her way out into the Bay of Biscay, where the long, flat, empty hull began to pound in the sharp, steep waves for which the Bay of Biscay is infamous. Andren, in his sixteenth summer and his second as a deckhand, was a junior seaman. He was ordered into the hold with a broom.

"I never forgot that," he said. "I had discovered girls and drinking in Aviles; I had a hangover and there I stood with a broom and a whole hold to clean in a Bay of Biscay storm. I loved shipping, but I said: 'What the hell am I doing here? Never again.' "

Young Karl Andren could afford to say "Never again." In one generation the opportunities available to able young Åland men had changed out of recognition, and there was no longer an unyielding need for any adventurous, ambitious Ålander to go to sea to find his fortune. Seagoing had also changed out of recognition in the fifty years between Gustaf Erikson's start and Karl Andren's first attempt to follow him. Romance and excitement at sea, as well as hardship and much of the danger, died with the sailing ships. A modern seaman, living in a one- or two-man cabin, with freshwater showers, more food than he can eat, an eight-hour workday at sea, and six months ashore each year, is immensely more comfortable than the fo'c'sle hands who had to bunk together, husband their drinking water, and beg for more food. He is also bored. Karl Andren hates being bored.

His decision to build a sailing ship twenty-odd years after the Bay of Biscay storm was carefully considered and weighed by all the modern means of market research. Sail, Andren said after he had made up his mind to gamble on being a pioneer, had struck him as a good, unexploited way to get into the overcrowded business of ocean cruises; a neat, new money-making angle, well thought through, and professionally analyzed. He resolved to build the first large modern sailing ship, he said emphatically, "to make money. Why else do you get up and go out the door in the morning?"

The king of the square-riggers would have approved.

3

CHAPTER

The New World

He left full of courage and garnered riches, far off in Greece, for his heirs.

—Viking runic stone at Veda

When he was fifteen, Karl Andren left his home islands and came to America by sea. He worked his passage across from the Baltic as a deckhand on a freighter carrying cars. His mother sailed as a passenger in the same ship, but they were denied the immigrant's gray dawn view of the Statue of Liberty standing at the head of New York harbor. The freighter went to Montreal. His father and older brother drove up to collect the boy who was still called Gösta and his mother. The youngest Andren first saw the New York skyline from Fort Lee, New Jersey, a town under the western end of the George Washington Bridge, where that broad steel ramp across the Hudson River to Manhattan begins. His older brother Anders, who knew his way around after a year in a bachelor apartment with their father in Fort Lee, first took Gösta across the bridge by bus and into the New York subways. Karl Gösta Andren was prepared to be unimpressed. After all, on one summer vacation he had been to London.

Anders Andren, who became a professor of oceanography at the University of Wisconsin, remembers their first trips together into New York as adventures to an odd and foreign land. As he remembers the excursions, they took the subway to Harlem, got out, and walked. They rode the underground trains to Greenwich Village and ambled for hours. They walked down Forty-second Street and were accosted by men and women, offering things they had never heard before.

"Learned about life," Anders remembers, when he talks about their first trips to New York. He recalls that the subway always smelled like a dry sewer to him. Not to Gösta.

"I rode downtown and walked. I rode uptown and walked," he remembers. "New York was really exciting. I walked around like a kid with his eyes this big. It was dirty; filthy, compared to where I had lived, but it looked great. Wide open. Thrilling."

Karl Andren recalls walking up Park Avenue and looking at the discreet façades of luxury apartment buildings, imagining the well-appointed life within. He remembers walking down Broadway, not Forty-second Street, and looking at the glossy still pictures of stars, not the freaks of urban sexual life.

For any traveler, some places are indifferent. Others never seem inviting. And some places appear to be open doors, inviting the visitor to come in, to stay and enjoy life there. New York was Gösta Andren's open door. He had found his place. He enrolled in the Fort Lee High School and, at fifteen, was tested and placed in the senior class.

"Finnish schools," he said, "were fairly aggressive."

"Talk about a melting pot!" Anders once exclaimed. He went to Fort Lee High School first. "Well, no; the difficulty for us was that it didn't mix at all. There were factions: a Jewish faction, an Italian faction, maybe even a black faction and a Puerto Rican faction. No Finnish faction."

Anders made it, though, and went off to Boston University with dreams of becoming a doctor. When it was Gösta's turn to finish school in Fort Lee he held his breath and went through high school fast, graduating on his Åland schedule, before his seventeenth birthday. Not having to pay too much attention at school suited him, because he was in a hurry to finish his education. School bored him, but then he bored easily, by his own admission. He liked the thrill of a new idea, any new idea, and was not enchanted by the effort of driving the new idea into a given order in the memory in preparation for an examination.

At Fort Lee High School, where he remembered the student body as "forty-nine per cent Jewish, forty-nine per cent Italian, and the rest was me," the youngest Andren changed his name. His teachers called him Gusta or Gawsta or Ghosta, so he announced to the family that he would adopt his first Christian name, left unused on an Ålands baptismal certificate until then. He would keep the name his family had always used, the name he had grown up with in Åland, within the family. In their new country, no one could spell Gösta unaided, let alone pronounce it properly. Henceforth, he said, he would be Karl, Karl G. Andren.

Taking a new name is a powerful way for a man to announce that he has become someone new. Karl's father had done it, too, dropping the family name Andersson to become Andren, when he was a young ship's officer in Åland. He had decided there were already too many Anderssons there.

Throughout the Åland years, Anders had been the student while Karl chafed at school, eager to be off doing things. After hearing a number of times that his youngest son had announced he would quit school to go to sea, Captain Andren hoped, in that spring of 1963, that Karl might stick with education long enough to enter and get through the New York Maritime Academy. The degree would at least start him on a seagoing career as a merchant officer. There were no parental constraints on his choice, however, and for that summer, Karl went to sea.

Captain Andren found a seaman's berth for his son and Karl signed on for the full summer. The sixteen-year-old worked on a Wallenius ship that plowed back and forth across the Atlantic carrying Volkswagens westward and coal to the east. He discovered, in that ship's dust-choked cargo hold off Aviles, that seagoing was not his calling. He came home and decided to start college as a physics major.

The question of college for both boys was resolved at a family council. Karl had visited Anders on the urban campus of Boston University and found the place too large for his liking. Anders was ill at ease there, too. He found it to be like going to school with a whole city at once. So mother, father, and the two boys settled together on Upsala, a small college named after the ancient university at Upsala, in Sweden, for both sons. The American Upsala was in East Orange, New Jersey, not thirty road miles south and west from the Andrens' new home, and the boys believed it would be comfortable to be that close to home and exciting to be that near New York.

Anders, by then, had found his vocation and was bound for a scientific career, mightily pleasing his father. He went through Upsala and on for his doctor's degree in oceanography. Karl had no such clear-cut calling. He only knew that he was an immigrant in love with New York, and dazzled by the opportunities that seemed to surround him in America.

At one time or another while he was growing up and becoming an American, Karl Andren started on the way to careers as physicist, petroleum geologist, shipping executive, and investment banker. He dreamed of becoming an archaeologist, a New York playboy and man about town, even a truck driver. On a northern island where only shipowners were rich, Karl had dreamed of being a shipowner. In the United States he saw that all sorts of people were rich and that the limited chances for shipowning were only one of many business opportunities. Still, his first dream seemed to pursue him.

As an undergraduate, he changed his major field of study from physics to geology, in order to get outside. But his highest marks came most easily in business courses, and he started riding the bus to a stockbroker's office in Newark. In a year, he tripled his initial investment of $100.

On his Saturday trips across the Hudson and into Manhattan, Andren had conjured up visions of himself as a young executive, single and free-spending, with a convertible, a downtown New York apartment, and a different date every night. But during his first year at graduate school, he married his father's secretary, a young Swedish woman named Louise Strom, who had dark blond hair and was tall enough to look any of the six-foot Andren men in the eye. Karl was twenty-two when he cut off his playboy options. He has a one-line explanation. "When I see a good thing, I grab it."

Having grabbed it, Andren needed a job. After graduating from Upsala with a bachelor of science degree in geology, he had followed a graduate program at Pennsylvania State University that combined geology and business. It was pointed toward employment in the oil business, and still his vocation dogged him. His master's thesis was entitled "Ocean Transport of Liquefied Natural Gas." He defended it on a Friday and went to work on Wall Street the following Monday, analyzing oil stocks. He had sent his résumé to every brokerage house he found in the Manhattan Yellow Pages, and had settled on Dominick and Dominick. The year was 1969 and share trading on the New York stock markets was booming. After inflation caught up with the boom and burned it up, the years of Andren's start in the financial world were known, with a certain nostalgia, as the "go-go years."

"They were go-go, all right," Andren recalled later, with relish. "Go and get it. Go and do it, do the deal."

"For some reason, I'm a deal-maker," Andren said. "I love it. It's fun. But I don't like running any company from day to day. I like to have the idea, find the elements, put them together in a deal, then look for another."

This was a description of himself as entrepreneur, born on his feet and running at the peak of the stock market boom that accompanied the American war in Vietnam like a brassy and distracting obbligato. It was one of several descriptions of himself that Andren made, then held up to look at and discuss, the first time we met at length to talk about his life.

It was July in New York, the season in that city when the population is stunned and impatient; stunned by the heat and impatient with each other. In July and August, if one walks westward off the geological spine of the island, away from the cars and trucks caught snarling at each other in the midtown grid of streets between Third and Eighth Avenues and toward the Manhattan bank of the Hudson River, one comes eventually into a cool flow of air from the river, tentative at first and then more pronounced. It does not do to rush toward the Hudson in a taxi. The sense of coolness will not penetrate the cab. And perhaps it is only a sense of coolness, not truly cooler air, but a sense that rises as one drops toward the water and the river horizon grows. Perhaps it is a sense that comes with turning back toward the sea in one of the great natural harbors of the world.

The farther west one goes in July, the cooler the air seems to be, until, at the riverbank end of Forty-second Street, one comes to Circle Line Plaza. The plaza is no more than a wide place in Twelfth Avenue, with turning space for tour buses and room for a rank of waiting taxis. Beyond the stained asphalt of Circle Line Plaza stands the façade of the city's old Pier 83, refaced not too long ago with tiles in the shade of institutional green that was once popular for hospital waiting rooms and public lavatories. It is a two-story front, at the river's edge, with ticket offices on the ground floor and Venetian-blinded windows above. The river floats, gray-green and disembodied, behind the galvanized mesh of eight-foot cyclone fencing.

CIRCLE LINE SIGHTSEEING YACHTS, the free-standing steel letters of a sign in red proclaim above the building. AMERICA'S FAVORITE BOAT RIDE. The sightseeing yachts, sturdy double-decker excursion boats with rows of slatted wooden benches above and below and polished brass fittings at their pilot houses, rub their flanks against Pier 83 beyond the fence. In July, people who are outward bound on America's favorite boat ride line up to talk through a grille let into safety glass at the ticket booth.

When he bought Circle Line and its affiliated boat tour operations in 1981, Karl Andren moved his New York office to the green Circle Line building at Circle Line Plaza. He was president, and figured as principal owner, but his office seemed to be an anteroom to the wood-paneled suite next door, belonging to the chairman of the board, the founder and former owner of Circle Line. The chairman had views south over downtown Manhattan from his corner windows, and west over the river to the Palisades that rise beyond it.

Andren's windows faced across Twelfth Avenue to the blank façade of a former hotel, purchased by the Chinese government to house its New York consulate staff. Like any other New York office worker,

Andren had a view of a dirty wall and a noisy street below it. The outside windows made one wall of his office. Two other walls were closely hung with two marine oil paintings and the photographs of a self-made man's career: a tank farm, a tugboat, his first vessel, the fuel barge *Joan K.*, and Karl grinning at the launching of the tug *Karl G. Andren.* The fourth wall of the office was a clear glass partition between Andren and one large room filled with desks for the Circle Line staff. Andren's glass cell had once been the bookkeeper's pen. He assigned the only other corner office in the building, at the water's edge above the river and the tour boats, to his executive officer, his personal right-hand man.

In effect, Andren had installed himself in the middle of the Circle Line office floor. When he arrived for our appointment, he did not close his door. I was told he never had. It is not that he wanted to watch each employee endlessly. He grew up impatient with detail and did not want to supervise, in any company, the details of tickets and tow ropes and toilet paper. He wanted to be free to deal, and his eagerness to deal led him to make his own telephone calls and, apparently, to ignore some of the trappings of American entrepreneurial style. He calls his open, all-cards-face-up-on-the-table approach to business a Scandinavian trait and sounds proud when he says it. The open glass office might be part of that approach. From that office, one cannot see Andren's gray Mercedes coupe, equipped with a telephone and leather-upholstered seats and parked in his marked space next to the door onto the Circle Line parking lot.

Andren came through the door like a puff of wind. When he moves, he stirs air. He wears investment banker suits in blue, with or without pinstripes, and patterned gray, and he was taking off his jacket as he came in. His hair is the color of polished brass, and heavy. He pushed it off his forehead, filled a cigarette case with unfiltered Pall Malls from the old red package, lit one, and started.

Ideas fascinate Andren. When he comes across a new one, he does not poke tentatively at it or roll it slowly around in his mind. He jumps to his feet and starts pursuing the idea with words and gestures, talking it out and shaping it with his hands in the air. The ideas were all familiar to him when we started talking. He recalled himself as a boy, in love with his island past but possessed by an ancestral ambition. We looked together at himself as an immigrant, in love with New York City. When we came, in time, to Andren as an entrepreneur in love with deals, he stood up and and started walking in the little glass-walled office.

For an idea man, he tells a story well. There was the one about his start in shipowning, after he had put in three years at Dominick and Dominick. He had left financial analysis behind quickly to become a bloodhound in corporate finance, sniffing out companies ripe to sell to other companies.

"It was 1974," Andren said. "I was having fun on the Street, making deals, but I came across a little company and finally I saw the picture. I saw the way to get back into shipping.

"The company was ripe for a buy-out. The owner was in his eighties and he had no children. It was called Manhattan Oil Transportation, Inc., and the price was one point seven million dollars. The only question was: Where was Karl Andren going to get one million seven?"

He went to Jacob Stolt-Nielsen, Jr., a shipping magnate from a more autocratic background, but another man who had made himself in his own image. The Stolt-Nielsens had been shipowners in Norway for three generations when they sent twenty-two-year-old Jacob to New York in 1954 to learn more of the trade. On his own in the United States, the young Stolt-Nielsen began to build a fleet of his own.

With American partners, he built one ship, then another. His new ships, which carried several chemicals in separate holds, were called parcel tankers. They became a trend. Jacob Stolt-Nielsen says without hesitation that he started the trend. One brief business biography suggests that less than ten years after he commissioned his first parcel tanker, Stolt-Nielsen bought control of his family's old firm in Norway.

When Andren first approached him, the Stolt-Nielsen empire included a multi-ocean fleet of tankers, tank storage terminals on four continents, North Sea oilfield maintenance companies, and an aquaculture conglomerate. Once, while bloodhounding on Wall Street, Karl Andren had tried to get Flying Tigers to buy out Stolt-Nielsen, but the Norwegian did not hold it against him. He recognized the pushing touch of another entrepreneur.

"He's bright, he's ambitious, and he has a nose for business," Stolt-Nielsen said of Andren. He was not surprised when the younger man, almost fifteen years his junior, came to him for financial backing. As Andren remembers the deal:

"I offered him a fifty-fifty split, without knowing where in the hell I was going to get my fifty percent. He took eighty percent and lent me the money for my twenty. And, boom, boom, boom. That was it. I was back in shipping."

Then there was Andren's story about Chemlink, Inc., the first company Andren started from scratch. It was founded to carry separate chemicals in barges on American waterways and grew fast from 1977 through 1980. Thereafter, the story was short and sad.

"The charter market started to fall, so I wanted to go to long-term charters and lock some rates in," Andren said. "The president didn't. We disagreed and that's not good for a partnership, so I sold our shares to him; mine and Jacob's. He stuck to short-term charters and they went broke."

And there was the success story of United Tank Containers, a company that built, sold, and traded tanks surrounded by rectangular steel frames that could carry any liquid anywhere container ships and flatbed trucks went.

"There's our terminal in Chicago," Andren said, pointing to the framed photograph of light-colored tanks by a flat lake shore. "It cost five million dollars. I put up ten bucks. That's what they call leverage."

"Finally, I had found a business I could grow in and I was having a hell of a good time," Andren recalled.

United Tank Containers, started just after Chemlink, grew well, while Andren also presided, in his own liberally delegating way, over Manhattan Oil Transportation and another tug and barge company he had bought on the coast of the Gulf of Mexico. With three businesses running in 1978, Andren started a long and complicated courtship of the original five owners of Circle Line. He hit it off directly with the founder, a courtly Irishman from Queens who was well connected in New York politics. But there were other backers and their relatives, five families in all, and many political connections to consider and appease. The documents for the 1981 final closing on that transaction sit on a Circle Line bookshelf, in a folio volume almost 6 inches thick bound in leather. Jacob Stolt-Nielsen came in on the deal for forty percent, and he and Andren set up a holding company together. Andren's stories were getting longer and more complex.

In those swift, acquisitive years of his, other businessmen began telling stories about Andren.

"You have to know that Karl is not a one-iron man," a ship broker in New York said. "He always has more than one iron in the fire."

As a negotiating meeting opened one morning in a New York conference room, a lawyer seated on the opposite side of the table announced: "Here comes Karl Andren again. He wants to buy the whole world with no money down."

Karl told that story on himself, and laughed at the punch line.

Andren was just one of a shoal of young Wall Street apprentices who grew up in the go-go years and swam out into the business world with what then seemed a new financial technique, buying companies without any money of their own. Andren was not even the most spectacular practitioner of the technique of buying something real with something imagined: credit. He bought with borrowed money that steadily had to be paid back and so just as steadily held down the profit he might have made, and he did not use the far-fetched credit instruments that later came into fashion, the bonds the dealers who sold them immediately called "junk." Andren was not a financial magician creating illusions and selling them. He was building real companies in a business that he knew, with Stolt-Nielsen, a very rich backer with a proven entrepreneur's nose, as his model and guide.

No one gets truly rich buying something for nothing, or real things like tugs and tanks and barges with borrowed money, unless someone else buys what one has bought for much more than one paid. The payoff in the debt game, as millions of American homeowners discovered in the same, inflationary years, comes only when one sells in a steeply rising market to a buyer with some cash. Andren's payoff came late in 1982 when the European oil giant, British Petroleum, and Jacob Stolt-Nielsen bought his United Tank Containers.

"They walked in and said: 'Karl, we'll give you five and a half million.' I said: 'Well, I'll have to think about that.' "

That is the way Andren remembers the meeting that gave him his own stake.

"Of course, I was ready to jump up and shout, but I had to show some restraint," he said. "I sold, as soon as it looked right, and I was left with money in the bank. I went back to the drawing board.

"That's when I first started to look at the cruise business," he said. However, his business analysis of the cruises Americans take on converted ocean liners or cruise ships built to look like them discouraged him. So did the price of the first passenger cruise liner he looked at. There were too many ships, Andren decided, and very little difference among them. The market was crowded and too expensive for a newcomer. He knew that from everything he had ever heard about shipping.

"Shipping is a lousy, small-margin business if you're a traditional shipowner with some hulls to charter," he says. "Everybody else has hulls to charter, too, okay? You have to find something new, somewhere to start, your own niche in the market. That's when I started thinking about sail."

The heat had gone from the afternoon when Andren reached the end of his string of stories about the deals that had given him his start. The July sun hung in a haze to the south and west over the tanker terminals in Bayonne and the container piers in Port Newark that had supplanted the port of New York. The dingy white brick of the converted hotel across Twelfth Avenue no longer appeared to glow with reflected heat. Andren sat down behind his desk in his shirtsleeves.

"I had always heard about sail, growing up," he said. "I knew it. It was, after all, in my blood."

It was late in 1982 when Andren paused to listen to his blood. He was thirty-six. He had made deals and money. He owned a house in the New York suburb of Greenwich, Connecticut, where the rich enjoy being discreet and many well-to-do Scandinavians with business in New York had settled before him. Stolt-Nielsen lived there and had built his world headquarters in Greenwich, on a sandy height by the shore of Long Island Sound. Still, although he never said it, Andren had been for years an extension of Jacob Stolt-Nielsen.

Stolt-Nielsen had developed subdivided oceangoing tankers for chemicals. With the Norwegian's backing, Andren built barges divided to carry several different liquid cargoes at once. Stolt-Nielsen diversified into tank storage terminals; so did Andren. A man's memory reflects something of events and something of himself. Andren, on that long July afternoon in his office, spoke of Stolt-Nielsen as a benefactor, a pioneer and an optimist always ready to go ahead on a new Andren project. Stolt-Nielsen recalled his first meetings with Andren, years after they had happened, saying: "We did some business together while he was at Dominick and Dominick. Later he worked here."

"No," he added, correcting himself. "No, he never worked for me. He has always been the promoter, from the start, and I his backer."

After British Petroleum, as part of a larger deal with Stolt-Nielsen, had bought United Tank Containers, Andren had money in the bank and time to plan a venture that might be his own. He wanted to think out something that, like Stolt-Nielsen's first divided tanker hold, would be wholly new and also needed.

"Success in business is always timing," Andren said. His voice was quieter than it had been, his manner less intense. Outside, the raucous afternoon rush hour on Twelfth Avenue had spent itself. "To make real money, you've got to be the first guy on the market with something new."

Andren decided then, in October 1982, that his novelty would be something very old made new. He chose to become a full-fledged oceangoing shipowner by buying or building a sailing cruise ship.

He was silent for slightly longer than was normal. Then he added: "Pioneers often get screwed, though, and the second guy in makes the money."

4

CHAPTER

The Dream Ship

I suspect that not before a case can be made out, on solid and practical economic grounds for the use of wind propulsion for some particular function, will any shipowner do more than keep an eye on the developments.

—Prince Philip, Duke of Edinburgh,
Royal Institution of Naval Architects'
Symposium on Wind Propulsion for Commercial Ships
London, 1980

Sail was not a silly choice for a cruise ship. Setting aside the deep appeal of going to sea gently and in silence, there were solid business reasons in favor of developing passenger ships with sails for ocean cruises. And in business, business reasons are reputed to be the only ones that count.

First, the idea of using sails on a new ship to take passengers on short, leisurely voyages promised an opportunity to blend romance and luxury, at a time when both were fading from conventional cruises—those crossings to nowhere on converted passenger liners, or on new motorships built to look like transatlantic liners. A sailing cruise liner would look and feel different and might be very practical.

The idea was not as new as Karl Andren first thought. Passenger steamers began the business of cruising for pleasure in 1844, but in 1884 the square rigger *Tyburnia* sailed with passengers only on a round trip cruise from England to the Caribbean.[1] The fare was a guinea per day, and included food and wine. On that trip, her only cruise, the fare also included a slow sail past the bellowing cannon of a fort on Madeira and interrogation by suspicious customs agents in New York. Neither the Portuguese governor nor the New York customs men could believe that the ship carried only pleasure-seeking passengers. However, by sailing in the trade winds to islands in the Caribbean, *Tyburnia* set the precedent for most subsequent cruises. British steamship companies had been carrying cruise passengers in the Mediterranean, but by

1895 the same companies had added pleasure cruises to "the West India Islands."[2]

Cruise passengers, like working sailors, prefer itineraries that take them to ports and islands in the trade winds, where the sea is blue, and surf washes gently onto beaches of white sand on islands full of fruit trees and tropical flowers. Trade wind weather is Hawaiian weather, Tahitian weather, the stuff of dreams. Over the trade wind belts, long stretches of ocean ten to fifteen degrees of latitude wide on both sides of the equator in the Atlantic and the Pacific, the breezes blow steadily from the east and inward toward the middle of the globe. The wind almost always blows and is almost never too strong. Any blue-water sailor who has been in the trades might gladly spend the rest of his life there, riding the long, blue ocean swells and counting clouds, waiting for the sun to set.

Life under sail in the trade winds is usually so blissfully uneventful that sunset becomes the most dramatic moment in the day. Young Åland seamen organized boxing tournaments on board their barks to stay tough while the ships rolled through the trades. The wind takes the sting from subtropical sunlight there and, if his ship is happy and well-found, a sailor's sense of well-being rises until it fills him to the throat, and leaves him smiling silently through every watch on deck. Sleep is like a long lullaby, because the ship makes only the most soothing of noises.

Columbus rode the northeast trade winds to his new world. Magellan crossed the Pacific from east to west using first the southeast trades, then, on the other side of the hot, fussy, and frustrating weather at the equator, the northeast trades. The nineteenth-century crews of long-haul sailing freighters saved their best canvas for the battles of the high latitudes, above thirty-five degrees north and south. In the gentle, steady trade winds they set old sails, soft and patched, and let the unvarying wind fill them for days and nights on end. So, for a modern cruise ship owner, sailing in the trade winds promised theoretical benefits in operating costs. The wind is free. Marine diesel fuel in 1980 had risen in price from $35 to $310 per ton in the seven years following the first Arab oil embargo, which shocked the industrial world in 1973.

In the early months of 1973, winter months in the developed Western world, the oil shortage that had seemed inevitable someday suddenly arrived ahead of schedule. In the United States, once omnipotent automobiles crept like puppies on their bellies into the long lines that formed wherever gasoline was sold.

After the sudden shortage of oil, there came an explosion of practical enthusiasm among marine designers and engineers who believed in using the power of the wind as part of a slow readjustment of human technology to less wasteful presumptions about the resources of the earth. The few who had worked, alone, at designs and projections for windships hoped that the tenfold increase in fuel cost might make new windships seem not only morally good, but also useful and financially practical.[3] The Organization of Petroleum Exporting Countries began to make their arguments to shipowners for them.

By the time Karl Andren began dreaming about sailing ships, in 1982, there was already floating proof of a prize waiting for shipowners who were willing to rig their ships for sail. A small Japanese coastwise tanker, launched in the autumn of 1980, had shown that savings of ten percent in fuel cost were possible if her two stubby sails were used to help the ship's main engine along, and then only when the wind was fair. The tanker, *Shin Aitoku Maru,* was an idea ship and a bit of an ugly duckling, but she worked. She hauled her cargoes steadily, her sails paid for themselves and saved some fuel money, and, since they were set and furled by machinery, the ship did not require extra sail-handling crew. In fact, the owners at Aitoku Line discovered, the tanker's sails steadied the ship's roll so much in heavy seas that one of the six crewmen aboard found he could master his chronic seasickness when the sails were set.

From the technical point of view, cruise ships were ideal vehicles on which to try modern sail propulsion systems. Cargo ships were much more demanding. The passengers on cruise ships make a light, easily-stowed cargo that pays very high freight, per ton, and is even appreciative. Cargo capacity does not determine the hull form of a cruise liner, so a passenger hull can be drawn long, deep, and lean enough to carry sail and develop speed. Cruise ports are generally open and easy to get into, without low bridges or overhanging buildings that would snag the masts of a sailing ship. A cruise ship needs none of the cranes, conveyor belts, or hose gantries that swing out over container ships, bulk freighters, and tankers to mechanize their loading and unloading, so that masts for sails are not, on cruise ships, a troublesome interference.

Modern commercial ships are designed to carry specific cargoes and to fit the machinery-intensive ports where they load and discharge these cargoes. Container ships, with loaded truck trailer vans stacked like outsized building blocks in their holds and in overhanging piles on deck, must go alongside docks at special terminals. Broad steel cranes reach out over them to unstack the containers. Masts and sails would forever be in the way. In fact, the short steel masts for *Shin Aitoku Maru*'s two half-metal, half-cloth sails that unfolded to the wind like the flaps on airplane wings[4] had to be placed at the two ends of the ship, in order to leave the low sweep of her tank deck free for the gantries that lower huge hoses onto the tank outlets.

The neat match between cruising passengers and sail propulsion had occurred to a number of naval architects who thought about bringing back sail, but most of the wind propulsion theorists wanted to build sailing cargo ships. They thought such ships more serious than cruise liners, and as businessmen, they were right. Airliners now lift the travelers that ships once carried to Capetown and Sydney, San Francisco, Bombay, Buenos Aires, and Hong Kong. Passenger ships make up only one percent of all the new ships launched each year on the world's seas.

However, by 1980, when marine fuel prices fluttered downward for the first time in seven years, none of the designers outside Japan's tax-subsidized program to develop commercial sail-assisted ships[5] had been able to convince any shipowner to build any kind of modern windship on a large scale. The return of commercial sail, which had at first seemed so inevitable to the windship designers, had been delayed by caution and conservation. Shipowners and seamen have always, as a body, been oak-ribbed professional conservatives. As a rule, they build only what already works. Steam engines only wholly replaced sails at sea some eighty years after their first successful trials. But after only seven years, high fuel prices, the sharpest spur for shipowners to try sails, or spinning rotors or upright wings, began to drop before new windships needed to be tried.

Some of the advocates of windpower turned almost querulous at the Symposium on Wind Propulsion of Commercial Ships in London, late in 1980. Although many of those there had met to discuss the future of windships in 1975 and again in 1976, there was no tangible sign that the world outside was paying serious attention to their ideas. The exchanges between engineers who had developed competing computer models of how large windships would work and had sailed them on a sea of electronic projections were snappish in London. Some of the question periods following papers were marked by the kind of ironic asperity used by scientists who know one another's ideas too well.

One British naval engineer lamented that only talking about ideas for commercial sail made it impossible to "distinguish genius from wishful thinking."[6]

A German engineer, representing the Hamburg Institut für Schiffbau, where serious design and wind-tunnel testing of commercial sailing rigs had begun in 1957, concluded his paper soberly by saying: "The technical possibilities have significantly increased since the decline of commercial sailing sixty years ago. Further development prospects are in sight. At the same time, we have allowed ourselves to become accustomed to the waste and pollution of irreplaceable natural resources. To make use of progress for a complete technical change will only be possible if we are willing to change our values."[7]

In 1980, then, when windpower designers assembled for the third time, there were already designs for sailing bulk carriers, modern square-riggers tested in computers and wind tunnels, on drawing boards in Australia, Germany, Great Britain, the United States, and Scandinavian countries. There were designs for ships with upright airplane wings on deck, and windmills, and spinning rotors. There was even a sketchy design for huge kites on cables to pull submarines. But there were still no shipbuilding orders for these designs. Two years later, when Karl Andren began looking for sailing cruise ships, he did not even consider the new and technologically resplendent designs of the windship engineers.

When he thought of sail, what Andren had in mind was the *Pommern,* the great black bark in Mariehamn harbor, or something like her. For years he had overheard men his father's age talk about putting *Pommern* back to sea. So, when the idea of a sailing cruise ship caught him, Andren thought first of a ship that would sail in the grand old way, and then of the passengers that might pay to go to sea that way. There would have to be cabins aboard, with basic hotel amenities, Andren thought, but he also believed there would be room on the ship he had in mind for a dormitory, a large communal cabin like the long, open space under the poop deck where cadets in sail have swung their hammocks on training ships for a century. And the cruise passengers, some of them, at least, would surely want to help with the sails occasionally, as passengers always had on the Cape Horners.

Gustaf Erikson, the Åland shipowner, had tried the idea. He had put a dance orchestra aboard *L'Avenir,* one of his grain-carrying barks, and partitioned the 'tween deck into cabins. He set her to carrying cruise passengers in the Baltic for the summers of 1935 and 1936 and ordered a tug to follow her and tow her through calms. Andren did not know about Erikson's attempt to make a cruise ship out of one of his sailing workhorses, but, just as Erikson certainly would have in his place, Andren initially looked for an old, used sailing ship that no one else wanted. There were none lying abandoned in near-working order, as there had been in Erikson's day. Almost all of those that remained at sea commercially, large old yachts and converted fishing and trading schooners, were already in the cruise business. Andren, the entrepreneur, found a way to look at their business figures and his interest in the idea quickened. On paper, the financial results of some sailing cruises, where passengers and crew went barefoot on wooden decks and worked together at sea, looked tempting. The boats, however, were too old and too small for what Andren had in mind.

Not wanting to appear too interested in a sailing operation that he knew was for sale, Andren sent his retired father and his right-hand man, a former merchant marine officer with a master's degree in business administration, to research sailing cruises. In selecting his spies, Andren chose two people with natural disguises. Captain Wikar Andren, then sixty-seven years old, was recently retired. Thomas Franklin Heinan, nearly thirty-eight, was of an age to take a first or second honeymoon on a sailing vessel in the Caribbean moonlight. They fit exactly the cruise salesman's description of a typical passenger list, in those years, for cruise ships catering to Americans. Among themselves, travel agents and cruise salesmen called their most likely passengers "the newlywed and the nearly dead."

Tom Heinan and Captain Andren were not honeymooners. They watched their cruises with the eyes of experienced seamen, and brought back lists of difficulties and drawbacks, most of them related to the age of the vessels in which they sailed.

"In their ad copy, the outfit said you could sleep on deck, under the stars," Heinan said, years later, of his yacht cruise. "It wasn't a matter of choice. The air conditioning didn't work. You had to sleep on deck."

Wikar Andren found it pleasant, but sad, to go to sea under sail again. The aging, yacht-built bark he cruised aboard seemed worn and fragile to him. "They couldn't drive her hard at all," he said.

There were legal and operational disadvantages to sailing old ships for modern cruise passengers: the cost of adequate insurance was high, U.S. Coast Guard certification would be difficult, and so would national registration for old wooden vessels. The headaches he could foresee caused Andren to give up the Erikson method of acquiring a sailing ship. He was relieved to return to the idea of building a new vessel that would seem traditional. His first, broad specifications, drawn up with Heinan in 1983, would have made a spartan ship. Following Andren's original idea, the one he had grown up with, she was to be a working sailing ship of traditional rig and traditional appearance, 250 feet long, with 100 cabins, each 8 feet broad by 12 feet deep. Ten feet by 12 makes a small bedroom for two Americans. There was to be a dormitory, too, and a common dining room for simple fare, cafeteria style. The ship, Andren and Heinan thought, would supply a better barefoot cruise. They thought of it then as a kind of Club Med afloat.

In the summer of 1983, after his cruise, Heinan started sketching profiles and plans for the deck and rig. Andren had looked at the only design for a modern sailing cruise ship then being offered to shipowners, a 297-foot-long schooner for 176 passengers which a Spanish shipyard proposed to build for $12.5 million. The shipyard, Astilleros y Talleres Celaya, S.A., in Bilbao, was one of only four in the world with recent experience in building traditional sailing ships. Since 1968, it had delivered square-rigged sail training ships to Colombia and Ecuador. However, Andren passed up the design. He wanted, then, something that looked more traditional and offered more passenger space. As he thought his way toward the ship he wanted to build, Andren was unaware that Finland's largest shipyard had a sailing cruise ship design, tested and developed to the working model stage, but no one to sell it to.

The Wärtsila shipyard in Helsinki has the heft and the feel of an institution. In a city of granite and monumental cement, with gray and often grandly oversized buildings and statues, Wärtsila's corporate and design offices are as massive as the climate and company solidity demand. The building even has doors like a bank's, a double, swinging set built of tempered glass and naval bronze that has been covered by a brown patina, except at the handles, which are polished by the palms of many hands every day. The offices stacked in the building above those doors, behind partitions of Formica in neutral tones, look either like well-lit mockups of functional office designs, or like greenhouses.

The naval designers assigned to the company think tank work in one of the greenhouses, with their ideas framed in pictures hanging on the walls behind the indoor plants. Their leader is a tall, quiet naval architect and cruising sailor named Kai Levander. The sailing cruise ship was his particular passion. He called it the Wärtsila Windcruiser.

For Levander, the Windcruiser was the most pointed proof of a thesis he had sold to the Wärtsila board of directors six years earlier: to sell its designs, a shipyard has to think for shipowners.

"No one had ever asked for a sailing cruise ship," he said. "No one thought one would work."

Even within the company, there had been skeptics. When he had first taken the idea before the Wärtsila board, Levander reached past their polite resistance to a memory held by all, but filed as ancient.

He showed one sketch of the Windcruiser, another of the *Nina,* Columbus's caravel with its three tall triangular sails.

"This is our rig," he said. "It got Columbus across the Atlantic. It will do."[8]

It might well do, but, three years after the board presentation, it had not yet sold. The shipping business had been so battered everywhere by high fuel prices, low freight rates, and cutthroat competition that very few shipowners were willing to try anything new. What Levander had was new. He had designed and tested, in tank and wind tunnel, a four-masted sailing cruise ship 322 feet long with luxury cabins for 130 passengers.

Other ideas from the Levander think tank were bought and built at the Wärtsila yard in those difficult years. P & O Lines built the cruise ship *Royal Princess* following the yard's design for a large passenger ship with all outside cabins. A Norwegian shipowner built Levander's idea for a small luxury liner for cruises like those of a large, oceangoing motor yacht, and called her *Sea Goddess.* But the first client for his windship had withdrawn and the second had gone bankrupt. Both had been large, solid shipping companies with cruise line experience. Still, Levander remained sure that his design would work and make money. That, he knew, was the only convincing reason to build a new ship.

"We went to all those nice conferences about sail power and told them sailing is a way of attracting people to a cruise," Levander recalled. "Basically, you had the square-rigger people who were there for the romance of sailing and the people who were there because they knew the aerodynamics of sailing inside out. We were not very popular with any of those people because we said openly that we were proposing a sailing rig not to save energy but to attract people."

It was an approach suited to this age and Levander knew it. He was not trying to sell anyone an anachronism. He had spent years building a computer model of the cruise market, the only market left for the new passenger ships that Wärtsila builds in Helsinki. He concluded that the cruise business was not a shipping business but a hotel and tourism industry. His windship was designed to please passengers, not theorists or romantics. The product, a modern marketing man might say, was wholly market-driven, meaning that the shipbuilder in Levander had looked beyond his eventual client to the real marketplace and had drafted something that would sell there. He wanted the windship to be built.

One of the testier participants at one of the conferences Levander had attended said: "Short of the collapse of civilization, there will never be a time when wind propulsion is inevitable."[9] The Finnish naval architect, an independent-minded corporate creature, appeared to have accepted that judgment. When I met him in Helsinki, Levander spent a dark winter afternoon and evening painstakingly laying out all the details of his market-driven design process. The central theme of that session was that his windship was not a dream but a workable, unobjectionable, and practical approach to the business problem of getting more people to take cruises. There had not been a great deal of invention involved, he insisted. The plan for the ship's sailing rig, a schooner with staysails only, that is, one triangular sail ahead of each mast and none behind any mast, had originally come from Dick Carter, an American naval architect and yacht designer who had used the rig on ocean racing yachts for single-handed sailors. It was simple and easy to handle. It looked right and that was important, Levander said, to lure passengers. The ship's sails were, in a sense, symbolic billboards advertising a new attraction.

The Wärtsila think tank had contributed new designs for the mechanisms that would handle sails, Levander said, but they mounted their sail-control devices on booms like cranes swinging from pivots on deck, an idea that had been around naval design since the 1920s. They also worked out a way to keep the hull from sliding away from the wind, under sail, without a full, sailboat-style keel, but their way was a scaling up of an idea that had already worked well in cruising sailboats. He emphasized that they had only worked continuously on details while under contract to a potential client. The clients, one after another, had paid for the development work in advance.

By early evening he had opened seven brightly colored plastic cages full of files, unfolded three stacks of plans, spread out two carefully labeled boxes of pictures, and dipped into the blue-bound degree thesis of a naval architect, which detailed the computer program that evaluated the windship's performance. On the varnished birch table in front of us there were also two mugs for tea and a wood box no taller than the mugs. Inside the box was a scale model of a carpeted passenger cabin, just big enough to stand a matchbox up in, with two portholes, two armchairs, wood paneling, and two bunks with patterned bedspreads. Figuratively, at least, it seemed that all of the cards were on that table. I asked Levander whether, business aside, he thought the rig would sail.

He took out of his wallet a picture of a cruising sailboat, her white hull moored close to granite boulders and fir trees, near the shore of a blue Baltic cove. She had a red boottop, for a stripe of color at the waterline, and two masts of exactly equal height, two rolled staysails, and two booms that pivoted on deck like cranes. The boat was a floating replica of the rig we had seen grow, all afternoon, in the plans on the table. Levander smiled.

"That is the first Wärtsila Windcruiser," he said. "I converted my own boat."

Levander, the entrepreneurial understudy, and Andren, the entrepreneur, first met after three other shipowners had given up on the Windcruiser. Karl had heard about the design, and at the end of a family summer vacation trip to the Finnish lakes, he went to Wärtsila and looked at it. "It looked like a bathtub with sails on it," Andren said.

"We were initially designing for Scandinavian companies," Levander said, defensively. "We used modern Scandinavian design. The Americans didn't like it."

Still, as Andren's New York ship broker Sven Hansen said later: "They spoke the same language, so to speak."

The two Finns had not only ancestry and language in common, and Hansen, who was Swedish, knew it. Andren and Levander also shared a sharp but well-contained sense of pride and a conviction that sail would work, which was based on a real grasp of the market for ocean cruises. And Wärtsila needed a client. Andren needed a ship. It was almost business at first sight.

There was another cruising windship in the works, though. At Andren's request, Frank MacLear, a New York naval architect who was also an advocate of commercial sailing ships, had been working over Tom Heinan's sketches. Early in 1984, MacLear delivered his design for a 320-foot-long barkentine, with a long, lovely black hull reminiscent of the Vanderbilt steam yacht *Corsair*, and square sails on the foremost of her three masts.

"The square sails were Tom Heinan's idea," MacLear says. "They were on, then off, then on again. What did not change was the traditional shape. We had to get the traditional shape, even though we didn't need it for stability." The design showed luxury cabins for about 150 passengers, and also, in deference to Karl, large cabins with domitory accommodations.

Sven Hansen did not like what he called "the better barefoot idea, with passengers working the sails and that sort of thing." Andren did not like all of what he read in the sixty pages of MacLear's specifications, which had cost $50,000. He filed that design in January, the same month it was delivered, and flew to Helsinki. There he made a deal with Wärtsila.

Andren wanted Wärtsila to redesign the Windcruiser so it would look more like his idea of a sailing ship. They asked for $25,000 for the design work. He said that if they wanted to be paid to redesign a ship that might well be built in their yard, he would put the final specifications out for competitive bidding. Wärtsila wanted the right to bid and royalties for their design if they lost. So it was set, and through the Finnish and New York winters, Kai Levander's crew reworked their ship to the size and shape and specifications supplied by Karl Andren, Sven Hansen, and Tom Heinan. Hansen, the most experienced sailor, urged them to add more sail area to the four bare staysails on the original design so she would look more like a ship and less like an experiment.

Eventually, Wärtsila added a bowsprit, with another triangular sail, a jib that Hansen had suggested, to set from it. Andren had the yard draftsmen draw in a normal, boomed sail behind the aftermost mast. With two sails set from it, that mast taken alone looked like the rig of a conventional, sloop-rigged sailboat. What set the ship apart was her size and the three masts in front of the conventional one. Using sea terms from the days of the four-masted barks, the masts from bow to stern would have been called the foremast, the mainmast, the mizzen, and the jigger. The sail on the last mast aft would have been called a spanker. For the sake of simplicity, the prospective owners called the mast and its new sail the mizzen and the name stuck.

Andren changed the lines of the hull he had called a bathtub. The main deck line in Levander's design drooped toward bow and stern from a high point amidships, where a glassed-in wheelhouse perched like the upper deck cockpit in a jumbo jet. The owner insisted on the classic deck line of ships: a gentle curving line that rises to the bow and to the stern. The line is called the sheer and looks like the long trough between ocean waves. At its most beautiful, it is a subtle and compound curve of a kind that was built by eye as early as 200 B.C. by Viking shipwrights. Andren approved a sheer line that finished on a long, lifting curve which flattened into the straight, aspiring line of the bowsprit. That line, intersecting a concave curve rising from the waterline along the cutwater, made what is called a clipper bow.

The result of the redesign was a three-quarter-inch-thick bid book, the size of a good paperback edition, bound in light blue and labeled:

Windcruiser for Circle Line
Project 1289
Wärtsila

Helsinki Shipyard
April 25, 1984

The bid book looked like an instruction manual. It amounted to no more than lists of generalities about speed, size and rigging, and specific descriptions of parts and machinery. Taken together, the lists described Andren's sailing passenger liner, but they did not tell anyone how to build it.

"We wrote it together," Andren said of that book, and the thought pleased him. The claim is true and it illustrates Andren's entrepreneurial style. He accomplishes more than he might be capable of doing alone by adopting the ideas of others without blinking if he likes them. Sometimes he adopts the people themselves, and makes them extensions of himself. Andren does not like details; Tom Heinan thrives on them. So Heinan, whose ambition had reached beyond the old Liberty ships converted to carry coal, where he started his seagoing career, eventually became the second man in Andren's two-man holding company.

"He's my operations officer, my engineer, my lawyer. He is the most versatile guy I know," Andren says.

Andren is not gregarious in the mass. He dislikes crowds and shuns public speaking, so he is not suited by temperament to take something new to market and sell it. He knew this, so for the sailing venture he hired a marketing man, who knew the business and spoke mellifluously in public in two languages.

Andren works his way from business inspiration to inspiration largely by intuition, but he holds onto reality through more experienced or more cautious men. He uses their views to expand his own and to produce a larger, more balanced vision of the whole. Sven Hansen, until his death in 1986, was Karl's guide on the search for his ship. Hansen had grown up in the cruise business, a shipowner's son. He had owned ships and sailed all his life. His gravelly voice was not pessimistic, but tempered. Heinan called him "our guru." He was Andren's friend.

"Sven," Karl would say on the telephone. "I've got an idea. We've got to talk."

And for years, while Andren started in the shipping business, whenever he bought or sold or had a new idea, they talked, the young man beginning his career and the older man at the end of his. Hansen sponsored Andren's application for membership in the New York Yacht Club. Karl loves the sedate Yacht Club building on Forty-fourth Street, enjoys the lofty ceilings, the wood paneling, and the marble staircases. It is the yacht club for the shipowner who also sails and Hansen knew that. He also knew that Andren liked quiet places as much as he liked the turmoil of business battle, loved the idea of maneuvering deal after deal into place and also loved being able to sit on a rock, alone and undisturbed, afterward. It was Hansen who had once called Andren "a more-than-one-iron man."

"Ideally, you know, as an entrepreneur you start a company and you're supposed to do everything yourself," Andren told me one afternoon when he was tired. "You mop the floor, you keep the books, you empty the wastebaskets. I can't do that. I have too many other deals going."

Hansen marked Andren as an intelligent man because he knew himself well enough to complement his ebullient business nature with the hard eyes of Tom Heinan, to extend his private business personality by looking for an outgoing, public-minded cruise line president. Hansen found that president.

Early in 1984, when Wärtsila's design was nearly complete, Hansen called a Frenchman he had known as the U.S. manager for French Line. He had no idea if the man would be willing to leave his comfortable seat as the president of a cruise line based in Florida to try to build and sell something as unconventional as a sailing ship. But Jean-Claude Potier, who had never heard of Andren, flew to New York the following Saturday.

The idea of a sailing ship gripped Potier immediately, but the new enthusiast quickly pointed out that the ship needed more luxury aboard if it were to pay for itself. For Potier, the economic steps of the argument in favor of building for luxury rose to a single, illustrative point: telephones in the cabins. With amortization schedules and cost projections in hand, Potier said he convinced Andren that he would need nearly $300 per day from each person to operate his ship and pay for it. Anyone paying $300 per day would want a telephone in his stateroom. QED.

A telephone system went into the design and the dormitory cabins for low-fare sailing passengers were erased. Heinan and Potier expanded and rearranged the public spaces for the new clientele.

Potier's first task, that winter, was a marketing study to discover how many people there might be in the United States eager to pay $300 a day to go sailing in luxury. The research was contracted out for $35,000.

"I don't need a marketing study," Andren once said. "I do mine like this." He stood up and slapped his left hand to his stomach, wet his right finger and held it aloft, testing the buyers' breeze. Then he sat down.

"But I'll tell you, I need it for the banks," he said. "When I walk in and give a bank a leather-bound marketing study, they say: 'Oh yes, I see.' " Andren stroked his chin. "And I'm serious."

The hired students of the market selected eleven American cities. They drove in vans to supermarkets, malls, and shopping plazas, where the $300-a-day people spend their money, and there they parked and asked questions. They showed profile plans of MacLear's barkentine and of the Wärtsila Windcruiser with its four stark sails. Neither one stirred great enthusiasm. Although the Wärtsila design got more votes, those votes were hedged. The ship in the profile plan looked too modern to be real. Andren and Heinan and Hansen listened to the market, and ordered the changes that added the mizzen sail, the jib, and the clipper bow. The researchers also discovered who might be most likely to want to go to sea under sail and they came back to report: "In short, the primary market is young, upwardly mobile professionals."

Levander's design process had come full circle to touch its starting point. Watching the cruise market from Helsinki, he had begun shaping ideas to fit each part of it. He found clients for the easiest ideas first, then, finally, for the most unusual and the closest to his heart. The client for his sailing ship went back to the market and found that, yes, there were people in it who wanted Andren's idea and Levander's ship. These were people who would not count themselves among the "newlywed and the nearly dead," and had not, many of them, been on a traditional sea cruise. In the terms marketers use when the euphemisms are boiled away, Andren's potential passengers were "the BMW drivers," the "me-now crowd." They wanted to go sailing, but with telephones in their rooms, and video cassette players, and large bathrooms stocked with perfumed soaps and hairdryers, and small refrigerators filled with drink.

In the end, the technical book of lists that described Andren's ship had very little of his initial dream left. The design was a mosaic of many minds and motivations. The square sails were gone, and the traditional rigging. No passengers were going to fist the tall triangles of dacron cloth as thick as plate steel and nearly as stiff. Even the crew was going to let hydraulic motors and steel blocks running on steel tracks do the sail handling. More efficient. Less expensive. And a computer on the bridge would sing out the orders to the sails.

Besides, there was not going to be that much sailing; at least not in the market that Kai Levander used to define his initial design. "The sails will be in use only part of the time," Levander had said. "And a short time at that."

"The rig is short," Frank MacLear said when he saw the Wärtsila design. That is sailor's shorthand. It means that the ship has less sail than her hull could carry. But MacLear added gently: "When the crunch comes, if he can give the same service he'll be ahead. For now, people will go to sea to see great, tall, white sails above them when they go on deck at night. Later, when the oil is gone, his may be the only way."

Others, around the world, were thinking that same way. More shippers had begun using the wind. In the three years since the dismal London conference on commercial sail, the *Shin Aitoku Maru* had paid for herself, according to her proud owner. He ordered two more sail-assisted tankers. A small Danish freighter built so her single cargo boom could be stayed erect and carry a sail had set that sail through both trade wind belts on a round trip to Paraguay with fuel savings reported at thirty percent. The Windship Development Corporation, a Massachusetts company, had fitted an auxiliary sail for the Greek freighter *Mini Lace* and the Massachusetts designer, Lloyd Bergeson, reported fuel savings of twenty-four percent. Jacques Yves Cousteau, after overseeing two French designers for several years in secrecy, had announced plans for a wind-assisted research vessel, with two fat, aspirated airfoils erected on its deck. He called them Turbosails.

None of these ships did away with engines. Not at all. The sails aboard were auxiliary power, the way steam engines were auxiliaries for the first twenty or forty years of their lives at sea. No one had been prepared to give up sails, then. No one was prepared to give up engines, now. All the sail training "tall ships" have been fitted with engines. Andren's ship was to have an electric main engine, powered by the electricity generated by three diesel engines. The engine would complement the sails, or, without them, drive the hull alone. Like many modern cruising sailboats, the ship would be what is called a full-powered auxiliary, with engine power enough to push the hull almost as fast as her sails.

In the new vocabulary invented by wind-propulsion advocates[10] who hoped that those years would see a transition to windships, *Shin Aitoku Maru* and *Mini Lace* were called "wind-assisted motorships" and Andren's design, at first, would be called a "motor-assisted sailing ship." So would all the sail training vessels that we know as tall ships.

In the Åland Islands, the Cape Horners, the surviving old hands in sail, would call her a *slättopare*: a flathead schooner, because of her masts of equal height. They had seen such ships before, schooners built in Maine and Nova Scotia and bought by Ålanders when New England Yankees thought they were worn out. Åland seamen nicknamed each three-masted schooner whose mast tops stood in a line a "one hundred eleven." Andren's design would be a "one thousand, one hundred eleven." In the building of ships and sending them to sea, there is rarely anything wholly new.

Andren did not care. He was satisfied with the design drawn for him by many hands, and in a hurry to build before some other shipowner got up the nerve to try to beat him to it.

"You don't build such a ship for yourself," he said. "That's what the dreamers do and they go broke. You build something for a market, not for yourself or your friends."

She still had the wood decks he had wanted from the start, however, and the clipper bow. And he made the designers draw in a bridge deck well aft, where the Cape Horner helmsmen stood, and specified a wood steering wheel there, where the passengers could stand and steer his tall ship.

2

PART

THE SHIP

5

CHAPTER

Bidding to Build

Will some brave entrepreneur step forward to try again to harness the enormous power of the wind?

—Frank MacLear, 1976

Karl Andren believes that the only thing that might distinguish him from other businessmen is doggedness.

"The secret to the way I get things done is persistence," he says. "The old Finnish *sisu.* That's what they call it. Once I've started, I do not let something go until it is done."

Persistence is his internal metronome, but it only begins to tick once he has decided that a deal will be done. While he is first exploring an idea, Karl's face is open and his eyes are wide. He listens with intensity, almost like a child at story time, to those whose opinions of his project he is weighing. Then, with figures to squeeze and a contract in sight, his face closes over the effort of concentration. His pace is then set by *sisu,* which is the quality Finns admire in long-distance cross-country skiers and men who swim for sport in holes chopped through lake ice. His words come faster and he even walks more quickly. It is as though Andren likes going uphill more than down.

Once he had resolved to build the windship, Andren began to move faster. The ship's technical description came back from Wärtsila's printer on April 25, 1984, and was mailed out within five days. Sven Hansen sent copies directly to four West European shipyards, one each in Sweden and Denmark and two in West Germany. All of them had recent experience building cruise ships. Wärtsila kept its own copy and held the inside track in the bidding. These were the yards invited to build the windship, but, at Karl's request, Hansen also sent bid books to two Korean shipyards.

"That was only to get a lowball offer and keep the European shipyards honest," Karl said. "They'd never built a cruise ship in Korea and I wasn't going to be their guinea pig."

None of the invited yards, in Europe or Asia, had built a sailing ship for at least two generations, but that did not bother Andren. His attitude was the reverse of that shown by other shipowners, then hesitating, everywhere except in Japan, over plans to use the wind. He knew the wind would work.

"I had the concept. I said I was going to build, come hell or high water," he said. "I figure that engineers are there to make it work."

So Andren's invitation to bid was first a professional dare. Any interested shipyard was challenged to decide, within a month or two, how it would build a ship type that had never been tried before. And the naval architects and engineers in charge of the bid had to estimate how much it would cost to build the ship and to guarantee that it would work at sea. There are three large steps to the design of any ship: preliminary design, contract design, and construction design. The first step describes an idea, the second spins the idea out into a web of specific characteristics and materials that bind both shipowner and shipyard. At this stage, a shipyard decides for itself whether it can build the ship the owner wants and stakes its professional reputation on that ship's life at sea. The third step, designing for construction, comes only after the owner has signed the yard's contract and made his first payment.

At the preliminary design stage, it is normal practice for shipbuilding designers to judge a new ship's characteristics by other ships like it. There were no ships like the Wärtsila Windcruiser, and no shipyard but Wärtsila knew the theoretical details of what might be involved in building one. Furthermore, Andren had invited experienced shipyards to build a full-scale prototype that would work reliably on the first try. Prototypes rarely do work reliably, but all of the shipbuilders knew that the windship would have to work well enough to make money consistently. They knew that they would be called on to share the risk with Andren in his new business, since new ships are routinely financed by the building yard, or its banks. If the windship did not work, whichever shipyard built it ran the risk of not being paid and, in the worst case, getting the nonworking ship back.

Although it was made up of elements familiar to modern shipbuilders, the ship Andren wanted made an unknown whole. The bid book showed a steel hull and subdivisions. It showed engine rooms, cabins, and air conditioning. These were ordinary enough; but the book also called for masts 150 feet tall, a sail for each mast, and automated machinery to control the sails. The bare specifications in the bid book called for the largest modern sail plan ever attempted; they described the first passenger liner under sail ever built. Andren made his request, then walked on. He was busy. He had work to do, a company to found, financing to find. Tom Heinan, however, waited with a certain apprehension and was relieved when the shipyard bids began to come back two months later.

"That meant ours was accepted as a workable project," he said. "Something they could and would do."

The response from shipyards was a relief because the approach of others then developing wind-propulsion designs was much more cautious than Andren's. In 1980, the Hamburg Institut für Schiffbau, where the world's largest concentration of theoretical work on windships was stored, began a project to replace coastal motorships in the Indonesian archipelago with modern sailing freighters that could use the winds of the annual monsoon for power. The project, called INDOSAIL, was a joint undertaking sponsored by the West German and Indonesian governments. The chief researcher in Hamburg described it cautiously, thus:

> As this is the first project of a newly designed cargo vessel with main propulsion by wind energy which is close to realization since [*sic*] 60 or 80 years, we cannot rely on any recent experience with a comparable development but have to go carefully and step by step through our own development process making our own trials and errors. This is a painstaking and time-consuming process, but in our view it is worth while in order to find an appropriate technical concept and to design a prototype ship and rig which is still in many aspects an experimental system. . . .[1]

When Andren called for bids, four years after INDOSAIL research started, German engineers had just started to design a 155-foot prototype hull. In Indonesia, they had begun testing a small model of the masts and sails at sea on a 60-foot Indonesian sailing craft. Meanwhile, Jacques Yves Cousteau had sailed a prototype of his wind-propulsion system, the Turbosail, made up of two airfoils joined together like an airplane wing so fat it was almost a cylinder erected on deck. The Turbosail, which was not a sail at all but an aspirated airfoil, worked through power-driven fans and slots that controlled the flow of air around the elliptical cylinders. The device is the kind of wing onc might put on an airplane designed to float through the air like a mechanical bumblebee.

In the autumn of 1983, Cousteau decided to cross the Atlantic on a

65-foot catamaran called *Moulin à Vent*, powered by one Turbosail and auxiliary engines. The Turbosail carried away at sea. Its welded supports snapped at deck level and Cousteau finished the voyage to the United States under power. But he declared himself content and announced plans for a still larger prototype with two Turbosails.

Andren did not intend to finance years of research, tentative trials, and step-by-step development. He had found enough of that to fit his purposes, ready-made in Kai Levander's offices at Wärtsila. Calling for bids, he wanted to talk only to shipyards that could convince him they would be able to build a sailing cruise liner that would work, in two years from contract to delivery.

The bids began coming back in midsummer and the Swedish shipyard's offer was by far the highest. Andren and Heinan understood immediately that the yard was signaling its disinterest. Other bids sounded more competitive, but were not detailed.

Quickly, the two men separated out two responses they thought worth pursuing, those from Wärtsila and Bremen-Vulkan, a German shipyard. But Bremen-Vulkan had a sailing ship design of its own, called the *Pinta,* which was a modern version of the square-rigged ship. That was what the yard wanted to build. Andren was tempted again by his original dream, but when he looked at the design, he thought the rig was complicated and not thoroughly engineered. Heinan found that financial arrangements to build the Wärtsila design at the German shipyard would be difficult.

Wärtsila, the Finnish shipyard where the design began, had started ahead of all of its competitors. The yard staff knew they could build the ship, even after Andren's changes, because models of the hull and a smaller rig had been tested there. They could start their contract design, the plans and specifications from which a ship is built, with confidence. Kai Levander and his development crew could predict how much the windship might cost. Wärtsila offered to build the ship at a cost to Andren of $21.5 million.

The highest bid had been $29 million; the lowest bid, from Korea, had been $14.5 million. Andren was not wholly satisfied with Wärtsila's price, and he was not pleased with the terms on which the yard asked him to pay it. They had asked for a twenty-percent cash downpayment, and that was not his style. He asked the Finnish shipyard to work on their price and their financing. They agreed to do so, and pared their offer to ten percent cash down.

On August 17, three months after he had called for bids, Andren telephoned Wärtsila from New York to say that he would build his ship in Helsinki if they ground down the terms and interest rates of the repayment schedule for the ninety percent of the cost due after the ship's delivery. Then he left for a sailing vacation in Maine, aboard the 60-foot schooner *Ocean Viking,* of which he was part owner. He was inwardly pleased at the way his decisions were linking together.

"It was boyhood dream stuff. You know: poor boy emigrates, then comes back years later and builds a big ship in his home country," he said. "Besides, I knew Wärtsila. They build Cadillacs and they never miss a delivery date."

Two weeks later, Andren got a message to call the Parisian ship brokerage firm of Barry, Rogliano and Salles. The matter was urgent. He called from a public phone booth in Camden, Maine, and listened. Then he left for London to meet the president of a small French shipyard who was most eager to build the windship, and had an offer of financial terms that sounded like just what Andren had been trying to draw from Wärtsila. The discovery of two truly interested shipyards, ready to bid against each other while he dealt one against the other, appealed to Andren, the entrepreneur, more than did boyhood dreams.

The Société Nouvelle des Ateliers et Chantiers du Havre had not been on Andren's short list of the shipyards he invited to build his sailing ship. No French yard had. But the shipyard in Le Havre, really a conglomerate of two small yards and an engineering works, was not even on Sven Hansen's list of possibilities. ACH, as it is known in Le Havre, had never built a passenger ship, and that was the minimum qualification Andren wanted in all serious bidders.

Gilbert Fournier, the president of ACH, first heard that an American had called for bids to build the Wärtsila Windcruiser from his ship broker at Barry, Rogliano and Salles. The bid book was circulating in the industry and Pierre Barry called Fournier late in May 1984 to describe it.

"*Cela vous passionne?*" Barry asked. "Wouldn't you love to build it?"

"*A priori,* yes," Fournier answered.

The approach was very nicely calculated. Barry knew his man, and asked first whether the project might absorb Fournier and please his sense of which ships were fit to build, whether it would challenge him and excite the kind of enthusiastic attachment of the whole mind that the French have taken to calling *passion.* Used in this sense, the word does not mean intellectual obsession or sensual abandon, but a kind of decorous devotion that might be called ardor in English. A man the French now call *un passionné de la voile* is an ardent sailor; *un passionné de l'informatique* is a computer enthusiast. Fournier was both. His lead naval engineers shared both those passions.

Barry's teasing question was the proper way to test Fournier's interest. It fit the manner in which highly trained intellectuals among French business leaders—and they are still in a majority in the uppermost reaches of many industries—think about themselves. They like to think of themselves as in business for the ardor it offers, not the money. Barry did not mention money, nor the fact, which both knew well, that the ACH order book was empty. After the truck ferry then building in Le Havre was launched, Fournier's shipyards would have no ships to build; they would face bankruptcy and might be forced to close. European shipyards, in a shipping market crowded with cheaply built hulls from Asia, had already begun dying. Yet money was not mentioned.

"The French, in such a project, would never speak directly of money to be made," Fournier's chief naval engineer and shipyard manager, François Faury, said months later. He explains the intellectual style in French business by drawing a contrast.

"When an American has told you how much he makes or how much he is worth, he is quite content to have fully identified himself for you," Faury said. "Now, in France, we might say that we will do such a thing, build such a ship, because it is a challenge, because we believe in it, and only then say that, perhaps, in the end, we hope to make some money doing it."

There was no irony in his explanation, and none in the way that it ignored his shipyard's desperate situation when the bidding began. Faury has the best intellectual credentials available in France. He is a *polytechnicien,* a graduate of the École Polytechnique in Paris, and is therefore highly trained in mathematics and logic. Irony is for politicians, not the paramilitary engineers trained at the École Polytechnique. Faury's wife Annick is the politician. The mother of four with a helmet of blond hair and a smile like a sunrise, she sits in the minority as a conservative councilwoman in the Communist city government of Le Havre and sees the irony in the stylized, apparently offhand French approach to the business of making and spending money.

"It is true, in France, that we would much rather be known for our books or our paintings, our wit, education, culture, or conversational arts than ever for our cars or bank accounts," Madame Faury once told me. "We would like the beauty of our houses to please more than their size, of course. But we all, with extreme politeness, ignore the fact that all of these accomplishments require money."

François Faury's passion is analysis, polite, punctilious, and constant. He brings it to bear on shipbuilding and on windsurfing with equal fervor. One can sometimes feel his intelligence swing like a searchlight toward some new idea, but it is highly focused. In two years of talking about the project, I never heard him mention the obvious foundation for his yard's bid: ACH had to get the windship contract to survive.

Gilbert Fournier knew that well, but his response to the ritual challenge from his ship broker in 1984 was stylistically deliberate. He made no commitment, acknowledged that the project lay within the realm of his enthusiasms, and started thinking. Bidding to build the windship meant directly challenging Wärtsila, a shipyard perhaps ten times larger than his own, for a share of its passenger ship market. Fournier found that worth doing.

However, he would have to talk money first. To bid well, he knew that he would have to catch Andren's attention with a better financial package and then convince him of the excellence of the shipyard at ACH. Fournier did not worry about that excellence. He assumed it. The yard was his creation, assembled from the wreckage of three failed shipyards and marked by a decorous devotion to making prototypes. The new and the difficult excited not just the president but all of his engineers, most of his draftsmen, and some of his foremen. If there were passion in the project, Fournier knew, it would spread. He left the bid book with the design staff and prepared for the task of convincing the three-year-old Socialist government of France that an American sailing cruise liner was worth an export subsidy.

To an outsider, he might have seemed unsuited to the job. Everything about Fournier puts him in France's merit-based aristocracy: the utmost in education, an outstanding career in business, good tailoring, and a formal, laconic cordiality. Fournier is a man of quite certain proportion and unswerving elegance. His gray hair is brushed away from a clear forehead made higher by baldness. The features of his face are well-defined and almost delicate. His eyes are clear blue and his long hands are well kept. His appearance and manner are a true picture of what he is: a graduate of the École Centrale des Arts et Manufactures, another of France's top technical schools, forty successful years later; the president and part owner of the largest surviving private enterprise in what was fast becoming a public sector.

Some, including Socialists, might call Fournier's manner arrogant. But Fournier's arrogance is so direct it is disarming. And he is always lucid.

"Not just lucid," one of his colleagues once said. "Lucid when looking backward and clairvoyant when looking to the future."

"This company is what it is today thanks to the character and efforts of its president," a designer nearing retirement said fervently one day. "Yes, sir."

"Old man Fournier," declared a Frenchman who had negotiated with him often, "is a wise fox."

While Fournier pondered business strategy, the job of deciding whether Andren's ship could be built, and for how much, drifted a bit until it fell to one of the most experienced men in the design department. Turning a list of specifications into a cost-and-feasibility estimate usually takes two or three months, with computer help. This one was done in eight days and delivered on June 29. It was a shot in the dark, illuminated by experience, and somewhat short of complete.

"They asked me to figure it, so I did. I left the accommodation and decoration line blank, then wrote in: 'To come,' " the senior designer, a man with the qualifications of a naval architect who did that first round of calculations recalled. "No one here seemed to take it too seriously, at first. After all, it was a sailing ship and how long has it been since anyone built one of those? Then I came back from vacation and found out we'd hooked something big."

While the senior man was on vacation in August, his colleagues in Le Havre began to redraft the sailing ship from scratch. One started on the fifth, drawing the lines of a hull to fit the engineering calculations. He worked freehand, on transparent paper stretched over a drafting table so large it looked like a movable piece of the wall. He walked around the table and sighted along each tentative sweep of his pencil, then extended it if he found it true. Drawing a hull in three dimensions, freehand, on an exact scale of 1 to 100 is a one-man job, and others left him to it in the long August days of northwestern France. Then, as they returned from their vacations in September, one after another of the designers picked up pieces of the job, extrapolating from the newly drawn hull, calculating the new volumes and the new weight. The feeling that they had hooked something big spread.

During the annual vacation season of July and August, Fournier had gone first to the bureaucratic niche he calls "my guardian ministry," the shipbuilding department at the Ministry of Industry. With their agreement that the sailing cruise liner qualified, in principle, for an export subsidy, Fournier pushed on. The largest French banks had all been nationalized and his subsidized offer to Andren had to pass two other ministries watching over the banks. Courting the bureaucracy was the only sure way of keeping his shipyard alive.

Finally, an interministerial loan committee, with executives from two nationalized banks, convened and listened to the shipbuilder from

Le Havre. In August that committee approved a subsidy equivalent to $10 million, but only if Fournier could sign a contract by October. The bureaucrats acted on the grounds supplied by two of Fournier's arguments: they would be supporting the shipyard to maintain several hundred jobs, and they would give ACH a head start in the technology of sail power.

Fournier felt later that the second argument was the most convincing. He believed it and so did the civil servants. Keeping a shipyard in business for the jobs it generated might be a political reason dear to the Socialists, but the pursuit of new, energy-saving technology was already a multipartisan goal. France has no oil and in the years of petroleum shortages and high prices the country turned decisively to alternate sources of energy. Nuclear power, solar conversion, even the elemental power of the tides at the mouth of the English Channel, had been researched, developed, and applied.

"We had no oil," a technocrat told a popular French magazine in those years. "We had to have ideas."

The French government supported Cousteau's research into wind propulsion for ships, and in 1985 the nationalized special metals company Pechiney announced that it would build the second vessel to use Cousteau's Turbosails.[2] The same prospecting attitude prevailed for Andren's sailing cruise ship.

It was the end of August when Fournier called his ship broker back with a deal. He met Andren in London on September 3 and offered to build the Wärtsila design for $19 million. On September 4 Andren signed a letter of intent to build his ship at ACH in Le Havre.

"Then I had to tell Wärtsila," Karl recalled, with a grimace. But the letter of intent was full of contingencies, and no one on Andren's three-man ship project team was convinced ACH could build the cruise liner. They hired Wärtsila engineering consultants to help them find out what the French shipyard might be able to do and to act as technical judges while the Americans and the French developed their final contract. Although Wärtsila knew ACH had a reputation for competence, the Finns still hoped to win the bidding and build the ship because they had years of experience building passenger ships. The French shipyard had never done it.

In early September, by Andren's calculation the two shipyards were seven percent apart in total price, but the French repayment terms were easier. Karl decided to push both of them hard. He told them both that if Wärtsila came within ten percent of the French, on comparable terms, he would build the windship in Finland. Simultaneously, he started a kind of technical examination of the French yard. Fournier and his staff flew to Miami, at Andren's request, to visit the kitchens, the cabins, the lounges, and the laundry aboard *Song of America*, a Wärtsila-built cruise liner. They were being shown what was expected of them.

Early in October in New York, Tom Heinan and a Wärtsila engineer drew up a list of standards, materials, and performance characteristics for the windship. It was the beginning of the contract specifications for ACH. Heinan was convinced that Wärtsila had already made their contract specifications, and that the engineer carried them with him, in a locked briefcase.

"He even slept with it, and no one ever got a look at those specs, not even me," Heinan said. He had to work out his own, tugging first at Wärtsila then pulling on ACH. Neither of the two competing shipyards was forthcoming. Wärtsila was still fighting for the contract. The ACH designers and draftsmen in Le Havre were trying feverishly to catch up with the inspired estimate made in June. Someone had to find out if they really could build the ship for the price they had offered. Just before the first hard session on contract specifications was due to begin, the French designers determined by calculation that the ship, as she had come to them in the bid book in the spring, was not stable. She seemed to be too narrow to stand up at sea, under extreme conditions.

François Faury, his car ferry launched and in her final fitting out, was about to take over the detailed negotiations for the French side. At forty-three, he was a compact man, and athletic. He looked rather like the center on a professional hockey team, the heart of the team's attack. He had the same air of controlled intensity, a neatness in bearing, and wide-set eyes for good peripheral vision. People say of Faury that he sees things quickly.

"We thought it was a design with great qualities, and some very fine ideas," he said of Wärtsila's preliminary design. "But we knew it would not work and we said so at the outset. We said the hull was not wide enough. This was a ship that would capsize." But Faury has a footnoting habit. Later that same day, he saw me and, without preamble, said, "You must understand that it would have capsized under certain specific conditions: with one compartment open to the sea."

The outset came in earnest on October 5, when Andren, Heinan, and their Wärtsila advisor went to Le Havre for the first time. Field harvests in the Norman countryside were complete and the coast and countryside were mantling themselves with gray for the winter. Andren's crew took the train from Paris and were driven to the shipyard. There, they saw a kind of functional austerity. There were no fountains, no statues, no designer signboards, no lawns or titled parking spaces. The entrance gate was attended by a middle-aged man in a cardigan sweater and tie, whose cozy office with one glass wall looked like an extension of his parlor, because it was. Most of the open spaces at the shipyard were paved with a haphazard mix of crushed rubble and dredged gravel.

Driving across the flat Le Havre dockyards to the ACH shipyard for the first time is like running a maze paved in cobblestones and set between railroad crossings and drawbridges. The most direct route from downtown Le Havre crosses three spur lines and one drawbridge and passes the longshoremen's hiring hall, the municipal garbage incineration plant, and the slaughterhouse. Through the last level crossing, squeezed between a wall and a short strip of rowhouses, the shipyard gate is right across the street from a neighborhood café and a dry goods store founded in 1887.

The yard was built immediately after the Franco-Prussian War, on the tidal flats behind the harbor at Le Havre, where the Seine meets the Channel. It was erected on the cold, hard edge of the city, in a neighborhood called Les Neiges because the snow stuck longest on the riverbank there. Les Neiges was, properly speaking, a part of Graville, a village where all the trails ended for centuries, until King François I, in 1517, decreed a new port in the salt marsh just beyond it, at the very northwest corner of the Seine estuary. In his grace, the first Francis called the new royal port Franciscopolis, but then relented. It became Le Havre de Grâce, and spread upstream slowly, over the centuries, eventually absorbing Graville.

Once the Industrial Revolution finally took hold in France and there was money to be made everywhere, the shipyard at Graville grew quickly. It became big and busy. Twice near the turn of the century, during a ten-year period of direct French government subsidies for steel-hulled sailing ships, the Graville yard launched four Cape Horn barks in a single year. At the time, it had eight of the long inclined ramps called building ways, each incorporating the slipways along which ships slide into the water when they are launched.

Those ways were made by the same local masons who built stone barns and turreted manor houses in Normandy, men bound by a regional tradition that building materials must contrast in color. They wanted dark colors for structural parts and light materials for the walls between. So the shipyard building ways were made out of brick laid up into barrel vaults and light brown Norman stone mortared into the yard-thick walls between the dark brick columns. The building ways rose gently from the low water mark to a height of almost forty feet, so that a new ship, at her launching, was poised on a slope of just under six degrees, which is about the angle at which a book will begin to slide along a smooth, tilted board—or a hull will begin to slide along a greased slipway.

Two world wars and the sharp increase in Japanese and Third World shipbuilding had left only two slipways in the Graville shipyard. The toes of those slipways touch the flat estuary waters opposite a landfill peninsula covered with pastel storage tanks for crude oil. Oceangoing containers are stacked two stories high like brightly colored blocks in the container-ship terminal next door. With a modern industrial desert across the water to the south and next door to the west, the antique building and launching ramps that Andren saw looked like long wedges cut from the Paris sewers and set out in Le Havre's hazy sunlight to dry.

On dry land, at their raised ends, three shop buildings enclosed the slipways in a U. One was a tall, modern industrial shed with a steel frame and corrugated steel skin. The walls of the other two were then over a century old. Some of the machinery inside them came to Le Havre as part of German reparations at the end of World War I. So did three of the four shipyard cranes.

The two negotiating parties began to talk out the ship's details in the shipyard offices, up a creaking wood staircase with a banister lacquered caramel brown inside a long, two-story building of brick with high ceilings and tall windows, backed up against the yard's west wall. Most of the second floor had once been devoted to the mold loft, where every important curve and form in each ship was laid out in full scale on a flat tracing floor. Long, thin battens of springy hardwood, pegged at intervals to that mold-loft floor, tested the truth of each line in shipbuilding plans then.

Andren, Heinan, and the engineers set out to do something similar, testing one another's capabilities and resolve, writing down small truths each day on the list of contract specifications. They worked for five days, then the Americans left to consider what they had learned.

"The more exposure we got to the yard, the more confidence we got in their ability to produce the product," Heinan said, looking back.

"Faury and Fournier said they would be building from the heart, because it was a sailing ship," said Andren. "They still negotiated hard."

The ACH executives pushed Andren for a signed contract at that session, even though they had not completed the ship's specifications. It was an appeal to sign on faith in the yard's ability to complete their own design. Andren refused to sign without complete specifications approved by Wärtsila. He trusted the Finnish yard, not ACH. The French, in the same room with a Wärtsila engineer, would not tell Andren all they had discovered in their redesign. The meetings trailed to a close, but not a definite end. Design work continued in Le Havre. Negotiations stopped for a while, and Andren began to have second thoughts.

François Faury said later that he saw Andren hesitate as the list of practical difficulties grew and the true extent of what he had undertaken became clear. The engineering details of the project were daunting. As they probed those details, all of the men felt sharply, for the first time, some of the age-old uncertainties and dangers of going to sea under sail. It was one thing to dream of doing something that had once been so commonplace as sailing across oceans in large ships, and another to build a large ship to sail across oceans when centuries of tested knowledge about how to do it had almost vanished. The certainties that come with experience had gone. All the modern sail-power pioneers—the Japanese, Cousteau, the Germans, the British, the Americans—had to design, test, and redesign windship rigs to establish new certainties. Without old certainties or new knowledge, there were really only worries.

Andren, as a boy in Åland, could have heard about the four-masted bark *Hougomont,* running the few hundred miles up the Chilean coast from Coquimbo to Tocopilla in 1908. The northbound Humboldt Current was too strong and the wind too light. The ship was swept past her destination and the captain's patience broke after days of trying to beat back against the current. He bore away for Australia and took eighty days to get there. Before she arrived her insurers had posted *Hougomont* as missing.

Or he might have heard of the time that a North Atlantic gale caught Gustaf Erikson's pride, the *Herzogin Cecilie,* north of Scotland on her way to Australia in ballast. A screaming gust threw the 315-foot bark on her side and the sand and rock ballast shifted, pinning her there. Her sails blew out and her decks turned into hillsides so steep the crew could only climb them on all fours. They spent forty-eight hours, without stopping to eat, shoveling the gravel and sand ballast back uphill, over ledge after ledge they had made out of boards. For another two days they pumped out the ship's flooded spaces. Then they bent on more sail and bore away for Australia, sewing sails for weeks on the way.

The French sailing engineers might have known how the *France I,* the first five-masted bark ever built and the biggest sailing ship of her day, was abandoned off the coast of Argentina in 1901, after the sudden, violent onslaught of the offshore gale called a *pampero* blasted her onto her beam ends and her cargo shifted. All of the negotiators in Le Havre that autumn would have read, earlier that year, about the loss of the 117-foot British training bark *Marques.* She was driven under by a squall 90 miles northeast of Bermuda, while racing with the "tall ships" from Puerto Rico to Halifax. She sank in sixty seconds and took nineteen of twenty-eight people aboard with her.

Andren admits wondering, in October, about his ship's sailing ability. What, he thought, if she doesn't move? Or what if she moves, but she's unstable? And would the rigging be strong enough? What if it would not stand in a real wind?

"There are moments in every project when you ask yourself: 'Why the hell did I get myself into this?' " he said later.

Andren's doubt passed. There was an electrical engine in the windship design that could run off any one of three diesel generators. The engine and propeller could drive the new ship and reduce the total frustration of calms for sailing ships, or of contrary winds and currents, like those that made thousands of ocean miles easier than a hundred against the wind and current for *Hougomont.* A computer aboard the new windship was supposed to handle dangers at sea faster than any crew. Kai Levander, a sailor, had designed the block outline of a computer program to run the hydraulic machinery that would control the sails. The program was laid out on a panic threshold equal to an angle of heel of eight degrees. To a small-boat sailor or blue-water yachtsman, eight degrees of heel is nothing. *Herzogin Cecilie,* after her 1928 knockdown, spent four days with her decks at an angle of thirty degrees to the right of horizontal and her starboard rail underwater. But Levander had made a fundamental design rule for the sailing computer program. If the new ship's decks leaned to eight degrees from the horizontal, the computer would have to release all the sails immediately, emptying them suddenly of wind.

"We've read the results of psychological tests which show that is the ordinary passenger's panic angle," Levander said. "Anything beyond eight degrees seems to set off a visual alarm in the head that says 'You're going over.' The computer never lets her go beyond that angle of heel."

The only action that can save a sailboat or ship overwhelmed by a sudden squall at sea is to spill the wind from all her sails at once. It can be done by casting off or cutting all of her sheets, the ropes holding her sails to the wind. Then, if she has not been crippled by shifting cargo, or water on board, she will come nearly upright. Without enough people on deck to do that, the training ship *Marques* sailed under, overpowered by the wind. Levander's computer program was designed to be the equivalent of a crewman at each sail, each with incontrovertible orders to let go as soon as a passenger felt uncomfortable. He had prescribed intermediate steps, as well, so that the windship need not get caught with too much sail set in any wind.

In fact, it was the marriage between a shipboard computer taught to sail and the hydraulic motors called servomechanisms that made the modern windship possible in principle. Enough professional crew to handle sail quickly and reliably enough for passengers who had never sailed in deep water would have made Andren's idea too expensive. Servomechanisms, of the kind that turn the heavy front wheels of a car with one hand on the steering wheel and translate a finger touch into tons of force, and a computer that needs no sleep, would make up a full, permanent sail-handling crew. That, at least, was what the preliminary design asserted. Making it work was essential, but not easy. No one had done it before.

ACH was eager to try. Gilbert Fournier had built his company by specializing in unusual ships that were difficult to build. His yards had built cable-laying ships too small to interest foreign yards but necessary for the French telecommunications monopoly, and cable layers handle huge weights with precision using the hydraulic power of servomechanisms. ACH had become expert in hydraulics.

Fournier's staff in Le Havre had also been quick to seize on the competitive advantages of computers in ship design and construction. Fournier himself was a programmer who had taught his first personal computer to solve differential equations, using only machine language, the abstract tongue that computers speak to themselves. Later, he wrote the yard's program to smooth the lines of a ship's hull by swift, repeated approximations, based on differential equations. Doing the same thing with agonizing care by hand had taken experienced draftsmen sixty to ninety days of work. While Andren was wondering about the strength of his ship's rig, Fournier wrote a computer program to simulate the stresses on masts and rigging and show the results on a terminal screen. He did it over one weekend.

Very slowly, Andren began to believe in the French shipbuilders. He had a twentieth-century businessman's confidence in engineers and heard no historical irony in the assurances they gave him. In effect, they said, everything we will use on this ship already exists in another application. All we will be doing is scaling up, they said, making everything larger.

However, scaling up in sailing ships had reached a definite ceiling early in this century. *Preussen,* the largest full-rigged ship, and *Thomas W. Lawton,* the largest schooner ever built, had both proven to be mankillers. But the financial negotiations were practically complete and it appeared that Wärtsila's pride in its design would move the Finns to be sure that ACH would build a ship to Wärtsila specifications. Karl went ahead.

"We gave the owner a very good price and we offered him good delivery dates," Fournier said, to sum up his yard's approach to Andren. "Then, we are all sailors and understood at once the problems that needed to be resolved. Finally, our specializations in computer technology and servomechanisms have direct applications to this project."

Andren liked having engineers who were sailors to build his sailing ship, but it was the financing package that determined his decision. Karl does not like being called a gambler, as he was after the windship project became more widely known. He sees himself as an optimist and a business mathematician who calculates every risk. He calls himself a "numbers man" and does not use outside financial advisors.

"When it came to the doomsday projection, it didn't appear to me the French government would end up owning Circle Line," Andren said, when he reviewed the decision. "I always do one of those. On every project, I figure out what happens if it doesn't work at all, and I don't go ahead unless I see we can start again. Maybe eat potatoes for a couple of years, but hold onto the house and the companies and start again."

Wherever he might build, Andren's financial arrangements would start on a foundation of ownership capital from himself and the Stolt-Nielsen family. Nordic Bank in New York had agreed to lend $10 million to start the new cruise line, with Circle Line for its guarantee. Either shipyard would finance ninety percent of the cost of the ship, so the difference between the two came in the personal stakes from Andren and Stolt-Nielsen. Andren figured, in large, round numbers, that if he built the ship in France and doomsday came, his loss would be $10 million. If the ship were built in Finland and became a total failure, his loss would equal $14 million. By his doomsday projections, the difference between the yards was forty percent.

The cost difference was less, expressed as a total that the shipowners would eventually have to pay. Wartsila had offered to build the ship for $21.5 million and ACH had bid $18.5 million. But the interest terms from ACH were substantially easier, and at the close of negotiations, the French yard offered to contract for two ships at the same price, one for delivery in 1986 and one in 1987. The government export credit had helped. It was an essential condition for Andren's commitment.

Two weeks after the first meeting in Le Havre, Andren was ready to close the deal. He was moving fast again, when he returned to France with Heinan on Monday, October 21. They met Faury and Fournier that day in the Paris offices of Fournier's ship brokers. In three days, sitting to negotiate all day, they settled the contract's technical specifications. François Faury and Tom Heinan signed the ninety-five-page book of specifications at about six P.M. on Wednesday. Their signatures were firm, upright, practically triumphant.

The next day, a Thursday, the two sides started trying to put their agreements down in contract form. Lawyers made drafts in many copies, then read them aloud for all. That day the negotiators made progress while nailing down large themes like the ship's performance characteristics and cruising radius. On Friday they met to specify the quality standards, the materials, and the costs for the ship's internal decor. There, the negotiations broke down.

The difficulty lay in the design and decoration of the passenger spaces. It appeared, quite pointedly to the French, that Andren and Heinan did not trust their yard to make a success of the essential interior of the ship, the places where passengers would pay to live. Fournier recalled later that Heinan had long lists of materials and standards and wanted each agreed to and included in the contract. The yard did not want to be pinned down that precisely.

"It was rather like the haggling of rug merchants, if I dare call it that," Fournier said. He found the session "quite trying." Heinan, looking back, called it "knockdown and drag-out." Each side got up and walked away from the deal at least once that day. Andren responded by declaring a marathon. They would not leave the office until they could agree.

"We worked day and night. It was like a conclave for the election of a pope," said Fournier. "It is very Nordic in style, though, this business of locking the doors until the business is done. I had run across it only once before, with Norwegian shipowners."

Just before dawn on Saturday, Heinan and Faury signed the contract. Their signatures on the profile plan of the ship, dated October 26, 1984, look tremulous. The usually erect backbone of Faury's *F* is leaning and

Heinan's slanting script wavers. No one was wholly satisfied with the details later. An outside naval architect who read them called the specifications "so loose they were laughable." Andren admitted ruefully that there were only two days for sea trials of the new ship in the contract and said that no one thinks best at four in the morning. Heinan, sitting one day in his Circle Line office where all the books are shelved, all the papers squared, and the only decoration on the sill of his window on the Hudson is an hourglass, said the document had flaws. He nodded at a New York lawyer, in a dark-gray, three-piece suit who had just come into the office.

"Which he has spent his time and lots of our money fixing," Heinan said.

The lawyer looked up from the files in his open briefcase and said, quite softly: "It wasn't dated."

In Paris, that morning, the worn negotiators were so relieved, however, that they drank champagne at five A.M. Fournier made what he calls his standard contract speech to owners, which begins "Your indulgence does not interest me in the least," and ends, "I do not want you to become such good friends with my engineers that you will, out of friendship, suspend your criticism of what they do. The errors we make and correct in the yard may cost *x*. Errors that are caught outside the yard cost ten times *x* and my reputation."

The Americans listened, and thought that they had saved Fournier's yard and made a good deal by doing so.

"ACH had to stay in business," Heinan said, months afterward. "The government wanted them to stay in business, that's what made the deal eventually so attractive: the yard had an empty order book, it had the technical capability, and the government had an employment problem. Those three things made the deal." It was eminently an American view, fixed on the bottom line.

The French shipbuilders preferred a longer view. The three facts were as Heinan said, but there were others, important to them. In fighting for the windship with a singlemindedness he had tried to dissimulate, Fournier followed his character and the path it had already made for him in his business. He pursued a prototype, as he had before, in order to learn a new technology while building it and to put his yard in the forefront of that technology. He was true to himself. Faury fought for the one chance a professional engineer may get in his lifetime to build from the soul and to leave his mark on the history of his profession.

Andren had found a good match for himself. Faury and Fournier had gambled just as hard as the Ålander. When they signed the contract, they did not know for certain, in detail, whether they could build the sailing ship for the price they had fixed. The designers in Le Havre had not finished the French version of the ship.

"We had to hurry so," said one of the designers. "In the end, we signed the contract first, and worried about what it meant afterward."

In the gray-black Paris dawn, the negotiators pulled on their coats and went back to their hotels. The first delivery trucks went by over the cobblestones in the streets with a rubber rumble. Street sweepers diverted water from the street mains into the gutters and swept ragged leaves off the sidewalk toward the moving stream they had called up. Heinan packed and left for London. Faury flew to Toulouse, where his wife was at a political convention. He could not find her that morning and lunched alone.

In Helsinki, Kai Levander filed away the contract specifications for his ship, the ones that the Wärtsila consulting engineer had carried through the losing battle to hold on to the Windcruiser. He had checked them against the specifications the French yard had accepted.

"Everything technical in the Andren ship comes from us," Levander concluded. It was true, then. Wärtsila was to get a royalty of two percent of what Andren would pay for the first ship and one and a half percent royalty for the second. That royalty recognized Levander's work. Nonetheless, he still felt the loss in his shipbuilder's pride, when I met him one year later.

"It was not easy to give up that ship. It hurts the soul, so to speak," Levander said.

6
CHAPTER

The Hull

Trop fort n'a jamais manqué, puisque fort assez a parfois consenti.

—French shipbuilders' saying, used today as a professional motto

There are places in the world where shipbuilding is as natural as the weather and where the shipbuilding trades passed, for centuries, from father to son. The coasts of the Baltic hold such places, but so do the shores of the North Sea and the Thames estuary and both coasts of the English Channel, including the deep eastward bight in the French coast where the Seine runs out to sea.

The Romans traded by sea from that estuary and the Vikings used every creek and crease in it, before and after they had settled there and become Normans. William the Conqueror's invasion fleet of 696 Viking longships was built and launched on the south shore of the Seine estuary between February and October of 1066, and the European discoverers of Newfoundland and Quebec sailed from the same shore. British shipwrights, late in the seventeenth century, copied their first fast fighting ships from those built on the Norman coast,[1] and the prettiest four-masted barks afloat, in the eyes of the last deep-water sailors,[2] were French-built. At least eight of them came from the Graville yard of the Société des Forges et Chantiers du la Méditerranée, where ACH proposed to build Andren's sailing cruise ship.

Since 1945, however, Norman shipyards have been dying. They have been gone for 150 years from Honfleur and Harfleur. Since 1970, they have disappeared from Fécamp, Rouen, Dieppe, and Caen, and four have collapsed into one at Le Havre, where the technical high schools no longer teach any specific shipbuilding skills. Yet men with the necessary gifts are still drawn to shipyards, where, the old hands say, it takes three to five years to make them shipbuilders, even if they arrive as graduate naval engineers. Apprenticeship has kept a tradition alive.

Gérard Jouan, the man who started the real construction of Andren's ship at ACH, began his shipyard career on his knees, watching out of the corner of his large, round eyes to learn the tricks of his chosen trade. Watching, he learned how to carry a curve in his pocket and how to pick up a flat measurement, ball it up inside his hand, then apply it exactly and without distortion to a curved surface. Jouan is a lofter, born and trained. Lofters once worked on blackwashed floors with chalk, waist-high dividers, and protractors as tall as doghouses. All of the lead foremen at Graville began their careers that way. They used springy wood battens to form curves and laid down full-scale patterns for every piece of a ship in broad, quiet rooms hundreds of feet long. There were mathematical rules, derived from solid geometry, to produce an accurate conversion of two-dimensional plans into flat shapes that would bend without distortion into three-dimensional hull plates. But the old-time lofters who taught Jouan preferred their own tricks and the traditions of centuries.[3]

A lofting floor was nothing more than an outsized drafting table on which the lofters knelt to work; their work was a mental preproduction of every step in the building of a hull. They thought their way from two dimensions into three. The name of their trade in English is taken from the lofts above shipyard workshops where they worked, tracing lines and making molds. Now, they use computers to aid in drawing and conversion, but lofters still use the kind of imagination that makes solid geometry an everyday affair.

Watching is the one indispensable skill of any apprentice, but vision remains the central skill of the masters in Jouan's profession. The first material step toward building any ship passes through the particular imagination of a man like Jouan—the lofter's imagination which lays the curved lines from paper plans flat and to scale, on sheets of steel plate, so that the plates will cut, shape, and fit together into the long curves of a fair hull. A lofter at work is like a tailor cutting a pattern except that the patterns lofters make come together in a steel skin large enough to contain a small hill and to follow all of its curves and hollows too.

Construction began one month after the ship's final dimensions had been fixed in a contract, which was tumbling haste in shipyard terms. When the engineers and designers at the building yard had mentally weighed and balanced, then mathematically stretched and tested the hull of the sailing cruise ship, they named it ACH Hull No. 269 and began giving bits of it to Jouan and his lofters. It was January 22, 1985, and the yard had contracted to deliver the ship on September 29, 1986.

Almost the full design and drafting staff of sixty-eight men and women had been working at the ship's plans since the previous August. They wanted still more time, but did not have it. The work force was idle outside and the deadlines the yard had accepted forced them to design on the fly and to build at the same time. They were pressed, too, by the peculiar nature of the windship. Since no one had built a modern sailing ship of its size before, the contractual requirements for the sailing rig were vague generalities, not detailed, step-by-step specifications of materials, construction methods, and performance of the kind yard designers normally receive with a contract. In effect, Andren and the shipyard had contracted to get along together well enough to work out specifications as the ship grew on the ways. Wärtsila's bid book had not been a cohesive whole.

"The design we got did not hang together. We had to start again from scratch," said the design team leader. He is a very shy and very precise former lofter named René L'Heryénat who has learned all the qualifications of a naval architect on the job. His section of the yard, where the light of preference for three rows of drafting tables comes from tall windows and the wood floor still creaks under new linoleum, is called the Bureau d'Études, the Studies Office. It is well named. The staff there prefers contemplation and calculation to production pressure. To describe the way they like to work, the designers and draftsmen in the Studies Office have a favorite phrase: "*On va se pencher dessus* (We're going to ponder that)."

That phrase comes from the heart of the nature of engineering, which is the art of thinking through a project before starting, and calculating the chances of success for each step.

"We made our own calculations, but finally had to get out construction plans without making as long a study as was our custom," L'Heryénat said one afternoon the following spring. He looked down at the surface of his waist-high drafting table as though what he was about to add might be a painful confession. "There was a hole in yard production. We drew some building plans before the hull form was final."

That form was straightforward enough to begin on faith and past experience. Detailed design of the masts, rigging, sails, and sail-handling equipment had to be undertaken slowly because no one knew in detail how the sailing rig could be made to work. The shipyard had said they could do it. Andren had hesitated hard, then taken them at their word. The central question about his ship from the start was: Will she sail? Starting from the familiar and proceeding to the unknown, the shipyard engineers began their answers with the hull. Their first decision was to make the ship 4 feet, 3 inches wider than Wärtsila had planned. It was a good choice for sail, because more breadth means more stability in a hull, more bouyancy in the water to resist the heeling pressure of the wind in sails. For centuries, sailors have called broad hulls "powerful," because they stand up to a lot of sail and a lot of wind.

The shipyard engineers made their second major choice in order to begin quickly. They decided to build a sailing ship hull, in the technical style of the last great sailing ships and of modern yachts, with a skeleton of frames that rose in parallel curves, like human ribs, from the keel. They chose transverse construction, with frames like human ribs for strength under the ship's steel skin. They set aside the modern method of longitudinal construction that places strength members lengthwise, like girders in a flat warehouse roof, within the rectangular steel hulls of supertankers and cargo liners. That choice made, the engineers authorized a start on construction.

Jouan, the master lofter, called in René Turquetille, the yard's master shipwright, and Turquetille came upstairs from the shops in his belted blue overalls, with a smile rising under his thin white mustache. For three months he had been building a *bateau mouche* for river tours of Paris, with half his normal work force and one hand behind his back, so to speak. The *bateau mouche* was complete and Turquetille was glad to get real work. The master shipwright is a tall, broad man of very succinct speech, with waving gray hair, a flushed face, eyes of Nordic blue, and a white mustache so straight it might have been shaved with the aid of a bubble level. Jouan, the last time he counted, in 1983, had lofted 110 ships, large and small. Turquetille is so unwilling to talk of his own accomplishments that he will not remember, out loud, how many ships he has built. He and the lofter took the first sailing ship plans in January and worked together, at first, because each has a unique way of looking at a hull and, together, they could imagine the whole task of construction before it began.

Shipbuilding is an industrial process driven by imagination, and a shipyard is a malleable sort of assembly line made up of permanent labor pools, each filled with a different kind of human imagination. Each one of the distinct forms of imagination is needed at a specific step in the building of every ship. Looking at a set of plans, the master lofter sees the pieces and the master shipwright sees the whole. The ship starts with one and ends with the other. In between there are special forms of vision, natural turns of imagination, that match the artist's sensibility at one point and the master carpenter's precision at another. Each ship is different, but the talents for building them remain the same; and, like a snake hunting on rough ground, the shipyard assembly line changes shape and contour while it holds to a constant purpose.

Construction begins with an act of imagination. At the building yard in Graville, early in 1985, the master shipwright went aboard the ship-to-be in his mind, and for days walked through the ship mentally, envisioning the practical steps for her construction. After forty years of building hulls, Turquetille can look at working drawings and imagine himself inside any part of the ship that the drawings represent. Once inside, he looks around in his imagination and decides how his shipfitters need to put it together so as not to trap themselves into odd corners where it would be impossible to work. Then he climbs out, mentally, and tells the lofters where they will need to divide each difficult assembly and how to number the pieces so that the steel will go together with the best possible welds.

"He made hand sketches for us, and we worked from his ideas," Jouan said. "He's the one who knows how he wants to do it. In our small shipyard, we do everything directly. No need for staff meetings and memos. We do it face to face and one's word is enough."

At the beginning, only four men planned the ship's construction: Turquetille, Jouan, a planning draftsman named René Charbonnier with a gift for organization, and their young boss, a Norman dairyman's son named Alain Adam, who has a civil engineering degree in the physics of ultraprecise measurement. Faury and the other managing engineers left the planning job wholly to those four.

They are plain men, competent and methodical. They have no frills. Frills, in France, seem to be reserved for some of the rich and for those born after 1960, when all of the wounds of World War II had finally scarred over. In Normandy at least, the war years sobered everyone who lived through them and some who were born afterward. Alain Adam was born on his father's farm in 1948, which he remembers as the year the sound barrier was broken for the first time. But Adam also remembers learning, as a boy on an eighty-acre farm inland from Dunkerque, the rules of life as it resumed after the war.

German army units retreating from Normandy in 1944 requisitioned and took with them all the draft horses from the countryside. The Germans with the horses from Adam's village were trapped and surrendered at the river Somme, 60 miles away. When they heard this news, Adam's father and his uncle left together riding their bicycles. They came back on foot, many days later, leading their horses and pushing their bicycles.

The horses could not be tired out by carrying men because they were the only motive power on the farm, and remained so until Alain went away to high school. His parents, with a family memory of two world wars fought over their farming country, pushed their bright son toward his chance at a technical career. They had every reason to believe that the opportunities which opened for him and others like him after the last war were an unprecedented stroke of luck that had no reason to repeat itself.

The other men in the planning group at Graville were of an age with Alain Adam's parents and had the same practical skepticism. They had seen the end of the war in Le Havre, when the Allied invasion swept past the city and the German garrison commander there refused to surrender. Paris had been liberated before the Allied command delivered an ultimatum to Le Havre. The German commander ignored it and began dynamiting port facilities. In eight days of saturation bombing in September, the Allied air forces flattened 4 miles of the city from the ocean to the ends of the port. More than four thousand French men and women were killed.

Turquetille had graduated from vocational high school with a lofter's certificate and started work that year, at the age of eighteen. What he remembered about the siege of Le Havre was that the German soldiers he saw all looked too old or too young to fight. Garrison propaganda called on them to surpass the sacrifices at the siege of Stalingrad. Turquetille said: "They only wanted to go home."

Turquetille, Adam, and Charbonnier planned the hull assembly following simple givens. The shipyard's prewar rolling press, which would shape the hull plates, had a hydraulic grip just over 26 feet long, so they divided the 440-foot hull into sixteen segments, each 26 feet long, with a seventeenth for the flare at the top of the overhanging bow. There were four decks above the double bottom, so each hull segment was limited to the 16-foot height of one deck, and that limit yielded a comfortably safe weight for the pride of the yard, an eight-year-old gantry crane painted white. The ship would go together on the slipway under the crane in prefabricated steel segments 26 feet long by 16 feet high. When it was laid out on graph paper, the plan looked like a middling complex project from a Lego box: apparent child's play, once the very precise work of preparing for assembly every steel detail in each segment had been done. Adam and Charbonnier left the detailed design of that puzzle to the imaginations of Gérard Jouan and Turquetille.

Jouan's professional trick of vision lets him translate any ship from two-dimensional plans to a three-dimensional mental image, then to divide that image into flat parts and determine how each part must be laid out and cut. Turquetille started shipbuilding as a lofter, too, and he works the trick in reverse, mentally assembling the images he sees in the plans. To ask them how they do it is to ask them how they walk. I once pressed Turquetille for an explanation and he said: "I have a good memory. That might be it."

Jouan thinks the ability to make and keep mental perspective drawings must be inborn. "I know that in the thirty-two years of teaching I have done, it has always been true that some apprentices have it and become lofters," he said on one reflective day. "Others don't and they can never learn; no amount of teaching makes any difference."

In French, lofters are called hulltracers, a name that describes more directly what they do today. Theirs is the trace that the builders follow through the assembly of the ship. They divide each hull into pieces, like the makers of a puzzle, then mark each piece with paint-stick glyphs and cold chisel marks that can solve the puzzle.

Hull No. 269 began with fifteen basic plans, from which the ACH draftsmen derived six hundred working plans. As these were slowly finished, the hulltracers next door broke the working plans into pieces and drew scale diagrams of each piece of steel in each working plan, as it had to be cut. They drew on a scale of one to ten, so that a 1-inch pen stroke meant a 10-inch-long cut in steel, and 32 inches of paper were enough to contain the full length of a hull-plate plan. Working from January to July, the hulltracers formed a catalog of 4,893 separate pieces, each with a distinct shape. Some shapes, like the flat, triangular gussets welded at intervals wherever horizontal met vertical in the ship, were repeated hundreds of times. Some, like the long, fluted roll of half-inch steel where the ship's bow would cut the water, were unique.

Jouan's assistants described each piece to the shipyard computer in three screensful of keyboard dialogue, and the computer held the catalog of pieces in its electronic memory. On command, the computer would outline each part, in ink, on 32-inch-wide tracing paper. Hulltracers cut out the computer's puzzle pieces by hand and pasted them onto scale outlines of the 26-by-8-foot plates in which shipbuilding steel was delivered to the yard. Then, using light-beam pens, they traced the outlines of their pieces, sheet by sheet, back into the computer's memory. The computer made the steel-cutting instructions by punching holes in long, creamy ribbons of stiff paper tape. The tapes, like computer punch-cards, drove the cutting torches of an automated machine to slice multiple shapes, in full scale, from two full-sized sheets of steel at once. Hulltracers working with a computer, Jouan has calculated, do the same work exactly fifteen times faster than lofters on the floor once did.

Hulltracers work like miniaturists and their computer scales the work up into orders that cut steel to ship size. The computer keeps the whole hull in its memory as an exercise in solid geometry, so that a master lofter no longer has to carry that hull constantly in his imagination and his men need no longer spend months on their knees in the loft, fitting and fairing every curve in the ship with hardwood battens. That fairing is also done now by the shipyard computer, which mutters over differential equations for days, in the program written by Gilbert Fournier. The machine finished smoothing out the hull form on February 8, but building had already begun. Two shipfitters started on the first segment of the bottom on January 28, one week after planning and hulltracing began. Seven others started on the sides a week after that. By the end of February, twenty-seven shipfitters were at work in two shops, putting the hulltracers' pieces together.

Computer-aided design and manufacture have become a passion at ACH, but the natural spring of wood still determines the curves in the hulls built at the Graville yard. Past the hulltracers' flat desks and the well-lit computer rooms, through the long, open spaces of the design office, and beyond an insulated wall, there is still a lofting floor, unheated and bare. Each curve in the 216 plates of the outer shell in Karl Andren's ship was laid out there, point by measured point, and trued between points by wood battens, then scribed into the green Formica floor. The three remaining true-scale lofters at the yard did the work.

"This loft," their aging leader told me, "once went all the way to the director's office. They still have to come here to be sure."

The men in the remnant of loft made flat wood patterns to fit the inside of each compound curve on their floor, and sent the plywood patterns outside to guide the ship shapers. Shapers, the shipfitters who bend flat steel plates into the curves of a hull, use the wood patterns as partial molds to check the forms they set in steel by eye. But it is a shaper's eye that makes his work possible.

"Shapers are sculptors at heart, really," a naval architect explained. "They are the secret of any good shipyard."

Shapers do daily what the Cubists presented as a discovery and historians mark as an epoch in the visual arts. They uncover, by eye, the formal geometric elements inside complex shapes made up of intersecting compound curves. The Cubists made their name by discovering that the curves along a woman's thigh or in the swell between her cheek and ear hid geometric shapes and could be painted as shifting cylinders or intersecting planes. A shaping shipfitter sees a hull that way every day. It is his job. I once heard a shaper say, of the turn of the windship's bilge where the form of her hull curved from the flat side to the concave bottom and rose on the long bend from bow to stern: "That's only two cylinders, really. They just have different axes."

Shapers work with hydraulic presses that crease or roll steel and the bending steel complains with a sound like the metallic grinding of monumental teeth. They sculpt a ship this way, piece by 26-foot piece, in two-man teams, an older man leading and his young mate helping. At work on Hull No. 269, they hardly talked at all, in a workshop booming with the noise from cutting, grinding, shaping, and shifting steel. The two looked at each plan together, fixed in mind the forms they saw, then bent a steel plate around those forms as though the final shape they sought were always present in the air between them. They worked as if the ovals inside a cylinder, the triangles underlying a pyramid, pressed out against the steel as they bent it.

René Turquetille believes that a shaper's eye is a gift that must be honed for five or six years at work; that it takes ten years to make a good plate shaper. There were six shapers at ACH for that hull, and a foreman, who said of his trade: "I think everyone has some form of gift. When you've found it, you're happy. This gift is like being able to look at a closed accordion and to unfold it in your head."

To roll the rising curve into all the plates that followed the turn of Hull No. 269's bilge, the Graville shapers used a 300-ton press that clamped one edge of a plate in place beneath a horizontal cylinder of solid steel then raised another steel cylinder, like a fallen tree from the forest floor, up to bend the sheet of ⅜-inch steel. Shifting and bending, they worked their way for two months along both sides of the ship.

No plate came out of the press perfect. The last slight tightening or slacking of each curve in the complex set rolled into a plate was burned in with a torch that carried a head of acetylene flame the size of a small cabbage. Heat, applied just so, expands the steel in patches. When it cools and contracts, the metal curls in those patches and puckers the plate. The senior shaper did the hot adjustments by eye, sweeping the flame in parallel arcs. Without speaking, the two shapers waited, then tested the curve with a set of wood patterns to see if it were true. When it finally was, they set that plate aside for the shipfitters, and took up another plate, another set of patterns. No one else checked their work. It passed on to the assemblers like an honest man's word.

No talking was the rule, also, among the shipfitters who assembled the ship's steel skin and put her bones, the shaped steel frames and the stringers that connected them, in place, block by shipbuilding block. Silence helps concentration. And concentration is the main virtue for shipfitters. In French they are called *charpentiers fer,* "iron carpenters," and one of their foremen told me: "To be good at it, they must love well-made things, things that are clean and square."

They are the puzzle-solvers, who put the steel pieces created by the hulltracers back into their proper places on the plans, but it seemed to me, as I watched on and off over the months, that the shipfitters spent more time thinking than clamping steel pieces into place and tacking them down with short, sparking strokes of their welding rods.

Shipfitters' work occupied most of the floor space in the two largest shops in the yard. The work came to them as a curved steel section of the ship's bottom or side and a bin full of pieces marked and labeled by the hulltracers. They approached it in a manner that made the shops look like large classrooms, on the day of a solid geometry test. Each time I went into the North Shop or the West Shop, during the months of hull assembly work, I saw shipfitters leaning over plans spread on tables next to jobs spread out in pieces on the shop floor. One would straighten and walk slowly in a tight circle, with his head tilted slightly upward and his eyes unfocused. A shipfitting foreman pointed out a circling workman one day in the spring. Nearly shouting over the shop din, he said: "Look. You see? He's fixing his plan. In his head. Got to. Before you start fixing pieces."

The shop foreman, another former lofter who uses the fragmenting bent in his imagination to look steadily two weeks into the future and see what plates and pieces his fitters will need then, guided me toward a 40-foot-tall opening in the shop door, where uncertain midmorning sun took the chill off the concrete floor. The shop noise subsided as we walked away from it.

"That's what really makes a good shipfitter: deliberation," he said. "It is not lost time. On the contrary. One must reflect."

Yet the fitters moved ahead, steadily, even swiftly, and hooded welders wrapped in layers of brown protective clothing kept the same pace behind them. The welders sealed each seam and joint with a bright, fat scar of new metal fused into place by electric current leaping across a few sixteenths of an inch in a blue arc. Grinders followed them, polishing and hollowing the back side of new seams into clefts of bright metal where the welders would make their final, covering pass. Inspectors checked each weld, once it was done, but the foremen rarely looked at the details of work in progress. They had work of their own and seemed to trust their men as much as they themselves were trusted by the shipyard engineers.

Through February and into March, the fitters and welders assembled the most trying blocks, the four widest segments of the ship's double bottoms. Following modern ship design principles, the hull was founded on two watertight steel skins, separated by a tangle of little tanks pierced by manhole hatches and pipe inlets. The shipfitters thought hard over the bottom tanks, to avoid trapping themselves and the welders into spaces too small to turn around in. Nonetheless, welders spent hours in the windship's bottom tanks, with legs drawn up and knees in their chests, welding with one hand and bracing the other against one steel side to take some strain off the cramped muscles in their thighs and calves.

The sailing ship frames had been spaced just under 24 inches apart, and anyone working in a nearly assembled bottom block had to find room to sit between the 6-inch-high frames. At the end of a welding day spent squatting or kneeling in the same small space with sparks and acrid smoke for hours, the welders regularly crawled out and began stretching twenty minutes before quitting time. Stiff and slow, they put away their tools and were finished ten minutes before the four-o'clock whistle. Then they gathered at the shop door nearest their locker rooms. So long as they did not step over the threshold before the whistle, the foremen said nothing to them. In return, welders and fitters worked throughout each day with no apparent supervision, and they began to gain on the construction schedule.

Early in March, Turquetille saw enough assembled steel to begin erecting the hull on the slipway. On a day so raw he wore a cardigan and an insulated vest under his blue overalls, the master shipwright drew the ship's straight backbone in the air above the slipway. His men had temporarily erected steel plates every 15 feet for 405 feet along the concrete strip at the center of the building way, each with a 1⁄10-inch hole at exactly the same height and each as plumb as a 2-pound bob could make it. On the appointed day, they put a bare, 100-watt light bulb on a steel stalk as high as the holes at the water end, where the ship's stern would be. Turquetille stood on the upper end of the slipway and sighted through the holes, calling for adjustments in the plates until he saw the light 400 feet away brighten into two horns like two small and separate flames. He calls this "shooting a light line," and that line in the air became the ship's axis, the conceptual, dead-straight line under her keel.

"We could use a laser," the master shipwright said. "We've got one. But we stick to the old way. It works."

He watched as the yard men built up plumbed piles of 6-by-8-inch wood blocks, where the sighting plates had been, to carry the keel. Then Turquetille and his principal deputy, a bluff man named Jacques Deporte with a jaw like a builder's square, themselves set an arc into the top line of 4-inch-square keel blocks. The arc was just over an inch above the line of light at its highest point of upward deflection. The hull, Turquetille explained, would settle as it grew. The increasing weight of steel would press down on the keel, and the steel would expand with the heat of welding and summer and contract on cold nights. She would flex on the ways until the day of her launching.

"The ship moves as she's building," he said. "Steel is alive."

On March 27, 1985, Turquetille called out the first two blocks of the windship and guided the gantry crane as it lowered them onto the slipway. The keel was laid. He walked away from the low, indeterminate shape on the slipway with his hands in his pockets. Later that day, two gloved reporters from a local radio station came to the shipyard and François Faury put on his overcoat and hard hat and went outside to describe the ship-to-be for their tape recorders. That was all the ceremony they had.

Shipbuilding steel was delivered to the yard with a haze of rust-protective coating sprayed on. It was cut, marked, shaped, and assembled in the three shops around the slipway in a steadily increasing rhythm. The rusty, rose-colored thin protective coat remained intact, except where the shapers had heated in a free-hand pattern and where the welders had burned in their seams with the precision of the plans. By April, assembled segments of the ship were being moved out of the shops to await mounting in the hull.

New rust formed in the spring rain on the welding and heating scars, and blended with the reddish coating. The waiting blocks looked like the abandoned armor of some defeated giant, but they signaled a return to work in earnest at the faltering Graville yard. Laid-off fitters and welders had been recalled and new welders were hired. On the eighth of April, Adam and Turquetille confirmed to the management that they would be ready to launch their hull at the top of the morning flood tide on the thirteenth of the coming November. Cutting had begun for the steel pieces of the second windship hull, set for launching six months later. There was evidence, before all eyes, of work for two years for the full shipyard complement.

Late in April, the shipyard chapter of the Confédération Générale du Travail, the national labor union dominated by the French Communist Party, called two strikes. It was time, the shop stewards said, for higher wages. The first strike was hesitant and lasted an hour and a half. The second lasted six hours and drew off almost half of the salaried yardworkers. Faury and Fournier, who are all the executive management the yard has, did not respond directly, but a nerve tightened throughout the building yard. Adam and Turquetille began to push indirectly. The shipwright started clumping upstairs to the design office once or twice a week. He stood at the elbow of the draftsman inking in the working plans he needed next and chided: "Come on, now, come on. We've got a ship building. I've got men to keep busy. Let's go."

Once or twice a week, Adam came to the yard in the dark at 7:00 A.M., when the fitters and welders punched their timeclock in the tiled hall of the workers' dressing rooms. He shook hands with every man who paused to say "Good morning," he noted the latecomers, and he walked through the locker rooms precisely at 7:30, when all were supposed to be on the job. Polite and smiling, he asked the occasional dawdlers if there was anything wrong. They rarely answered directly. They always heard about their tardiness from a foreman later in the day.

By American standards, the French shipyard was an immensely polite place, where every man and woman shook hands at the first meeting of the day with another employee, regardless of rank, every day, without fail. Adam, the engineer in charge of the hull, knew every man's name and addressed each, from the newest grinder to the foreman, as "Monsieur." First names were never used on the shop floor, except between friends of the same age and salary level. At the same time, working relations were so informal that there were no staff meetings and no weekly or monthly reports. Foremen, engineers, and workmen worked in what appeared always to be an atmosphere of mutual regard. They spoke of and to one another with an undertone of pride, as shipbuilders first, and as employees divided into a clear and static hierarchy only as a matter of course. But the hierarchy, marked first by education, then by earnings, and finally by achievement, was clear and the economic and political tension in French society at large pulled across its divisions like an undertow. The yard union was Communist, the yard owners were the largest surviving capitalists in the shipbuilding business, and no matter how considerate each might act, they had been cast as enemies in France. The political recoil following the dissolution of a governing coalition between Socialists and Communists sharpened the enmity as the windship advanced into summer. Without mentioning that enmity, Adam and Turquetille picked up the building pace.

The hull had started at the midpoint and was put together by two teams, one working forward, the other toward the stern. The builders laid down the bottom first, then the sides on each deck. Then they tacked the divisions and stiffeners on that deck into place. Finally they covered the assembled insides with a sheet of ⅜-inch deck plating like a flat mantle of steel from side to side. Given the midship start, the ship rose first in the middle and then at her ends.

By the end of June, the first two segments of the third deck, where the passengers would eat, had been erected and the middle of the ship showed over the soot-stained walls of the shipyard. More than half of the final launch weight of the ship had been placed on the slipway. Jacques Deporte, Turquetille's deputy and the shipwright who put the hull together, reflected: "It's a well-oiled machine. Design, cutting, shaping, prefabrication. As long as all that rolls along, we have no problems on board."

The builders' first constraints had come from the Study Office. There they could pressure their own colleagues. But late in the spring they began to feel the effects of changes that were outside their reach. Interior design decisions had been made and unmade at meetings between the owners and the shipyard management. Once in March, twice in April, and again in June the positions of portholes in the ship's side were changed. Turquetille resolved to erect the sides without the doubtful openings. They could be cut in later.

Adam had hoped to put aboard, deck by deck, all the sanitary installations for passengers and crew. The bathrooms had been designed outside the yard to be one module incorporating toilet, shower, and washbasin and were all to be cast from the same mold in fiberglass. He wanted them in their places on each deck before the deckplates closed above them. But in May decisions on the details of the modular design froze, for reasons that the hullbuilders could not see. Those reasons were aired at meetings each month, when the shipowner came to the yard, with his interior designer. The hullbuilders heard only the outcome from their engineers.

In June, the engineers reported that the details of the ship's stern ramp, from which the passengers would swim and sail and water ski, had not been resolved. Early in July, Turquetille decided to build the stern without the ramp. It too could be cut in later. He wanted to get as much ahead of schedule as he could, just in case. Just in case, Faury agreed. As a matter of conviction, confidence, and management principle, the shipyard manager left the hullbuilding to the master shipwright. Faury thought of his yard as small, and was proud of its flexibility, but he believed that everyone there had one truly proper function.

Engineers made design decisions and resolved construction problems by calculation in advance, in Faury's view. Shipwrights built hulls, once their shape had been settled, and engineers left them to it. His confidence in his foremen was a matter of course and he spoke of his frequent visits to the hull as "quality control." Adam and Turquetille worked together every day, each apparently comfortable on his own side of the line dividing engineer from craftsman. Adam was surprised when I asked why Turquetille and Deporte had set the arc in the keel alone, unaided by engineering calculations.

"They know how to do it," he said. "It's their profession."

Block after block swung onto the hull. Deporte aligned each huge assembly and leveled it with precision. The shipwright worked to a tolerance of 1 millimeter. He made adjustments where the welded steel segments came together with orders to men swinging 8-pound hammers and the adjustments rang with a clangor that suppressed conversation for 10 yards around. Cutting torches burned away the 3 inches of overlap built into the edges of each block, then grinder wheels spun the last hundredths of a millimeter off in sparks. Seen from inside the hull, the final joints between blocks as long and as heavy as eighteen-wheel trucks showed before welding as thin stripes of ground-out metal. Daylight gleamed through those joints only when the sun fell directly on them outside.

On the eve of the annual French summer vacation, which occupies the whole month of August, the ship had reached two-thirds of her launching weight. There were more shipfitters aboard than in the shops, and thirty-five welders worked in all the ship's corners like brown moles in the interior gloom. Day by day, they sealed the hull together. The shipwrights had gained a solid month on their construction schedule.

"This ship has a simple, I'd say even classical hull," Deporte said one day. "It poses no problems."

Turquetille was standing nearby. He grunted. "Not the hull," he said. "But wait until we start with the rig."

While Turquetille built, the engineers spent most of their time thinking through the rig: the masts, rigging, sail-handling machinery, and sails. Faury himself led the effort to design the sailing part of the sailing ship. It began to absorb him and, as time went on, he absorbed more and more of the task.

The hullbuilders heard little about the rig. They were told that the mast supports to carry the weight and strains of each mast down to the ship's keel would be built and installed after she was launched. The supports were still under study. They heard that the first test of a scale model of the sailing ship, in a wind tunnel in the French Alps, had provoked rethinking among the engineers. The builders learned that the masts, the funnel, and the deckhouses would all have to be made of aluminum. Steel above the main deck, as originally planned, would put too much weight too high up in the ship. High weight makes a ship less stable and affects her movement at sea. The change meant reordering metal; it meant requalifying welders to handle aluminum at the highest insurance standards; it meant the hull would be launched less than complete.

Turquetille had planned to complete the major shipfitting on Hull No. 269 in September. What was in his power slid together smoothly. The ship's bow went on in a 100-ton block on September 26. The stern had been propped into place the day before. The second deck was fully covered at the beginning of the month and the third at the end. The fourth was the last, the main deck, and they left it open, waiting for deliveries that were outside the shipwright's control. The three diesel generators were delayed. There had been a strike at the shipyard where they were made. The cast-iron casing of a huge ballast pump had cracked in its mold on the supplier's casting floor. It would be delayed. Most embarrassingly, the ACH machine shop downtown was very late in work on the two hydraulically driven fin stabilizers that would steady the hull in cross seas.

Sticking to their own schedule, Adam and Turquetille began the long preparation for launching on time. Launching has always been a perilous moment for shipbuilders. The hull, firmly fixed in place and erected like a building ashore, is cut loose on launching day to slide under its own huge weight into a different element. Swiftly, violently, and irreversibly a hull is transformed from a building to a ship afloat. For the minute or more a launch lasts, no man is in control and engineers detest that. They have technical explanations for the physics of the changing risk at every second of the launch; but the hull-builders know that what they really do that day is gather up a year's work, together with their reputations, and throw the whole into the lap of the gods, for a moment. They prepare for that moment with meticulous care.

They greased the slipways under Hull No. 269 and covered them. They built launching cradles and assembled them under the hull. They tested every compartment below the waterline, first with compressed air, then with water under pressure, looking for leaks. They found none. In the second week of October, the diesel generators came and were lowered aboard, then the electric motor. Pipefitters from the ACH dockyard, just upstream in Harfleur where the ship would be finished after launch, began to work on board. The port stablizer arrived and took two days to jockey into place with 25-ton chain hoists and 5-ton come-alongs. Finally, on October 21, the starboard stabilizer arrived from ACH downtown, one month late.

The hull would be ready and the yardworkers began talking about the launch. There had been stories in the papers. Hundreds of people were coming. The Le Havre municipal band would play. There were plans for special trains from Paris for guests from as far away as California. There was even a yard rumor that the U.S. Marines would be on hand to present arms when the Americans' ship slid down their ways.

On Monday, November 4, six working days before the launch, the shipyard's Communist union threatened to strike on November 13. In a truculent flyer passed out at seven by the shipyard gate, the CGT said its people would picket the shipyard on launch day unless ACH agreed to a general raise in pay, a shorter work week, guaranteed employment, and a new wage scale. CGT men, the flyer said, were not going to pay for American celebrations nor "dance to Washington's music." A copy of the flyer hung that day on the wall of the office used by the foremen. Someone had written in, with precise inked lettering: "They prefer Moscow's?"

Faury returned on Tuesday and told the shop stewards that negotiations on that list were out of the question. The yard was fighting for its survival, he told them, and was in no position to pay for a workers' utopia. Besides, no shipyard would live long past a strike on launch day. Adam and the foremen quietly tried to determine whether enough qualified men would cross the picket line to launch without the CGT. They needed sixty hands, but did not find enough in advance of the launch. The yard management refused to negotiate and the union refused to drop its wage demands. For two days, there was an impasse.

On Friday, Gilbert Fournier came to the Graville yard with a rented public address system and called the whole work force to a meeting in the cold November air. French industrial workers almost all come to work on one large cup of milky coffee and a piece or two of bread. They bring half-loaf sandwiches and a bit of a bottle for a true breakfast at the scheduled midmorning break, which usually falls two hours into the working day. Fournier caught them before the break and challenged them on a collective empty stomach. He said he believed the union did not speak for the majority, because everyone at the yard must know that if one ACH launch were delayed by a strike, no shipowner would ever again order from that yard. The world, as they well knew, was overfull with competitive shipyards where strikes were unknown. He called for a vote by show of hands. If there were a majority in favor of the strike, he said: "I will not launch."

Adam watched the vote from a vantage point where he could see his people and later estimated that seventy percent of the weekly wage earners voted to strike. Less than half of those on monthly salaries, he thought, raised their hands. Those were the section foremen and draftsmen, the junior designers and office staff. Fournier watched the arms raised in front of him and said:

"The launch is suspended."

He whirled and went upstairs to call the shipowner. Adam saw men crowd around the two Communist shop stewards. Many others walked back to the hull and the shops in gesticulating groups around their foremen.

It was nine on that Friday morning in France, which made it three A.M. when Fournier's call woke Jean-Claude Potier at home in Miami. Potier had a large public relations operation poised to begin the following Monday. Journalists, selected travel agents, and guests would begin leaving that day for Paris on their way to see the sailing ship launched. The invitations had been issued and accepted. Reservations for planes, hotels, and special trains had all been made, but Potier, Fournier recalled, was understanding. He told the yard president that he would abide by Fournier's decision but that he would have to begin canceling all his arrangements at two that afternoon, just after business lunches had ended on the Eastern seaboard of the United States. He would not start until then. Perhaps there would be some change. Fournier told Potier he would confirm his decision before that hour, which would be eight P.M. in France.

When he hung up, an engineer told Fournier the shop stewards wanted to see him. The two men told him that what they needed to call off the strike was a written promise from Fournier that the yard president would meet them following the launch, to negotiate new wages only. Fournier told them he would not negotiate under duress and would promise no such thing. If they wanted to reconsider, he said, he had been given until two P.M. by the owners. Without a change in the CGT attitude by that time, he said, his decision would stand although the yard might fall. He urged them to consider their responsibilities, but did not tell them his deadline was two P.M. eastern standard time, six hours later than two in the French afternoon.

At 1:45 in France, Fournier's gambit appeared to fail. The stewards told the shipyard president that he himself had seen the strike vote. They could not cancel the strike without something substantial to offer. They needed his promise to talk about wages. Fournier said he would not give it, and left for Paris. The launch, as far as anyone at the yard knew, was off. But the president had told his "guardian ministry" of his decision, and as Fournier drove that afternoon, the shipbuilding deputy to the Socialist minister of industry called the CGT in Le Havre.

Gilbert Fournier drives a Citroën, of that model which has a long, drooping hood. The car has a telephone and the ministry reached Fournier in his car, heading east in the hills above Rouen. The CGT wanted his promise to negotiate. Again Fournier refused. The telephone trilled ten minutes later, as the long car drummed over the bridges at the Seine above Rouen.

"What if I promise them that you will meet with them after the launch?" the bureaucrat at the other end asked.

"What you do is your own affair, entirely," said Fournier. He was racing through the beech forests at the western edge of the Île de France on the A4 *autoroute* where the speed limit is 80 miles per hour. "If you want to do that, go ahead."

The official hung up. When he called back Fournier was driving in the dusk past the bare fields of the Île de France and large old trees in artful woodlots, clinging to their last autumn leaves. The impasse had broken. The CGT had accepted the ministry's promise and would call off the strike.

Fournier drove on to his apartment at the eastern edge of the Bois de Boulogne, in a row of buildings made early this century to look like those of the last. Dead leaves had drifted against the building's 6-foot-high fence of black wrought iron and tangled themselves into the box hedge behind it. Fournier was admitted to the underground garage, climbed the stairs into an entrance lobby paved with large polished squares of black and white marble, and let himself into the apartment. He telephoned Potier and told him the hull would be launched the following Wednesday, after all. It was 5:45 P.M. in Paris, 11:45 A.M. in Miami.

There was an overcast in Paris so black and low on launch day that sixth-floor windows seemed to fade into the underskirts of the clouds. A cold and spiteful rain started just as the shipowner's party left a chartered bus at dawn, to walk across the flagstones to Saint-Lazare station. Potier led the party, like a confident scoutmaster, through the voiceless rush of inbound commuters. He had chartered two cars on the 7:05 businessman's express train to Le Havre, and they filled with a hesitant mixture of reporters and cameramen, French ship brokers, bankers, travel agents, and the radiant Andrens, surrounded by family and friends. The train rolled west along the Seine without a sign of sun. The grass on tunnel embankments had frozen, stiff and white. There was snow to the north and east, in Holland and Champagne. Away to the west, a winter gale whirled up the Channel along the coast of Britanny. But Le Havre was embayed in a hazy calm.

At 7:30 that morning, in the cold weather that drifts in gently on the second day after a gale, Turquetille ordered the keel blocks broken out from under the hull he had built. Along the broad keel, men swung 4-pound hammers simultaneously from both sides and long steel wedges split away the topmost block of 4-by-4-inch wood, the blocks that held the keel in an arch above the shipwright's line of fire. To be exactly on its designed line, once in the water, the keel needed to hold a barely measurable concave flexion when the blocks were gone, almost as if the hull were holding its breath. Six launching cradles took the full weight of the hull's steel—1,496 metric tons—and Turquetille walked out astern.

"There was this much left," he said, holding up thumb and forefinger with just enough space for daylight between them. He ordered five long steel shores cut away from the ship's sides. Two box beams on each side and one I-beam astern, they had been the third and final level of lateral support for the hull as it rose on the ways.

"In case of earthquake," Turquetille had said.

At half-flood, when the gray-brown estuary water covered most of the long double track of the slipway out into the ship basin beyond the yard, Turquetille ordered the bilge shores removed. These shaggy pine trunks had been blocked under the turn of the hull on both sides to keep it from rolling off the keel blocks. His men drove the leveling shims out and lowered the 15-foot pine trunks. Only four dog shores, pointing up into the hull from the direction of the water, well aft, and a plate of 1-inch steel welded between the launching cradle at the bow and a steel girder set in concrete at the head of the slipway held the ship back. With the long rows of bilge shores gone and all the debris and stages cleared away, the hull looked clean and purposeful. All unpainted, except for a coat of anti-fouling paint on the bottom to the waterline, and marked by the scars of welders' burns and shapers' torches, still she looked like a ship for the first time to the layman's eye. The plate shapers had known the ship's underwater form for months, and loved it.

"She is superb," the shapers' foreman said. "Truly. I can't pass her without stopping to admire her lines. I can't get enough of her."

The hull revealed, the underwater hull, looked like the body of a baleen whale. It was deep and sharp forward to cleave the water, then full and almost round, like the whale's belly. Behind the midships belly the underwater body rose slowly and shrank to a point like the shaft of the whale's tail. That was the vanishing point for any perspective drawing of the hull, where the curves all died in one thickness of ⅝-inch steel. That point, on a ridge between the bright, bronze blades of the propeller and the dull mass of the rudder, was where the shaper foreman stood to admire her in the afternoon calm that fell fifteen minutes before quitting time each day.

On launch day, beyond that point, divers backed into the water at 9:30 to make sure the underwater extensions of the slipway were clear. Two tugs were on their way up the harbor. The shipowners' train broke into the sun on the plateau just above the 3 miles of railroad-marshaling yards outside Le Havre. The Andrens looked out the windows and smiled. They nodded at Jacob Stolt-Nielsen and his wife Nadia, across the aisle, who smiled too. Good weather at a launch means good luck for the ship.

Just before ten, with the top of the flood one hour away, Turquetille and his men took away the four dog shores. The master shipwright walked slowly up the slipway, looking at every block on every cradle. When he reached the head of the ways under the bow, he was slightly below the christening platform, erected 90 feet closer to the water. The municipal band played at his back. The owners had arrived. The shipwright nodded at two welders in the slipway pit beneath him and they lit their cutting torches. One stood on each side of the 3-foot-wide holding plate, in broad notches where it had been cut away to leave a 12-inch-wide tongue. That tongue was all that still held the ship on land.

At 10:15, the scheduled launching time, Louise Andren began her christening speech, first in French and then in English. Her voice echoed from high loudspeakers to the shop walls. Her words were not wholly clear until she paused, took breath, and said: "Fair winds and following seas to this ship and to all who go in her. I christen thee *Wind Star*!"

The christening bottle of champagne swung from her outstretched hand, at the end of a pendulum of ribbons. It smashed and the band began "La Marseillaise." Then the musicians played "The Star-Spangled Banner." A tug drifted into line with the ship's launching run. Faury, on the edge of the christening platform, spoke into a walkie-talkie. Water boiled under the tug's counter and she moved. Faury pointed to Turquetille. The shipwright dropped his right hand.

"Cut!" said the welding foreman below him, and the torches bit into the steel holding plate. Their flames ate steadily in from each side and spat out the burned steel in molten, orange drops. The band had ended both anthems and the foreman saw light growing between the cradle and the slipway head. The last 3 inches of the holding plate snapped and the crowd fell silent. The ship began to move.

She slid at first in the same kind of sudden, huge silence that fills the instant before an avalanche or the seconds just before an earthquake. That is a windless sound, as if the mountains were drawing in breath before letting it all out in a huge and rumbling sigh; one of those sounds that are not noise, that are felt more than heard. At the launch, the instant ended when the cradles hissed past and the ship's stern took the water, shoving back the flood tide. Two ship lengths of 4-inch anchor chain, laid out below the cradles to slow her rush, rattled down the ways after her and the ship genuflected to the land, pivoting on the bow cradle as seawater bore her up from the stern.

The whistles of the two tugs screamed as she floated clear and the water displaced by the new ship foamed back up the slipway, breaking in waves on the empty slope. Four thousand, six hundred balloons that had been released from a breach in the main deck floated off like a brushstroke in the air, echoing the shape of the ship's launching rush.

Wind Star turned on the water and changed from rusty red to black as she crossed the low sun. She had gone into the water unpainted, unfinished, unmasted, and the two tugs took her in charge. One at the bow and one at the stern, they towed her away up the harbor for the year-long job of finishing. The guests climbed down from the platform, wrapping their overcoats tighter. With the excitement gone, the cold had returned. Only Karl Andren wore no overcoat that day, although his breath sometimes condensed before him. He was, perhaps, demonstrating what the sons of Åland could do.

"I liked her lines on the water," he said.

"She's going to be pretty," his banker, a guest at the launch, put in. The two men walked together to a press conference presided over by Jean-Claude Potier. Andren's father stopped and looked east, after the slowly moving ship.

"She bends her knees as she takes the water," he said. "That was a good sign."

In fact, every bit of the traditional launching ritual went right that day. Every augury in the seaman's lexicon pointed to good luck for the new ship. The weather cleared before launching, as though just for that event. The ship did not hesitate on the ways: one says then that she is eager to take the water. She took the water well and floated quickly free of the land, balanced high on her lines. She did not list or roll or heel but stood proud on the water. The foremen who had built her gathered and sat in a shop office out of the way, while the band packed up and the crowds went away. They talked about the launch until slowly their conversation came back to the business at hand. The cradles would be recovered this afternoon? No, tomorrow. And tomorrow, we'll want a full complement on the second sailing ship. Don't want to get behind on that. A passing man leaned in through the open office door and said:

"Congratulations, gentlemen." The foremen stirred, and answered: "Thank you, sir."

That afternoon, as the propitious tide selected seven months earlier for the launch ebbed away from the land, the owners and the yard entertained 250 guests at a three-hour luncheon in a high hall overlooking the beach beyond the harbor entrance: container ships and coastal freighters, trawlers and oilers left on the ebb, slipping between the two gray stone breakwaters outside the windows while the lobster was served, and roast beef, in a Norman cream sauce, and two wines.

Shipbuilding, it seemed, might go on forever. The owners toasted their builders. The builders toasted back. Conversation rose in a clatter and settled politely when Louise Andren rose to speak for Karl and thank the builders. As she spoke, the dessert was carried in, like the tenor in *Aïda,* riding in a sedan chair. It was a cake made to look like a layered ship in the Windstar company colors, white and Caribbean blue, and the shipowner's wife, her speech of gratitude cut short, presided while the baker's apprentices lit sparklers at every corner of the cake. Her last thought was lost in the rising noise of anticipation.

"Our venture, or adventure, if you want, has now truly begun," Mrs. Andren had said.

7

CHAPTER

Decision by Osmosis

If I believed in metempsychosis, I could see myself in one of my incarnations as a sea captain or, more likely, a shipwright.

—Marc Held, to essayist Gerald Weissmann

When she was towed up the harbor after launching, *Wind Star* was an empty shell of heat-scarred steel. Two tugs jostled her alongside the dockyard pier in Harfleur where the bare hull was to be turned into a passenger ship and rigged for sail. Yardworkers tied her to the land with double ropes of steel wire. She had been proud and imposing, floating in the estuarine salt water off the slipway at Graville. In the flat, brackish water behind the locks in Harfleur, at the very back and landlocked corner of the saltwater port at Le Havre, the ship might have been mistaken for a forgotten hulk. She lay at the quiet end of an inland barge canal, just upstream from a tank farm and a concrete depot. Her bow faced the continent, which was no more than a low and brushy bank there. When the S.S. *France*, perhaps the most beautiful passenger liner ever built, spent years laid up nearby, Le Havre natives named her berth in the brush behind the port the Quay of Oblivion.

No ship is at her best just after launching. Poised between building and fitting out, while the workmen who know her leave and new men move loudly aboard, any ship looks as dirty and abandoned as a house in a war zone. Aboard *Wind Star* at her first berth, the boots of pipefitters, electricians, and mechanics coming to work in the dark at 7:30 echoed with a dull and gritty sound from the steel stairs. Cables from the shore looped through the empty decks and along the passageways in black tangles and spilled down ladders to feed welding machines and bare worklights that only pushed the interior darkness back as far as the nearest corner, even at noon. There was nothing inside the ship that was finally hers except the main diesel generators, three of them, mounted but still in their plywood packing, the main electric motor, some lumps of crated machinery in the laundry forward of the engine room, and the reverse osmosis plant, squatting in the engine-room alleyway. This machine, piped and cushion-mounted, would make the ship's fresh water by putting sea water under extreme pressure on one side of a set of membranes, to force only water slowly through them into fresh water on the other side, leaving salt ions behind.

The unpainted wood toolboxes of the dockyard workers, with rope handles at each end like the sea-chests of a century earlier, were stacked squarely against bare steel bulkheads, promising a transformation to come. Jean-Claude Potier, the president of the new cruise line without any ships, had already made that transformation in his imagination.

Seven months earlier, when the keel had just been laid, Potier had seen the ship in his mind's eye, finished and afloat. With all sails set and drawing, she was driving for an anchorage in Antigua on a Sunday, in Potier's dream. All the largest cruise ships were there, in his vision, and Potier said he could hear the sound of a thousand jaws dropping as his ship hove into view. He could hear a murmur on many decks and, listening closer, distinguish words. "Look!" people said. "A sailing ship! That's what I want to go to sea on. Give me that for a cruise."

Potier had spent years in the passenger-shipping business becoming a master of imagery, who could weave a new impression of luxury around an old ship, an honest, working passenger liner, then sell that impression to cruise passengers, people with no fixed destination and leisure time to get there. When the chance came for him to shape a new ship that would fit inside an image of his own creation, Potier seized that chance. It is fair to say that the chance also seized him. By his own account, he was possessed.

"I was not looking for this job. I did not know Andren from Adam when he called me," Potier said, just after *Wind Star*'s keel was laid. "But when I saw the project, I said to myself: 'This is it. This is what I have always wanted to do.' "

That was a figure of speech, because Potier had never been a seaman or a sailor. He had pursued a business career as a hired executive as if he were training to become the chairman of some board. He had been married four times and hospitalized once, sick nearly to death with heart disease. He once remarked that if anyone had told him, when he was twenty-five and a good beginning bourgeois, he would marry four times in thirty years, he would have thought that person crazy. But he had married and remarried, changed countries and changed jobs. In personal matters, he had adopted the view he once heard expressed by a very successful French industrialist: "The only thing one can count on is one's professional life. Private life is so volatile."

Potier is a Norman by birth, a Parisian by training. He was born in Saint-Lô and raised on the Cotentin peninsula, the nearly square northernmost thrust of France that juts into the Channel athwart the gales from west and east. His family, as he remembers it, prized education and was careful about money, of which it had enough. Potier showed talent for music as a youth but was given a traditional education in law in Paris and history at the University of Montreal. With an M.A. in history, he went to work for the French Line, the Compagnie Générale Transatlantique, which is known along the whole Norman coast and well into Brittany as "la Transat."

He rose in la Transat, was transferred to New York in 1960, and stayed. After a quarter century in the United States, Potier speaks wholly fluent English, with great flair and a French accent that is just short of theatrical. The right corner of his mouth rises in a small, permanent muscular tuck of the kind that only strenuous work with French vowels will develop. Still, he is so American a Frenchman that he was outraged when a Parisian policeman stopped him one evening and demanded his identity card.

"I told him I was terribly sorry, but I did not have an ID card," Potier said the next day. "Such things are unknown in the United States, where I live."

Living in the United States and selling a luxury service in what he always calls "the cruise industry," Potier developed a creed. He came to believe that vacations for high achievers had become a necessity almost equal to food, clothing, and shelter. Such people, he thought, who drove themselves daily in pursuit of an abstraction, required a true rest in surroundings that contrasted with the noisy, low-quality, harried, and polluted life that money earners live in modern cities. His creed had a sharp point of personal conviction. Surgeons sewed five coronary bypasses around Potier's heart in 1980, while he was chief executive officer of Sun Line Cruises. Four years later, through Andren, he discovered sailing, which is the calmest way left on earth to travel long distances.

"*Mon vieux,* you should get interested in sail," I once overheard Potier tell another survivor of cardiac surgery on the telephone. They had recovered in the hospital together and had kept in touch. Potier gestured at me to stay and listen.

"*Enfin,* I don't mean go sailing, but find something you love to do. I passed my last stress test two months ago with better results than the year before. One can work ten or twelve hours daily as long as one avoids stress. I avoid stress by working at what I like, this sailing ship."

Potier tested his new affection carefully, between May and October 1984. He arranged Andren's marketing study and read the results. Privately, he did earnings and expense projections. He made sure of his deal with Andren and wrapped it in a tidy legal package. Then, one weekend, he left his job and went home to start the company that would operate Karl Andren's new ship. He installed an extra telephone in his Miami apartment and opened the company bank account with $500 advanced from New York. For months after that, even in rented quarters overlooking a sea of green treetops in Coral Gables, Potier and an elegant, protective secretary were the entire staff of the new company. He was proud, looking back, that they were taken seriously from the outset, even by the San Francisco designers who created a corporate symbol and company colors. The designers, he was sure, would have recognized a con man or fraud.

The new president changed the ship that Andren and Heinan and Hansen had planned. A contract addendum in early December, after Potier had been at work for two months, added a little length, as well as three feet of extra beam to accommodate more hotel staff in the crew quarters. On the new plan, the public rooms were moved up to the third deck and a glass-walled discotheque was drawn in above them on the main deck. At the same time, luxury became the aim in planning cabins and public rooms. Andren's dormitories disappeared and the idea of a windjammer cruise with working passengers died. Potier's experience, summed up in business arguments, prompted the changes.

The change in *Wind Star* was personified for the shipyard when Potier brought them Marc Held, the Parisian industrial designer he had chosen to plan and decorate all the places where passengers would live on the new ship. The yard knew of the designer. He had worked on remodeling a ceremonial hall at the Élysée Palace, the residence of French presidents. He had done buildings for IBM. Once, only, he had redecorated parts of a French cruise liner. This innocence of ship work was what Potier wanted, in order to get a new start. He wanted to create a cruise that he would take himself, with his friends; not the sort of sea vacation he had been selling before Andren called him.

"The cruise industry," Potier was fond of saying, "is perpetuating a tradition that has no living roots."

Caribbean cruises were not North Atlantic crossings, he said, so they had no business feeling like such steamship passages. Potier wanted no more cruises on converted transatlantic liners, where closed decks and grand hotel decor had once made passengers feel safe on the North Atlantic. He wanted no featureless hallways with fluorescent ceilings like those on new cruise liners. On Potier's ideal cruise there would be no more Italian nights with singing waiters in the dining room or horse racing, with betting on cardboard cutouts advanced by dice around the salon; no more passenger talent nights with paper hats and party favors; and no more captain's cocktail parties with receiving lines that might advance for hours at the pace of three steps, a handshake, and a Polaroid flash. All the sea cruises Potier had seen reminded him of his eldest daughter's report on her first meeting with Santa Claus at Macy's in New York.

"What did Santa Claus say?" Potier asked.

"He said: 'Keep moving,' " his daughter answered.

The ship arriving in Antigua in Potier's dream was to be a sailing ship, a ship with a naturally leisurely pace, and, below decks, a cruise ship like no other he had seen: "Open to the sea, the wind, and the sky," he said she must be, when design work started. To make those openings, he chose Marc Held.

"Held was brought to us by Tom Heinan and Jean-Claude Potier as their baby, the apple of their eye," François Faury, the shipbuilder, said. "We were ready to do anything for him." What could have been left to do?

First Kai Levander, then Faury and his technical assistants, had done the work that would determine the nature of the new ship at sea. They had chosen length and breadth and hull form and calculated the weight and placement of her machinery and her masts. These decisions, made years before she would sail, set the limits for the ship's performance. Such choices determined how she would roll in a beam sea and how she would turn and handle. The unadvertised and constant concentration of René Turquetille and all his men on the hull made her sound in advance. The workmen at Harfleur, running pipe and stringing wire, would settle how hard the ship would be for her crew to work, whether she would be simple and reliable or a cranky prototype requiring constant attention.

For a seaman or a shipbuilder, the important work had all been done. There remained only the passenger spaces, cabins and lounges and restaurants and bars, which occupied two-thirds of the ship but would cost only one-tenth of her final price to finish and decorate.[1] Passengers, however, would be the ship's public. They would judge the windship's success by paying to sail aboard. If passengers were not pleased by the ship, she would fail. Accordingly, the design and decoration of the ship's internal spaces, undertaken last, assumed first claim on the time of the owner and the builders until the very end. As in so many other modern endeavors, the public's perception of the project became its essence.

Marc Held was the last in a cast of strong-willed men brought together to shape the windship, each according to his own vision. First there had been Karl Andren, whose business vision was laid onto a deeper ancestral dream of sailing ships. Tom Heinan stood in for him, almost as Andren's alter ego, with a passion for detail and real control over the millions of dollars committed to the project. It was Heinan who said, over and over again, that the accommodations generated the revenue and that they had to be right. Potier looked ahead, to the marketplace, trying to foresee what would please the people driving BMWs, all unaware that Andren and Potier wanted them to go on a sailing cruise. Gilbert Fournier and François Faury had a technical vision of a new ship type, one that might mark their places in shipbuilding history. Held came in last, with the artist's conviction that it is the artist, and the artist alone, who signs his work before it is presented to the public.

Marc Held is a nut-brown man. He has hazel hair, chestnut eyes, and skin the color of almond hulls. He moves and talks with purpose and conviction, is articulate in French, English, and German, and dazzles even his enemies with his charm. At times, when he is at home by a table on the top floor of his Paris studio, in the same Left Bank building where Picasso painted briefly in the deep depression of his Blue Period, or performing before hesitant clients at a meeting, rearranging color swatches and material samples swiftly to keep ahead of ideas as they change in committee, Held might be a beneficent and practical elf: wise, creative, and adaptable. At other times, when he advances his own ideas or shakes off criticism, one notices how like a boxer he is in body and manner. He bounces on his toes, moving like a bantamweight in the ring as his own sentences peak. When others speak, his calves work and his feet move slightly, staying square. By preference, he moves to and from the crucial moments on any job surrounded by a following of friends and assistants.

Held was fifty-one years old when he got the *Wind Star* contract, and looked fifteen years younger. In the fall of that year, male fashion in Paris demanded a tailored version of the English country gentleman, with fitted tweed jackets and gray flannel trousers. One year later, the Paris look on billboards and in the best cafés showed pleated pants, broad-waisted shirts, and bow ties. Held wore both styles in their seasons, before they appeared on billboards.

Held is a self-made man in the most radical sense. He was originally trained and certified as an instructor of gymnastics for the French public-school system. It was his father's insistent idea of a secure career for the first French son of two immigrants, a Hungarian father and a Polish mother. But Held taught himself industrial design, won a contract to design furniture, and left his gym-teacher post. Without formal architectural training, he practices building design and lists both professions on an embossed business card that reads:

Marc Held
Architecte
Designer Industriel

However, he thinks of himself most often as an artist and sees time and mortality as enemies of his work. The advance of age, Held says, enrages him.

In the winter before *Wind Star,* the Held family vacationed together in the Austrian Alps, where it is possible to spend a full day skiing across several mountains with linked trails and lifts. Marc set out one morning to do that with his eldest son, who was then twenty-two.

"He is stronger than I, or his endurance is better, but I have the advantage of better technique. The tour became competitive," Held said. "We were quite even all the way through, but at the end of the day I found I could hardly breathe. It made me furious."

François Faury was forty-four years old and had four sons when he started to build *Wind Star.* He had been a competitive boardsailer for seven years and had reached the national championships in his age group. However, his eldest son had begun to surpass him on some points of handling a sail-equipped surfboard. One afternoon, on the way to lunch, he spoke of the seventeen-year-old's expertise to a visiting shipping inspector.

"Your son beats you?" the inspector asked.

"At certain things only, for now, but it is bound to happen," Faury said. "I fight like a fiend, when they start to compete with me, but I am very happy when one of my sons learns enough to beat me at something."

The shipbuilder was a self-disciplined, rather than a self-made man. He had been trained for five years at the graduate level, in the schools that make the French elite, and members of that elite do not scramble for their social position. They take it for won, by competitive education, and granted, by society at large. As a *polytechnicien,* Faury knew the form and order for any social ceremony and was connected to an old-boy network that extended to every power center in France. He was also a shipbuilder by choice, who had broken with a four-generation family tradition, forgoing a career as an army officer to follow his heart into naval engineering.

At Potier's insistence Faury and Held were brought together to build *Wind Star* and bound together by a contract in which Held, the owner's choice, became a subcontractor to the shipyard, responsible for the design of all passenger spaces. Faury, the yard manager and director of shipbuilding for the ACH group, signed as Held's taskmaster at the foot of a contract that included stage-by-stage deadlines, with firm dates and penalty clauses for late work.

The relationship began uneasily in November 1984, at the first of a steady series of monthly meetings between the shipowner, the shipyard, and Marc Held. The three parties had to work out the ship's interior as they went along, because no firm interior design work had been done when construction started. The shipyard engineers anticipated no difficulties. Although ACH had never built a passenger ship, they were confident that they knew how. The engineers saw Held as a decorator, who would choose colors and materials for the cabins and corridors, lounges and halls that they would build. At that first meeting, they showed Andren and Heinan passenger cabin layouts proposed by their design staff and asked for the owner's choice. It was as if the owners had not heard them. Held was in charge of passenger accommodation and decor, they said. He would design. The yard would build his design, space layout, steel bulkheads and all. The engineers retreated, recognizing that Held might be financially responsible to them but would take orders only from the owners.

Marc Held's studio delivered its work on schedule through that winter and into the spring. Coordinated samples of color and materials mounted on white cardboard plaques came to the joint design meetings first, then sketches, and finally perspective drawings. Potier saw the inside of his dream ship filling in before him like a portrait painted in several sittings, and he was enchanted. The drawings were full of natural wood and stainless-steel trim, with broad glass expanses giving onto sails and sky and sea. The ship would look like a large and luxurious modern yacht. The shipyard engineers nodded politely as they heard the plans and looked at the sketches. They said they were not sure they could get insurance approval for the use of wood, or for the large glass openings. Wood carried a large risk of fire; big glass windows were not considered safe at sea. The shipbuilders would see what they could do, but, their attitude said, they knew the rules and exigencies of their profession. They might well, the shipowners responded, but the owners knew what they wanted and would insist on getting it.

By the time the keel was laid, the two parties to the shipbuilding effort, owners and builders, had begun to speak of each other as "the Owner" and "the Yard." In a manner so traditional it has been reported for centuries,[2] they had identified each other not exactly as adversaries, but as rivals for perfection in the enterprise. Each knew how to build the ship best; each group felt the other group seemed slow to understand.

At the monthly design meetings, the yard was always represented by Faury, his donnish-looking assistant Antoine Castetz, also a *polytechnicien,* and René L'Heryénat, the chief of the Studies Office. They often called in others. The owner came to the early meetings in the persons of Karl Andren, Tom Heinan, and Jean-Claude Potier, and they were counseled by consultants from the cruise business and advised by friends and family. There were many opinions before every decision and the yard and the owner became quite carefully slow.

At least as I saw it from the outside, the business of designing and building the cruise liner's interior got a brisk start then suddenly slowed in the spring of 1985. Months later, Heinan said he thought that design decisions had only formed by osmosis, drop by drop, under pressure.

The yard fretted over its deadlines, the owners refused to be rushed, and Held occasionally stormed at both parties, at least as I heard them all by turns after their monthly working sessions. I was not, at first, admitted.

"You can't come to a meeting!" Potier exclaimed with alarm, when first I asked. "We shout at each other!"

"Shout?" Held said. "I shout. Sure I shout. And carry on. Life is short. The life of an artist is brief. Time, the time to make things, hurries us."

Held worked in an ill-defined gap between the yard and the owner, and, in his own judgment, he was slow to recognize the real, multipersonal nature of the two. "I thought at first that I had one interlocutor, Jean-Claude Potier, a man of taste," Held said. "That is normal in design work. One man has the power to decide."

Held and his associates worked on that assumption, he said, until the spring of 1985, when they were suddenly brought up short. In May, Jacob Stolt-Nielsen, his wife Nadia, and Karl and Louise Andren reviewed his design work in Le Havre. In the narrowest sense of the phrase, those four were the owner. They had decided to build the ship and had made the down payment together.

The two shipowning couples, one experienced and the other just beginning, together saw a passenger cabin roughed out by shipyard carpenters in bare plywood and reviewed all of the perspective drawings from Held's studio. They made many reservations and suggested a long list of changes. Andren later said there were too many sharp corners in the furniture as proposed. Passengers might have hurt themselves as the ship moved at sea. And the cabin design was full of dead corners that would be difficult to clean. Some of the materials Held had proposed for the cabins looked too delicate to stand up to years of hotel use, with baggage lugged in and out twice each week, parties inside, and spills in the halls. The owners also required some changes in the passenger bathroom design. The designer was not present, but he learned later he would have to start over. His first flash of resentment escaped not directly at yard or owner but sideways.

Andren had hired, as construction supervisor and therefore the owner's daily representative to the yard, a Danish naval architect named Kell Guldborg Andersen. Andersen had begun his career with a four-year apprenticeship during which he became a journeyman wood boatbuilder on his home island of Hirsholmen. Then he started his studies in naval architecture. He was precise, tenacious, and proud to the point of sensitivity of his twenty-two years in the passenger-ship business, perhaps because, in the year *Wind Star*'s keel was laid, his home firm went bankrupt and he became, at the age of forty-nine, an involuntary consultant. Andren, in May, directed ACH to involve Andersen constantly in their work and told Andersen to get, from Held, the changes the owners wanted in the molded fiberglass bathrooms.

"The first design of the sanitary module had many practical things wrong with it," Andersen said. "It was very handsome, of course, but who was going to sit on a toilet and put his feet up on a coaming five inches high? Things like that."

With limited French, the new consultant telephoned Held just after the May inspection and asked for a design meeting. He used Antoine Castetz as an interpreter.

"He got silent and finally just handed me the phone," Andersen recalled. "Held told me to go fuck myself and to go back to my little, lost country." The Dane blushed as he said it. Castetz, whose steady-running wit was of the dry, lofty, and slightly fey variety, stumbled a little over the same two phrases when he recalled them. Such talk was "inadmissible" in the view of a *polytechnicien.*

There was some sympathy for Held among the owners, however. Andren said, soon after the bathroom incident, that Held was an artist, after all.

"And you can't tell an artist exactly what to do," he said. "It's like commissioning a painter for a mural and telling him, 'You can do anything with that wall, just so long as you paint it red.' "

"I would rather be a nuclear engineer, running a neighborhood reactor, than a designer," Potier said fervently. A nuclear engineer, living near his own reactor? "Yes. No one has the faintest idea about nuclear physics, but everyone, absolutely everyone, thinks he—or she—is an interior designer."

The shipyard managers watched the debate over design with the kind of tight politeness that covers growing desperation. They said nothing. The shipbuilders were falling behind schedule too early and the most experienced men, just below managerial level, saw it happening. They did talk.

"It seems as though people don't know what they want anymore," Jouan, the head hulltracer, said one afternoon. "We'll have done this ship three times over, there have been so many modifications."

The practical difficulty, from the shipyard point of view, was that each change in interior design brought with it two immutable consequences. The first was a dead-time delay, for new calculations and new working drawings. Each interior change had to be accommodated to the whole, and some changes were easy to work in while others meant large upheavals. Furthermore, the time and concentration needed for completed working drawings of the inner workings of the ship could be staggering. The final, all-encompassing drawing of one compartment in the uncontroversial engine room occupied one draftsman for nine months. He had to place every machine, then imagine every pipe of every size that would run through the compartment, every wire of every planned thickness and every valve and switch and panel and place them all on paper, in advance of any installation, so precisely that no element would interfere with any other.

The second result of any substantial modification was a linked chain of changes that spread for decks away. The owners found out they could not, on second thought, change the perspective in the ship's dining room from partially closed to wholly open without changing the steel structure of the ship. They resolved to make the change anyway.

Andren, Heinan, and Potier discovered that they could not move the main lounge bar without changing the piping and the drains that ran through three decks below the lounge. They could not implement a new idea in lighting without changing deck-length wiring diagrams and, eventually, the whole electrical load of the ship. But they ordered both kinds of changes. So many electrical afterthoughts were added, even after electricians had begun to run the 120,000 yards of wire and cable diagrammed for the hull at Harfleur, that one of the supervising electricians there remarked that the owners might find they could not undock and run the ship's air conditioning at the same time.

"That's a joke," he said. "I think. We will see, someday."

All during the first year of their project, the hullbuilding year, the shipyard and the shipowner came ever more closely to grips with the immense complexity of building a passenger ship. On both sides, the early assumptions that the job could be quickly done evaporated. The chief of the machinery designers and draftsmen at ACH confessed that he had thought *Wind Star* would be easy.

"Today, I would never think it simple," he said. "Take refrigeration alone: there are six cold rooms, each with a different temperature, and a refrigerator in every room. That means a cold-water conduit to every one of seventy-five cabins on two decks."

The section chief had pinned a drawing of *Wind Star* heeling under sail to the door of the machinery drafting office. The caption said: "Remember! Everything has to work at ten degrees of heel."

There was no simple way of reminding the shipowners to make quick decisions. In January of the hullbuilding year, Andren and Heinan had resisted shipyard pressure to decide the size and location of all the ship's windows and portholes, once and for all. They wanted more time for the interior design, but windows and portholes required structural calculations for every change and insurance approval of every new plan. It was September before the window openings in the ship's sides were all finally sized and placed. Over that and other decisions, there was irritation on every side. The owners' party thought that getting technical commitments and plans from the yard took too long. Shipyard men said the owner was indecisive.

Decisions come most easily when they come from experience, and a lack of experience means hesitation. The shipyard engineers avidly accepted all the advice the owners bought from outside consultants who knew, from experience, how to lay out cruise-ship galleys and bars and passenger cabins, and how to comply with all the minute regulations of the United States Public Health Service. But the French engineers never so much as suggested that they could not have done it all themselves. Their assurance made a stylish cover for real engineering hesitations and occasional indecision. The owners were not so defensive about their lack of experience.

"Hesitant? Of course, we're hesitant," Tom Heinan said when he heard that word applied to the owner's decisions. "This shipyard has never built a passenger ship and neither have we."

In their joint hurry to qualify for the French government's export credit and settle a contract, the shipyard and the owners had accepted contract specifications that were vague, by the usual precise standards of modern shipbuilding. That meant that they needed to design details together, so, no matter what the irritation, they had bound themselves to get along for a year or more. They worked together in a conceptual space like a corral, with distant but inflexible fencing.

Each of the parties had deadlines. To survive, the shipyard needed to deliver the new ship on time. Andren had Circle Line under mortgage to start up his new cruise line, and he planned to spend several borrowed millions before the line's first sailing ship was even finished. Only when she was completed and working could he start to repay the start-up loan. Yet each of the owner's changes, as one after another was accepted by the shipyard, held a potential for delay in completion of the ship. For human reasons at first, and perhaps for legal reasons, someone had to be held responsible. After the inspection in May, Marc Held made an obvious candidate. His designs had not been accepted by the owners and his work had begun to arrive late.

The deadline for ordering the bathroom units had been April. After the changes provoked in May, the final design was not available for order until June. The first detailed mockup of a passenger cabin, with its Held-designed walls, doors, lights, wallpaper, rugs, curtains, and bedspreads in place, was expected in June. It was ready at the end of July and still the owners did not like all that they saw. Held came away from that presentation with the impression that something new, something more daring and modern, was wanted. He was given until early October to come up with it. He made the deadline with conceptual drawings but not working plans.

Faury began to apply the penalties contained in Held's contract with the shipyard. He delayed partial payments to the designer's studio every time a portion of the designer's work was late. To Held it seemed that the shipyard manager treated him as though he were a tradesman or delivery boy who was only welcome at the back entrance. He fought back, challenging the yard executives to reopen the late summer bidding on the construction and decoration of the ship's public rooms because he believed they could be built for less. He insisted that they get insurance approval for the use of wood in the decoration on board. After all, he pointed out, Wärtsila knew how to do it. When the second round of bids for the lounges, bars, and dining room produced a large savings, and the insurance inspectors finally approved a process for gluing wood veneer over sheets of galvanized steel, the designer felt he had humiliated the shipyard and rejoiced.

"We were," he said later, "at war."

"I have understood, finally, that building a ship is something tremendously emotional," Held said. "Those shipbuilders are putting their hearts, their very guts into this ship. They do not accept some landsman coming in among them and saying, 'I'm in charge here. I'm the father of this.' You see, there can be only one person who gives this ship its final shape—at least inside—and that one is me. When people ask 'Who did this?' the answer will be 'Marc Held.' And they cannot stand that."

The shipyard manager never accepted the designer's declaration of war. Faury looked through Held to the owners for decisions and continued to apply the terms of his contract with Held. The designer's working drawings for the cabin were late; so were his payments.

The practical deadline for the third model cabin for *Wind Star* was the day the hull was launched. Potier had invited his sales staff, travel writers, and wholesale travel agents to Le Havre that day to see the ship and a mockup cabin. One month before the launch, Potier and Heinan approved Held's perspective drawings for a corridor lined with corrugated stainless steel, like a railroad passenger car turned inside out, and a cabin with wood walls, rounded metal furniture, a broad mirror, and spotlights. They also approved a bid for the cabins from an old friend of the shipyard, a decorating contractor named Pierre Gravé, who had started his working life as a draftsman in a Le Havre shipyard with one of the old-line engineers at ACH.

Gravé received the designer's final scale drawings and material specifications twelve days before the launch, and there were two mandatory French public holidays between him and his deadline on November 13. He ordered the materials, including wood veneer from Finland and textiles from Marseilles, and sent his own trucks out to get them. He divided all his shop employes into two shifts, so that work could go on from six A.M. to ten P.M. each day. His staff developed the working drawings for the model cabin, then built every piece of the full-scale mockup, from the walls in to the bedspread, and finished it with varnish, paint, rugs, lights, drawers, latches, and mirrors at two A.M. on the thirteenth. Held himself worked with the assemblers on the last two nights and left at two, when the mockup was finished.

After *Wind Star*'s triumphant launch, the invited guests moved in a broad, chattering stream into the West Shop to see the ship's only completed cabin. The mockup stood on a platform of structural steel, lifted on 3-foot-long legs painted primer red. The outside walls were blank, unpainted fiberboard, and the only warmth in that corner of the shop shone out through the cabin's double portholes. In the dull, watery light inside the high, empty shop, the mockup looked like a lunar lander on a gray plain. All the life was inside.

The owners, the engineers, and the guests stamped their feet on the concrete shop floor to stay warm. They looked up at the cabin on stilts, waiting for a chance to peep in through a porthole or to walk up a ramp and through the cabin door, one small group at a time.

In Held's third version, the cabin had been finished with one curving wall of dark wood veneer that surrounded a large mirror and ended in a wood console by the bed. Beyond the bed, two large portholes with shining brass hinges were set into a fiberglass mold of eggshell white. Opposite the bed was a flat wall covered with white, sound-absorbent material. A television set in a black plastic case hung in one high corner, poised on a bracket. A bright metal lamp, shaped like a long dentist's light, was clamped to the wall with its back to the room. Below the mirror stood a gray array of vinyl and aluminum that looked like two steamer trunks placed head to head on their sides. It unfolded upward and outward in three places to act as dressing table, bureau, and desk. The master joiner who had put the thing together in ten days was awarded a medical leave of absence for nervous exhaustion after launch day and never worked on that part of the cabin again. He refused to.

Marc Held himself, wearing a white shirt, bow tie, and suit, stood in the cabin door as guide, and the shipowners, Karl and Louise Andren, Jacob and Nadia Stolt-Nielsen, were the first to enter.

"The reactions," François Faury said later in his mild and moderate manner, "were extreme."

The Stolt-Nielsens hated it and said so immediately. One of Potier's guests, a travel agent specializing in the cruise packages that large corporations offer as incentives to their sales staffs, left the cabin saying: "We can't possibly sell that." One of Potier's marketers walked alongside the agent saying: "We'll change it; we'll change it."

The news that the cabin design had again failed an owner's inspection spread slowly through the launch-day luncheon. On the special train back to Paris, the Stolt-Nielsens sat in silence, several rows behind Andren's cheerful party. That evening, in a rococo private dining room off the Champs Élysées, where the Andrens and Potier had invited their guests for dinner, Held saw Jacob Stolt-Nielsen approach him. The designer was talking to another guest.

"He was circling like a shark and I knew he wanted to tell me off," Held said. "Finally, he stopped, looked down at me, and said: 'I don't like your cabin and I won't put any of my money in a ship that has it.' "

However, at the end of that dinner, when Stolt-Nielsen rose to give a speech of thanks on behalf of all the dinner guests, he did not mention the cabin. He spoke of the good omens for the ship that day, wished her well, and congratulated Karl and Louise. Then he reminded the party that the soul of the enterprise still lay ahead. There were, as yet, no answers to the essential doubts about the new ship.

"Will she sail?" the senior shipowner asked. "Will she be a clipper or a barge? And the computer? Sometimes I wake up at night and ask myself: Will that computer work?"

Still, design and the designer had to be dealt with. Andren and Potier met Held for breakfast the next day. He declared himself willing to leave the job. They brushed off his offer. At midmorning, Held called Le Havre, looking for Gravé, the cabin contractor. He found him at the shipyard in Graville.

"He's started a new design," Gravé reported, in the yard manager's office after the call. "The steamer trunks are out and he's settled on a new piece of furniture under the mirror. It will be Scandinavian. You know, rounded, dark wood trim on a light wood background." The contractor looked from face to face, then added: "He has understood very well where his difficulties lie."

"What about the lamp?" Faury asked.

"No change yet," said Gravé.

"And the stainless in the corridors?"

"Not mentioned."

One of Faury's designers spoke up. "But we've got to order material. If that changes later, we'll fall behind." The others in the room nodded. Faury looked at them.

"We must leave Andren and Potier a few days to digest it all," he said. "They've faced the most pressing problem and now we will give them time to reflect."

Andren needed no time to reflect. The most pressing problem he saw was not design but power. Who was going to be in charge of building the new ship, Karl Andren or Jacob Stolt-Nielsen? I met Andren ten days after the launch in New York and he had already attacked the issue of power.

"Jacob didn't like the cabin," he said. "Actually, I didn't think it was so bad. But we worked it out, he and I. We played a game of golf up in Greenwich. It was a hard game; he took some money from me." He grinned, but did not make the business outcome of the game clear.

He suggested, instead, that I join him at a meeting of all the parties to the interior design work in Miami the following week.

The Miami meeting was a marathon that started at 9:30 A.M. in Potier's new corporate offices in a single-story business complex smelling of fresh paint and new asphalt under the subtropical sun and the main landing approach to the Miami airport. Potier and Andren presided. Stolt-Nielsen was not there.

Faury and Held had flown in the day before, each with his own accumulated set of doubts awaiting decision. The engineer brought a list of 126 detailed questions, covering sixteen typewritten pages, and insisted that even one more day of delay on any item, whether the design of a door handle or the shape of one-third of the ship, under the lounge, could delay the final delivery date. He apologized for that insistence. The designer brought two leather satchels unevenly filled with samples and sketches, set aside his copy of the shipyard list, and opened the meeting by asking Andren for a résumé of the objections to his design.

"Well, the stainless-steel corridor has been called a walk-in refrigerator," Karl said. "I thought it was pretty original myself. Then, in the cabin, we have to work on that damned trunk. On the whole, people found the cabin too dark and too modern. The bathroom unit is fine. There was not one negative comment, which is an achievement in itself." He stopped and looked at Held.

"I do not wish to be stubborn," the designer said, speaking English. "But we must beware of making a design by cutting and piecing ideas from everyone and everywhere."

Andren, his hands clasped loosely in front of him at the table, looked up at Held. Heinan had been lightly tapping the eraser end of a pencil on the table. He stopped. There was a sensible straightening of backs in every chair around the table.

"If we use pieces from everywhere, if one person is not in charge, we get, we get," the designer went on, switching to French, *"on a un bâtard."* Everyone understood.

"But I have a proposal," he added, fishing into one of the bags behind him. "Let's keep the wood, work on the wall fabric, and, of course, the trunk."

Held looked at, then flipped over to display, a drawing of a low table in white, with teak-dark trim and drawers outlined in teak. It was a picture of Scandinavian design and relief ran around the room with a rustle as people resettled themselves in their chairs. From that moment onward, for hours, the designer performed a one-man show. He was a virtuoso using sketches, swatches, and tufts of wool, bobbing and weaving verbally to win his audience. The performance was directed at Louise Andren, sitting tall, attentive, and smiling next to her husband.

"Karl is a decisive type," Held said in an aside, when the main conversation had wandered to another end of the conference table. "I have the impression that he's going to use his wife to convince the other wife. She was the violent one. Her criticisms went beyond the permissible, into personal considerations. I think we have a contest of wills, here, between the two men, the two chiefs. One knows it all, has done it all before and is used to being in command, but the younger one is trying to rise. Karl does not want to give in and Louise, you will see, will be his delegate."

Held blended wool samples before their eyes to make a rug pattern that Louise Andren liked. He fanned out bedspread samples and Louise remarked: "This one is Swedish."

"Why, yes," Held said, turning it over to read a label.

"He knows his audience," Andren said. "Nice touch, Marc."

"It's the war," Held answered, translating directly from French. And, as the hours wore on, he began to win it. Heinan supported him, from time to time. Potier spoke only rarely. Faury was practically silent as Held performed, blending, reshaping, presenting, and changing, then re-presenting his ideas. He yielded to Formica in the corridors, trading that concession for leather on the lounge chairs. During a general debate on wall coverings, he palmed an eliminated sample and held it.

"What's that you've got in your hand?" Andren asked suddenly. "I like that."

It became the wall material, although Potier and Held had wanted a neoprene sheet with raised, round welts of the size and shape of smallpox vaccination scars. Andren dismissed that sample, saying: "That looks like the floor at Charles de Gaulle airport."

Held ducked hard questions and charged into every opening. There was hesitation over the shape and color scheme for the swimming pool. Held said he would design it and the owners agreed. By the time Faury took the floor it was five and the day had been carried.

Held, for months, had forced Andren to go against his swift-moving, generalist's nature, had pressed the shipowner's nose into the details that he detested. Andren had delegated first Potier, then Heinan, then Kell Andersen, the Danish naval architect, to deal with the designer's details. Held had overreached Potier, fought with Heinan, and blasted Andersen, looking beyond them all to Andren. The shipowner had counted on the shipyard to keep Held on time. Held had rejected controls and had danced around deadlines.

At the Miami meeting, planned as a general showdown, Held chose his ally in Louise Andren. Potier and Andren nodded occasionally in approval, as if they had planned it, while the alliance formed before them. At Miami, the shipyard had hoped to nail down the owner's decisions on its list of pending questions and to eliminate any further delay for study by the interior designer. After the third failure of Held's cabin, they had thought that he was cornered. The engineers, looking ahead to their deadline, believed that the owners could only share their view that, as Faury put it, "no decision is the worst decision. Any further waiting for a choice that might be better is worse than a choice made now, even if it is not the best choice."

Pushing for decision after decision on his long list through the evening, Faury found the owners testy. Choices were deferred, or referred to Held. Held smiled, but never at Faury.

"Please do not do any decoration," the designer said sharply to the engineer at 7:30, when Faury suggested that the cabin portholes should be curtained with the same material as the bedspread. Held had resisted curtains twice during the day, successfully. He wanted to put wood blinds at the portholes.

"Stay on your side, the technical side," Held said rapidly, in French that only Potier, in the owners' party, could follow. "I love everybody. I have accepted the idea of working with Mrs. Andren and we have worked well together. But you, no. You stick to the technical. Leave design to me."

Shortly afterward, at the shipyard's Item 63, Andren burst out: "What the hell am I doing here designing door handles at quarter to eight at night?"

He took the meeting over from Faury and whipped through the pages, but the engineer, his face stretched with the effort of staying awake, hung on to settle the total electrical demand in each cabin, the material to be used in corridors, the depths and lighting required in the swimming pool. For the French, it was 1:45 in the morning on their jet-lagged internal clocks when the last item on the yard's agenda flipped through the meeting. The gym would not have a wood floor. The designer would choose the surface. The yard would supply the weight machines. Held was ready to go dancing, he said. Faury packed his files in silence.

Andren declared: "That's it. I'm going home."

The shipowner's solution, however, did not hold. Ten days later, Held missed the monthly meeting in Le Havre. He did not deliver the drawings and specifications he had promised in Miami. His contributions to the December design meeting had to be pulled out of him in telephone calls. Then, just before Christmas, Held resigned. In a letter to Andren, flashed across the Atlantic by facsimile transmission, he said he would not work under the original contract any longer. It appeared that Held, having won a substantial battle in what he called "the war," wanted to sue for victory.

His letter changed no opinions. The yard engineers hoped Held meant it. The businessmen looked right through his dramatic phrasing, searching for a business solution.

"I think he just realized he had underbid the deal," Andren said afterward. "I got quotes from two other designers, both around $330,000. Held was way below that. If he were Scandinavian, he'd have come to me and said, 'Karl, I've got a problem,' and we would have worked it out; boom, boom, boom. But he's not, so we had to go through this stuff about how I did this and I didn't do that and he could not be responsible for delays in the ship because we had not listened to him."

Gilbert Fournier, directly involved again by the new crisis, agreed with Andren. He suspected that Held had come home from Miami, done the arithmetic in his contract, and seen how much money he stood to lose. Fournier hinted that, by that December of 1985, the designer's final proceeds under the contract stood to be almost wholly eaten up by the accumulating weight of the penalties Faury had applied at every missed deadline. Each penalty bore interest until the deadline was met.

"Held is a diva," Fournier said. "He is always on stage, performing. And for a diva a contract means nothing. It is a mere basis for discussion. Deadlines are lamentable constraints on creativity."

Fournier, it appeared, was willing to make a new deal with the designer. He had thought of some ways to bring the prima donna in Held under control.

Potier, who said that he had known his choice of Held might bring with it severe production difficulties, was adamant. He would not permit any change of designer at that juncture, he said later. Only Faury made no remark on the crisis either then or later. François Faury presumes that all idle talk about others, all personal reflections without a purpose, is gossip and he believes that gossip is not a fitting diversion for a professional man.

8

CHAPTER

Abstractions

Je pense, donc je suis.

—René Descartes, 1637

By midwinter, every working engineer and many of the foremen at the shipyard knew about Marc Held and could sum up what they saw as his fatal failing in one scornful phrase: "Held can't read a plan."

For them this meant that he could not reduce his inner visions to a flat sheet of paper in accurate scale, as even the lowliest draftsman could. It meant he could not see, in his mind's eye, the spaces inside the ship that had been drawn out for him in plans, as even an apprentice shipfitter could. They believed it meant that they had to build full-scale models to show him the effect of his ideas, before he could judge them himself or decide to change them. In their eyes, that meant unnecessary delay and needless work. It meant that Held, by their standards, was simply not professional. He could not think or talk in meaningful abstractions, the kind that other technically trained people could readily understand.

The representation of reality in abstract symbols is the main mental skill of the engineer's trade. If an engineer wants to build an idea, he or she ever must first reduce the idea to mathematical symbols, then discipline it by calculations on paper that will test its strength and forecast its performance. Finally, the engineer will have to lay the tested idea out in plans, flat drawings full of conventions and symbols that builders can understand and follow. To talk an engineer's language is to speak physics and mathematics and to be able to draw. These are the three disciplines in which the candidates for admission to L'École Polytechnique are tested, in a full week of examinations that are given once each year in Paris. Those who attempt the exams have spent two years after high school in special cram courses, preparing for them, but in some sense, every educational choice for a French student with mathematical talent is made for a chance at that week of trial. François Faury faced it in 1957 and passed. He had not been born to abstraction, but he had prepared for it quite singlemindedly for most of his youth.

Faury was born in the country, in the war year of 1941, but he grew up in Paris along the Avenue Breteuil, which starts at the back of the Hotel des Invalides and is thus anchored on Napoleon's tomb.

"It was an old-fashioned childhood," he once told me. "Strict and well-ordered. Which was fine. I spent my youth in studies and scouting. Were you ever a scout? Scouting is great fun."

He was raised and educated in the two most essentially Napoleonic quarters in Paris. Home and high school both lay in the rhomboid street plan between the Invalides and the École Militaire in the Seventh Arrondissement, a genteel neighborhood of high-ceilinged apartments where families in the military and government, families loyal to the idea of French glory, might live with the assurance that French arms once ruled the world and could do so again, when the wheel of history turns. His professional school was in the cluster of Grandes Écoles in the Fifth Arrondissement.

One might translate *Grandes Écoles* as "Big Schools," or "Higher Schools," or even as "Great Schools." The most likely translation, however, is "Grand Schools," because Napoleon formed them and placed them at the pinnacle of his postrevolutionary, rational reform of French education. These schools still train the French elite. They are all professional schools on the graduate level and were founded, in part, to replace the old aristocracy with a new meritocracy. At the beginning, the intellectual premise behind the Grand Schools was that all the world would eventually be explained with the precision of mathematical expression and that, in the interim, much of the world could be engineered to fit French purposes. In the schools' corner of the Fifth Arrondissement, even the streets have names with a rationalist ring.

The École Polytechnique, Napoleon's favorite, faces Rue Descartes and, at the back, touches Rue Monge. Those two men, born 150 years apart, were the fathers of French practical abstraction and gave the mathematical structure of modern engineering to the world at large. René Descartes was the first to apply algebraic symbols to problems in geometry, so that they could be stated and solved without compass, protractor, or ruler. Letting x equal the height, y the diameter, and b the base of a cone made it possible to try out an abbot's idea for a bell tower without building it. Abstraction made the fundamental disciplines of building a school subject, and took them away from their roots in experience alone.

Gaspard Monge was a military draftsman who became Napoleon's engineering amanuensis, developed analytical and descriptive geometry on the foundations left by Descartes, and invented the mathematical rules for accurately representing the three-dimensional curves of a ship's hull in two dimensions on paper. He also founded L'École Polytechnique, and helped it become Napoleon's central school for military engineers.

The Fifth and the Seventh Parisian Arrondissements, Faury's neighborhoods, are Napoleonic home places, not display fields or parade grounds. They are orderly, restrained, hard-working, and assured. Between them lies the Latin Quarter and the undisciplined ebullience of the oldest faculties at the Sorbonne. That is a political neighborhood, and Faury came of age in a highly politicized time in France, between the aborted Franco-British occupation of the Suez Canal and the bloody French war in Algeria. But François did not play at politics at all.

"We were a military family," he said. "The military has no politics. At least, that is the rule."

His grandfather and his uncles were graduates of the French military academy at Saint-Cyr who became army generals. A more distant relative, Simon Bernard, was in the first graduating class at L'École Polytechnique and became a general of engineers under Napoleon. After the defeat of his emperor, Bernard took his knowledge and his rank to the U.S. Army and served on a commission that fortified the American coasts. He is personally credited with the design for Fort Monroe,[1] at the mouth of Chesapeake Bay, which was so strong that the Union held it, in Confederate territory, throughout the U.S. Civil War. He returned to France to serve a restored king as minister of war and was made a baron.

Faury's father, an infantry officer, was posted to elite units as a junior officer and sent to the United States, just before World War II, on a mission seeking military aid to resist the coming German invasion. After the fall of France, he served his country in the other camp, commanded a company of Tirailleurs Marocains resisting the American invasion of North Africa, and was decorated with the Legion of Honor.

"They were one hundred fifty and took two hundred prisoners," Faury said. "Apparently, it was quite a feat."

His father was captured in Indochina, where the French fought the North Vietnamese before the Americans, and he died a prisoner of war. François grew up with only the army tradition before him and had to ask an architect, who had married one of his aunts, if there were any noble careers at all outside the army.

"I did not wish to be a military man," he said.

Instead, he went to the École Polytechnique, which lay only halfway over the boundary between military and civilian life. Students there wore uniforms, lived by military etiquette, and were obliged to serve in the armed forces. Faury went to the navy, as a student officer, and returned as a graduate naval engineer. But L'École Polytechnique was the central influence on him. He and all other graduates call the school *l'X*, "the X," as though it were an unknown to those outside its walls. *Polytechniciens* call themselves *les X*, as if, collectively, they had become unknowns at the school, by passing into a caste beyond definition by their countrymen. They have a kind of assurance that may not be aloof by intention, but imitates intellectual arrogance well.

"For *polytechniciens*, there are only other *polytechniciens*," Potier said once, trying to explain their attitude to me. "The rest of us are rabble."

Mathematics is the central discipline at the school, and it seems that every Frenchman who knows a *polytechnicien* has a favorite story about their tendency to calculate everything.

"To be a *polytechnicien* is a deformation of character," the father of one told me. He was not an X himself. "A *polytechnicien* can calculate the effect of a hammer blow on a one-hundred-meter tube, allowing for windage, temperature, and the twist of an individual wrist, but he cannot use a hammer to hang a picture at home."

The *polytechniciens* call themselves Cartesians, because they subscribe to Descartes' fundamental premise—that the sound human mind is the only reliable touchstone for any analysis of reality—and to his method of reducing every search for truth to its smallest elements, then using mathematical rules to pursue that search.

"Cartesianism implies giving reason precedence over your feelings, always," says Annick Faury, who married François, the *polytechnicien*-turned-shipbuilder. "For example, when all the evidence available to you supports a rational conclusion that a certain person is honest, then that person is honest, no matter what your intuition may be telling you. When, three months later, that person has disappeared with your life savings, then your Cartesianism allows you to conclude that the person is dishonest."

When I cited that definition to her husband later, Faury thought in silence, then accepted it. After two busy days he reversed his acceptance. On reflection, he had found that his wife's example did not allow for the way intuition functions in engineering minds at work.

"The human spirit is not Cartesian," Faury said. "Minds work by analogy and the accidental connection of ideas not connected by logic. After that, one applies Cartesian rigor." Absolutely without excuse, in Faury's view, one must be able to rein in the leaps of intuition with the disciplines of mathematics and logic. To do otherwise is sloppy, risky, and unprofessional.

"One must calculate the results of an intuitive solution," he said. "Calculation is a form of forecasting."

In Faury's view of the world, calculation defines no more than the risk. It draws the edges of the door that intuition would pull you through. He resists the central Cartesian assertion that logic alone leads to truth, so he resisted his wife's definition by example. After two years of postgraduate specialization in naval engineering, three years of studies in law and economics, four years building nuclear submarines for the French navy, and fifteen years in charge of shipbuilding at ACH, he did not think his intelligence was so limited as to blind itself to potential fraud out of loyalty to pure reason.

Faury is an eighteenth-century humanist, courteous, disciplined, and in love with the rational achievements of the human mind, whose limits he almost welcomes. Twenty years after graduation, he met a Polytechnique classmate, whose ambition at school had been to reshape human beings genetically through scientific method, and asked if he had been successful. "He said he had failed," Faury recalled. "And I congratulated him."

"*Les X* are completely theoretical," Faury said, and, after designing life support systems for nuclear submarines and building many ships that have made money for their owners, he had come to think of himself as practical; practical, but still an X. He admires, in anyone, a Cartesian ability to think by the rules of logic and to calculate the results of ideas. He only talks on terms of full equality to those who can do that. He admires even more the person who can make an intuitive leap, then calculate and pass along to others the trajectory of that leap. He recognizes that ability in Gilbert Fournier and admires him. He saw none of it in Marc Held and treated him as he would have treated any subcontractor; as he treated painters, electricians, and the manufacturers of stoves and garbage grinders.

Of François Faury, Marc Held said: "I found him the pure example of a nineteenth-century French industrial employer: cold, remote, and pitiless. I get along with presidents and working men. Never with the managers."

Faury, as part of his education in practicality, had learned to enjoy working in a team. Before he was required to share his ship with Held and work on the same team with the designer, the yard manager had developed three rules for successful teamwork:

1. Anyone in the team has the right to speak out on any doubt whatsoever on any subject, to any other member.

2. The rank of one member does not define his share of the truth. No one is right because he's the boss.

3. Avoid intense personal conflict. One person who will not admit error can spoil the work of all.

The naval engineer practiced those rules and held his employees to them. Held, by the end of 1985, had broken all three. Held's approach, perhaps more suited to this age, established his own intuition as the truth. Those who worked with him said he held to his own vision with absolute conviction. Faury held convictions of an older fashion. He was convinced that the new ship needed to be a happy ship and would not be if it were born in conflict; therefore, he avoided conflict. He was equally convinced that his staff could finish her decoration unaided and on time, using Held's original designs, approved in October, questioned in November, and thrown out in December. Potier said no; he would not let the designer go. In January, Fournier found a solution to the impasse.

"We all went to Fournier's beautiful little apartment in Neuilly, by the Bois," Held recalled. "Fournier, Faury, Jean-Claude Potier, and I. We were all very correct, very worldly and polite."

They struck a deal on Held's terms. The shipyard would release him from his first contract and he would return to work with them as a consultant, at consultant's fees for every visit, every sketch, every telephone consultation. The yard would supply the draftsmen to draw working plans from his sketches, and ship designers from the Graville staff would run down the material, make out the orders, keep the budget, and supervise the decorating subcontractors. Held was free.

"Monsieur Fournier did that job with all the grace and efficacy that he can bring to such things when he wants to," said Faury. "I followed without a shadow of hesitation." But those immediately beneath him, wrestling with a growing potential for delays in the contracted delivery date, were dismayed.

"I was sick," Antoine Castetz said of Held's new contract. As Faury's main technical deputy, Castetz had been named project engineer and given responsibility for the details of interior design and fitting out.

He was an executor. Faury reserved decisions to himself; still, Castetz said, "I did not sleep that entire night. We could have done it, and done it on time."

His was a cry of loyalty to Faury and his method, and that attitude ran deep at the building yard in Graville. It is an older place than the dockyard in Harfleur where *Wind Star* had tied up for fitting out. The Graville building yard has an air of austerity, leavened only by intellectual excitement. The foremen and engineers there are all equally grave, considerate, and formal; the designers and draftsmen are subdued and correct. The Graville yard has much of the monastery about it. The ACH yard at Harfleur is more like a bowling alley. I once remarked on the contrast aloud and said it seemed to me people laughed more often at Harfleur.

"We have to," Michel Lesage shot back. Lesage was the boss at Harfleur, where he had come up through the hawsepipe as draftsman, designer, foreman, shipwright, and then engineer in charge. His father had been a shipyard riveter and Lesage grew up at the beach, before the war when it was not fashionable. His closest neighbors made their livings gathering beach pebbles into mounds that they piled up by the basketload and sold to truckers as building material.

"Those hullbuilders in Graville take themselves too seriously. They ought to try fitting out for a while. That'd teach 'em a sense of humor. Outfitting, you either learn to laugh or go crazy."

Working through *Wind Star* for eleven months, Lesage appeared to use both those approaches; sometimes he laughed; at other times, he appeared to go mad in judiciously timed fits of anger. Fitting out a new ship is a tremendously intricate process that involves plumbers, mechanics of three types, electricians, air conditioning specialists, plasterers, painters, carpenters, joiners of two descriptions, riggers, and welders. There were hundreds of men aboard *Wind Star* each day in Harfleur, and at each place in the ship, one set of specialists had to finish before another might begin. A detailed choreography of effort was required.

In theory, outfitting proceeds deck by deck from the bottom up. The steel skin of the ship is insulated inside first, while the plumbing goes in overhead, then the wiring. The finish goes onto decks and bulkheads and overheads last, once all that needs to run behind them is in place and tested and inspected.

At the Wärtsila yards in Helsinki passenger ships have been built in substantially finished modules, whole chunks of ship lifted into place on board, each with its piping, wiring, lighting, ducting, and basic finish work in place. Using the modular system, each passenger deck can be sealed when all its blocks are in place and the ship can be delivered one deck at a time. At Harfleur, the ACH outfitters worked everywhere at once. There was a plan, but Lesage kept it himself in the lower right-hand drawer of his desk and, since the left side of his desk faced his office door and there was no room behind his chair, only he could get out the outfitting plan. In January, after Held's return, he declared that unless the owners made all their postponed decisions that month, the ship would be late. But he would not show his plan to explain how late or why.

There was a daily abstract from that plan, which Lesage wrote out in block letters with a black marker on ruled paper snapped onto a clipboard. The Graville engineers, designers, and foremen all used graph paper in their clipboards, so that they could sketch quickly and accurately to scale. They used the sketches to communicate new ideas and to propose solutions. I have a collection of graph paper sketches covering turning points in the ship's construction, because any Graville hullbuilder started sketching at the first sign of incomprehension. Lesage effaced his daily list item by item as each was completed, with furious sideways strokes of his felt-tip marker, as though he were covering his tracks. But at the Harfleur dockyard there was a man named Yvan Martin, the Turquetille of the outfitting yard, who carried the whole endeavor in his head and updated it several times daily as he walked through the daily changing ship.

Martin had come to the yard as lead foreman after retiring from the French navy, an engineering warrant officer. In the navy, he had qualified as diesel mechanic, combat diver, refrigeration mechanic, steam-fitting engineer, nuclear technician, and parachute jumper. He was a submariner who had come ashore reluctantly at the end of his twenty-two years in service, and snapped up the job at Harfleur in 1980.

"It was because I couldn't leave the sea," he said. "I had to stay in touch with the sea somehow." His new attachment to the sea proved bittersweet.

"Fitting out is like raising a child," Martin said during a morning lull on a weekend of continuous work at the dockyard. We drank coffee he had made just before dawn. The flavor held up well after sunrise and the warmth of the coffee came through the white glass cups to take the lingering night cold out of our fingertips. "You see a ship start, small and unformed, and it changes, grows up in your hands. Then one day, it's grown up and it leaves; well . . ."

Martin hesitated, rubbed his cheek and started again.

"You see, during fitting out I've got the keys to everything. I put the ship together and when the crew comes, I show them how to treat her, how to use everything. Then one day, I turn my keys over. One evening, we have a farewell drink, the crew and some of my guys. Next day, they leave. Well, I'll tell you, when you watch the ship get underway, well . . ."

This time his voice broke, although he was smiling.

"It does something to you," Martin said. "It does something."

Martin's memory and his disposition, which is a blend of tough humor and the resilience of a seasoned pine plank, took the place at Harfleur of the kind of detailed engineering plan-by-abstraction that has made possible the modular assembly of passenger ships at other shipyards, and therefore simultaneous building and fitting out, with running forecasts of every step along the way and the final delivery date of each ship.

"When Wärtsila tells you they will deliver a ship at 1615 on Sunday afternoon," a cruise-ship caterer who had taken delivery of two cruise liners there told me, "you had better be on board by 1614. She'll sail without you."

That kind of precision is built on the analytical method first proposed by Descartes: break each problem down into its smallest element, then proceed by mathematical rules to a solution, testing each step as you go. At shipyards and civil construction sites, the process of assembling each element of construction is done in the abstract long before steel and wire and pipes go together. Calculating the time needed for each job within each element and generating deadlines for each major step is now handled by computer programs that plot the critical path through very complex jobs. Programs for critical-path analysis of projects are even sold for microcomputers.

There is no more Cartesian tool than a computer. It breaks down every proposition into values of zero and one and operates on strings of propositions in the abstract language of mathematical logic. But at ACH the Cartesians in charge did not use computer programs to oversee the fitting out of their ships or to predict the effect of delays on their delivery dates. At Graville, Adam and Turquetille reported their progress weekly on each hull, coloring in the blocks on their construction diagrams and updating their flow charts. But at Harfleur, there was no such continuing report abstracted from the many jobs of daily work.

Faury and Castetz, both programmers, and Jean-Eric Enault, the junior engineer in charge of the shipyard computers and their programs, all said they had looked at critical-path method programs for use at the Harfleur dockyard and decided not to use them, on the grounds that they were too detailed and therefore too expensive to use. Lesage said flatly he would not have them. They would not work. Ship outfitting was too complicated to fit in a computer program.

"They update the delivery date, don't they?" he said. "And push it back every time you slow down? Now that is what you don't want. That changes the goal, which is the one thing you never want to change. If you do, the goal gets away from you and recedes forever. Use one of those and you would never deliver a ship."

The decision not to use computers at ACH for project planning and tracking had long since been made when fitting out began on *Wind Star,* and the absence of a computer plan surprised outsiders when they joined the windship project in Le Havre. It seemed almost inexplicable to some subcontractors, to managers working for Andren and Potier, and to the new ship's officers and engineers, several of whom had taken delivery of new ships at foreign shipyards before. All of them were used to regular reports on where construction stood and what would need to be done to complete it on time. Even Marc Held, in his letter of resignation in December, complained of lack of detailed planning and forecasting at ACH. He said, later, that he had been told every week exactly where construction stood on the IBM office complex he had designed, and when his next contribution to that project would be needed.

The naval engineers at ACH used computers for engineering calculations and mathematical lofting. They were particularly proud of the elegance of the programs their president himself had written for the fairing of curves in a hull and, for the windship, his dynamic simulation of the stresses on the ship's masts. That program was based on mathematical assumptions and logical sequences, but it forecast the future.

Enault and his even younger assistant, who tended the shipyard computer in its plain, air-conditioned quarters at Graville, had even developed a simulation program that projected what *Wind Star* might do when she finally went sailing. On a monitor screen in a moving perspective drawing, the ship's six booms swung and adjusted as she changed heading and her wake flowed out behind her in two jagged lines that shifted on the screen. That was a program Faury loved to show to qualified visitors. It even came quite close to predicting some of the results of wind tunnel and tank tests of the rig and hull in 1985.

There was no such prediction, however, for the millions of steps in the conversion of the ship from bare steel hull to Potier's luxurious dream. Perhaps as a result, Andren and Heinan and eventually even Potier ignored the shipyard's pleas for quick decisions on the plans for *Wind Star*'s interior decoration. Faury first pressed hard for decoration decisions in January and February of 1985. The owners then took their time. In July the yard announced that it would have to order the galvanized steel panels for internal walls by August, or risk seriously delaying delivery. The panels were ordered on December 13.

In October, one internal report showed that the owners had approved the fundamental interior design. But that design was overthrown by the owners in November and, in December in Miami, Faury found himself pressing again for decisions on matters that had accumulated like jetsam on his sixteen-page list. And there was no firm reaction. It was as though the owners would not believe Faury's assertions without a computer-generated, up-to-date forecast. He had none. For them, he might have been a shepherd crying "Wolf!" from behind a sand dune by the estuary.

Still, the yard manager left the January 1986 design meeting with a smile of satisfaction.

"We had a little explosion in there just now," he said, on his way out to lunch. "I told them we could not deliver the ship on time and Andren blew up."

The reinstated designer had not delivered the revised sketches and perspective drawings he had promised in December. Piping below the dining room and wiring and piping in the lounge could not proceed without a plan approved by the owners for those two large rooms. The wiring for cabins below those rooms and the building of the cabins themselves could not proceed until the piping overhead was complete and tested. That much was evident. But what would the exact delay be and why? Faury could not specify. So, when Tom Heinan left that same session, he said blandly: "We're going to get the yard to work a little harder on getting the right solutions in place. They can do better."

Andren went aboard his ship that afternoon for the first time since the launch. There had been a break in the winter storms and it was a soft afternoon, full of light amplified by the moisture hanging in the air. The windows for the open dining room had been cut out according to Held's October placement, and the light streamed into that broad, empty space. The window openings offered a clean perspective from side to side and pushed out the darkness for good. The resulting space was clear and well-proportioned.

It seemed, for the first time, that the ship had a human purpose beyond the work of finishing her, and Andren's spirits lifted. He left Le Havre after one day there, and Heinan stayed to finish the working meetings. The organization of design work for the shipowner's party had finally been settled. Louise Andren, as Karl's deputy, would oversee the interior design and Marc Held. Heinan would continue to do the rest.

Karl thought he had finally found the combination of personalities to supplement and extend himself well enough to permit him to finish his first ship. His second, a sister ship to *Wind Star,* was already building in Graville and, urged along by Potier, Andren was thinking hard about building another two just like the first: big, four-masted cruising schooners with electric auxiliary power. He swung his attention to the problem of raising money to finance a fleet, instead of a pair of prototypes, and effectively faded from the monthly effort to finish *Wind Star.* For the rest of 1986, Tom Heinan regularly filled the part of the shipowner, and the yard was relieved.

"We've never had a shipowner like this that I can remember," one of the yard's senior designers said late in 1985. He had been yarning, over lunch in the shipyard cafeteria, about shipowners and captains he had known. "We're used to sitting down to discuss stability and performance, technical details; but it's the color of the swimming pool and the lighting in the disco that interests this crew. If you talk strength and structure, you've lost them, except for your Tom Heinan, there."

Andren's right-hand man was "their" Tom Heinan by the beginning of 1986. They accepted him at his word when he stood up through a babble of argument at one meeting and said in a loud, hard voice: "We'll do it this way because I say so, and I'm the shipowner."

Technically, Heinan owned less than one percent of the shipowning holding company, but the shipyard men thought he owned five percent and, in any case, had long since accepted him as "owner." For months, Tom had been what the yard required, indeed almost yearned for, in order to build well. He was the knowledgeable exigent shipowner, who kept them to the mark and occasionally smiled at the ingenuity of one of their solutions to a technical tangle. He took their project as seriously as they themselves did, and drew his own designs for the cabins, the foredeck, and the engine control room. He was a seaman, a licensed master for "unlimited tonnage, all oceans, any horsepower," in the words of the U.S. Coast Guard license. He had been a chief mate for three years, and he held a master's degree in business administration from New York University.

The yard leaders had learned to overlook Heinan's macho American meeting style and to work along with him on his workaholic schedule. When the visiting Americans descended on the yard each month, the French engineers were ready to meet them at an eight A.M. train from Paris, work through lunch and well into the evening, then take the whole group out for a restaurant dinner of four courses and two wines that night, go to bed at midnight, and start again the next morning. Potier recalled that he had once seen Faury reach for Heinan's suitcases on the station platform, and carry them to his car. He was astonished that a *polytechnicien* would do such a thing.

Seen from within the shipyard, the monthly meetings in Le Havre were a sudden suspension of normalcy. The Americans blew in like a Channel gale. They smelled of jet voyages and Paris hotels. They had tight schedules and did not quit at four. Working-level Frenchmen, settled in routine, were shocked. Against the austere background in Graville, they looked big, sounded loud, and seemed rich. Looking up from his work, a yard draftsman might catch a glimpse of Andren's broad back in pinstripe, or Potier's in a tailored suit, passing quickly in the creaking hall. That was all anyone but the yard manager and his immediate assistants saw.

The shipyard bosses who usually did almost all of their work out in the shops or design offices, thinking out loud, sketching, and deciding among their employees on the job, disappeared for two or three days at a time when the Americans came. They reappeared, at the end of each visit, a little haggard and sometimes just slightly hoarse, with dark shadows under their eyes.

"They've all left today," Alain Adam said at the end of the January sessions. I had spent those days in the Graville shops and at Harfleur on the ship, and Adam had been my host. During meeting periods, he stood in for the others and handled everything but the visiting Americans. "Things will be calmer now."

Faury, Castetz, and L'Heryénat, the design chief, spent all their time with the owners when they were in Le Havre. The visiting cast changed month to month, but Heinan was always there. He could not speak French; they spoke English. He mistrusted their explanations and assertions; they let his mistrust flow during a meeting, then saw to it that they all passed what they had been talking about on the next tour of the ship. Heinan could read a plan and he saw things in place quickly. The engineers liked that. Slowly and with extreme tact, they had even begun to change some of his habits.

In the first meetings at the yard, Heinan had made it clear he would not break for a long French lunch. They were free to go ahead, he told

Faury, but he would stay and work. Would the yard manager please send in a sandwich and a bottle of mineral water? Faury enjoys playing working host on his own terms. When he takes business visitors to lunch, Faury's preference is to drive across town to the Club des Regates du Havre, the oldest yacht club on the continent of Europe.

The glass walls of the plain dining room on the second floor have views across the yacht harbor to the main harbor entrance, a narrow slip of water between two stone towers like medieval bastions. The shipping comes and goes below those at lunch in the club. The walls are hung with photographs and sailing prints, and every midday, beneath them, there are two long tables full of everything that comes out of the sea beyond the windows. There are four kinds of oysters and two kinds of clams, lying open in their shells. There are three sizes of cold, cooked shrimp, and boiled freshwater crayfish. There are boiled crabs and periwinkles and mussels; a choice of pickled, creamed, or salted herring and smoked eel. Then there are salads. This buffet provides only the first course at the yacht club.

Closer to the shipyard, there is a restaurant across the street from the municipal slaughterhouse, much favored by working men wearing open collars who laugh a lot and talk loudly. The butter there is served in bricks with knives stuck into them at an angle. The oysters come stacked six deep on stainless-steel platters 2 feet long, and the steaks are of Kansas City size. But Heinan wanted a sandwich sent in.

"To please him, we ordered sandwiches from the company cafeteria and joined Tom," Faury recalled. "Then our canteen cook thought that he could probably do better than cold cuts and cheese slices on bread."

It was a polite way of saying that the chef, a cook for years on a French Line passenger ship, had taken offense. He started responding to sandwich orders with arranged plates of cold cuts, platters of selected cheeses and fruit, and baskets of fresh bread. Then one month, the chef suggested a hot lunch—at the worktable, of course. By the November meetings, just after *Wind Star* was launched, Heinan had consented to eat both courses of a prepared French luncheon, served at the meeting room table, and cheese, and dessert. He even asked for more wine.

With Faury, Heinan went antique shopping and learned his way around French menus and French wines. And as the ship grew, so did Heinan's confidence in the shipyard's technical ability. In January, that confidence was reinforced by the views of highly qualified outsiders. Just before that month's meeting, Andren and Heinan had expanded an agreement with the Norwegian company that would supply the ship's officers and crew.

The company, Wilh. Wilhelmsen Ltd., agreed to help with technical supervision at Harfleur during *Wind Star*'s fitting out and sent along an experienced chief engineer and chief electrician. Their arrival in January coincided with the monthly meetings, and the first visit of *Wind Star*'s Norwegian captain to his new ship. Within hearing of the yard engineers, the captain told Heinan that ACH was giving him better workmanship than he had seen in a ship he had watched go together at Wärtsila in Helsinki. That was how the engineers heard the comment, and it pleased them profoundly.

It must also have pleased Heinan, because he beamed at Faury and the captain as the two talked; and sketched, and talked again all through dinner that evening.

"These guys think they punched out two hours ago, when we left the yard," Heinan said in one smiling aside. He helped the newcomers pick among the Norman specialties on the menu: duck livers, roast duck, duck pâté, and braised duck fillet. He tasted the wine, approved, and then listened to the technical talk.

Faury had been captivated that day by the captain, a Norwegian named Johan L'Orange, whose Huguenot ancestors had fled France to settle in Protestant Norway centuries before. The captain was a sailor, with extra expertise on boardsailers, like Faury, and, like Faury, he sketched constantly to explain his ideas. The two of them discussed sailing dinghies, spinnakers, rigging, ship maneuvers, and square-riggers. L'Orange had first gone to sea as an apprentice aboard *Sorlandet*, a Norwegian sail training ship that, in his time, had no auxiliary power. He remembered enough to be able to sketch all the lines controlling a square sail and remembered sailing across the North Sea from Norway to England in forty-eight hours. But he was a realist. He had been at sea under power for thirty-eight years and had been a captain for twenty-one of his fifty-three years. His hair was completely white.

"It was a great sail," he recalled of the boiling trip across the North Sea. "We sailed sometimes at seventeen knots. That was something, but then it took us nine days to sail back."

Faury, sketching, showed him how *Wind Star* would tack through the wind. For the first time outside his own offices, the yard manager discussed the details of the yard's computer program for sail control aboard the new ship. He spoke so enthusiastically one thought the computer might be at the same table.

"The computer will do that," he said, when L'Orange spoke of the need to bring the sails across in a certain order. "And the computer will do that," he said, when the captain spoke of the need to reduce sail quickly.

"You are going to like this," he said often, before he explained another feature of the program. During the dinner, which lasted until just after midnight, the engineer and the master used up the slips of graph paper from Faury's pocket calendar and the unruled slips from mine, and started on L'Orange's business cards.

Faury spoke confidently of his sail-control computer that night and discussed the ship's rigging for hours. But detailed composition of the computer's sailing program had not begun, and did not start until February 1986—the following month. The orders for sails and rigging were then well behind the engineer's orginal schedule. He had counted on raising one of the ship's masts during the Norman winter and setting a sail on the rolling furler that would carry it, to test sail, mast, and furler under severe conditions. When the sudden Channel gales blow into Le Havre from the southwest, the wind whirls around corners and hums under doors and windows. Flags whip out straight as though they had been painted on the sky at right angles to their staffs, and parked cars do little jigs in the strongest gusts, bouncing on their shock absorbers when the wind shakes them.

However, no mast had been made. The furlers had just been ordered between Christmas and the New Year, and the sailmaker had not yet been chosen in January, only nine months from the contracted delivery date. The shipyard had asked for bids for the sailing computer program from a specialized software company. That company reported that it would take three of its programmers three years of work to develop the program, and quoted a price that the head programmer in Graville called "astronomical." The Cartesians at ACH resolved to write the program for *Wind Star* themselves. It was what Faury and all of the mathematically trained and eager young men on his staff at Graville had wanted to do from the outset.

"After all, it is only the masts and the sails and the computer that makes this ship any different, and interesting," said one of the five young men who ached to work at the heart of the project, designing the sailing rig and its controls. "Monsieur Faury has kept that part of the project for himself." It was not quite a complaint.

In February, the shipyard assigned one young programmer at the group's engineering headquarters to begin writing the computer instructions, using Faury's list of requirements, functions, and priorities. Two months later, in April, another programmer, Enault's assistant from Graville who had compiled all the data from four wind-tunnel tests of scale models of the windship's rig, joined the first. The two programmers had never sailed or been to sea when they began writing together, and they had only five full months before the sea trials.

"In the end, the work of three men for three years was done by two men in six months," Enault said later. "It was terribly exciting."

In the last months of that winter, excitement flagged elsewhere around the project. Andren tried for several months to interest other shipowners in co-ownership of the third and fourth ship on his own terms, and failed. The effort tired him. From month to month there seemed little progress in the cold, grimy steel hull in Harfleur. But he had settled his differences with his partner, Jacob Stolt-Nielsen.

"Karl has wanted to be a shipowner forever," the older man said, as spring drew close in 1986. "He's an Ålander and he has it in his blood. Now he's a shipowner and he wants it to be his own way. I have decided to leave it to Karl. Two cooks are bad for the soup."

Andren put it more directly. "I'll build these ships, okay?" he said, when I asked him if the decoration difficulties had been solved. "Only one man can do these things."

Held's bet in December had been well placed and the designer was happy with his new boss and his new contract.

"All told, it was like a happy ending in the theater," Held said, looking back at the end of the crisis he had provoked. "Louise arrives and everything goes better." He was ready with a new cabin by April and it was approved.

The warmth begins to come back to Normandy that month, although it can still be put to flight by a passing cloud. On nearly cloudless days, the women who work in Le Havre push the season to put on their cotton dresses. They are all so tired of winter. But they have to hurry through shadows, where the winter chill holds on, and they all seem to have jackets and umbrellas within easy reach. The weather changes fast.

A lift always comes with the returning warmth, and in 1986 it coincided with a joint announcement by Andren and Fournier. ACH would build a third sailing cruise ship and Andren had an option for a fourth. There were still no orders for other kinds of new ships, but with one more sailing ship to build, the uncertainty that had hung over the shipyard jobs, as gray and depressing as the Channel winter weather, lifted too. At Graville, the managers authorized a new coat of paint for the faded walls of the main staircase and their offices, and ordered new linoleum laid, in the same cold-oatmeal shade of gray as the old floor.

At Harfleur, the subcontractors working on wiring and air conditioning and accommodations were so emboldened by the prospect of more work to come that they asked for a meeting with Faury and

Lesage. If the owners made any more changes, the subcontracting firms declared, they would not be able to deliver their contracted shares of the new ship on time. Faury listened and later circulated a memo asserting that the shipowners' interests were no longer served by flexible accommodation to changes suggested by the owners' representatives. Andren was now represented at the yard by Andersen, Captain L'Orange, and two Norwegian seagoing engineers overseeing technical installations for Wilhelmsen. All of them had ideas. All of them made suggestions. Faury wrote that the shipowners' interests now lay wholly in getting their ship finished on time.

Alongside the dock, *Wind Star* had a new coat of primer, the traditional brick-dust color of red lead, from her waterline to the main deck, and her name was picked out in raised white letters at the bow. There were cabins and doors in the crew's quarters and stacks of stainless-steel counters and machinery in the galley. The passengers' bathrooms were in place on two decks and the galvanized cabin walls had begun to go up. The ship was due to be delivered on October 3 and, for the first time, it had begun to look as though she might make it.

The meetings in May at the shipyard went along as gently as the warming weather. Even Tom Heinan had relaxed noticeably. The shipyard men, who always used both names, said he was not the same. He was wearing new tailored shirts, with his initials embroidered just below the left breast. He was drinking less coffee.

"You don't get the feeling that you're pushing back chaos here now," Heinan said during one session. After two working days in Le Havre, the owners and the yard went to Paris to meet Marc Held and there chaos threatened again. At the end of a long day, a shouting Held expelled Faury from his office forever. But the designer no longer held center stage and the incident passed.

"I have a fairly thick skin," Faury said, the day after he returned from Paris. It was after five, a time when Faury, Castetz, and Adam returned to their offices in Graville almost every afternoon to read and sign correspondence and to think. The upper floor was silent then. On that warm day, the voices of children playing behind the rowhouses over the wall came through an open window. Faury sat with his back to a table in Adam's office and almost dismissed Held's explosion in Paris.

"Such things are personally unpleasant, even hateful," he said. "But I can absorb them. I worry about the ship. I've told you before that a passenger ship must be a happy ship; she must be happy while she is building, with no psychological strains or tensions. There is much still to be done and this will make it difficult."

He mused a bit.

"If I must, one day I will fire him," Faury said, without naming Held. "It is never good to fire a person. But if it becomes necessary, I will do it."

It never became necessary. Louise Andren made herself the bridge between the precise and formal Faury and Held, whose mood and manner were unforeseeable. Faury would not go to Paris; Held would not come to Le Havre. From May to October, at least once each month, Mrs. Andren went to both cities and made the owners' choices. The three shipyard designers who did the detail work that was required to turn Held's designs into walls and lights and carpets on board were deeply grateful.

"She has a very sure touch in matters of taste and she is quite willing to decide and stand by her decision," one of the designers said. "Besides, I've liked working with her. She is a person whom one just naturally wants to please."

And then, by midsummer, Held's designs began to take shape inside *Wind Star.* If the designer could not read a plan like an engineer, it appeared that the engineers had not all been able to envision what Held had in his mind when he had showed them sketches, perspective drawings, and material samples. They were sometimes surprised by the real interior finish as subcontractors erected it in the rough steel spaces inside the ship. On the afternoon that the first two pieces of the wood paneling he had initially resisted went up on the dining room walls, Faury was on an inspection tour of the ship with Tom Heinan and Gilbert Fournier. He broke away when he saw the wood and stood looking at it as the others walked on, businesslike.

"The wood is beautiful," Faury said, his voice dreamy and pleased. "Truly beautiful."

Captain Johan L'Orange, a Norwegian whose ancestors fled France in the Huguenot diaspora, on the bridge of Wind Star. *(*Joseph Novitski*)*

Alexander Maresca, the first mate. Wind Star's *chief officer was born in Switzerland but moved to Norway as a small boy when his sculptor father got a commission there. The sea captured him and he returned to it on a Norwegian shipping line as a teenager. (*Joseph Novitski*)*

*René Bernard, seventy-eight, a retired professor of physics and the designer and manufacturer of the windship's roller furling stays, in his working rig. Bernard described himself thus: "I am not an intellectual who is clever with his hands. I am an artisan who was intellectually trained." (*Joseph Novitski*)*

*ABOVE: Jean-Eric Enault, engineer, degree in subatomic physics, violinist. Computer director at Graville. (*Joseph Novitski*)*

*AT LEFT: Antoine Castetz, graduate of the École Polytechnique, naval engineer, racing dinghy sailor, wit. Project engineer for the windship. (*Joseph Novitski*)*

BELOW: "Farewell, France. Bon Voyage, Wind Star.*" A crowd of between twenty thousand and fifty thousand people gathered at the edge of the harbor in Le Havre to watch the first large windship built from the keel up for commercial purposes in sixty years sail on her first ocean crossing. (*Joseph Novitski*)*

Gérard Boulenger, designer. Professional certificates in mechanical drawing, sailing instruction, ski instruction. Professional ocean-racing skipper who returned to Graville for the chance to work on Wind Star. *(*Joseph Novitski*)*

*Jacques Bouché, engineer, degrees in industrial engineering and civil engineering, seated by his sailing computer with the sail control console behind him. Lead programmer for the windship's computer. (*Joseph Novitski*)*

The shipbuilder. François Faury comes aboard for Wind Star*'s maiden voyage. (*Joseph Novitski*)*

Sail trials. Captain L'Orange reduces power to the propeller on the morning of October 15, 1986. Wind Star *sailed without her motor for the first time that day in the Portuguese trade winds. (*Joseph Novitski*)*

Sail trials. The containership Presidente Ibanez *passes astern of* Wind Star *as the windship maneuvers under sail for the first time. The slick water between the foam and the ship's side indicates that the sailing ship is slipping sideways, away from the wind and her bow wave. While she was in shipping lanes, fishing boats, a few ships, and one navy helicopter detoured to see what manner of ship the tall, white* Wind Star *might be. (*Joseph Novitski*)*

ABOVE: *First port. The windship tied up at the breakwater in Ponta Delgada, São Miguel, the Azores, with the colonial center of the town behind her.* (Joseph Novitski)

AT LEFT: *Motorsailing.* Wind Star *boils along the coast of São Miguel island in the Azores at 12 knots under sail and power. The open steering wheel on the flying bridge, which Karl Andren put into the design as a recollection of traditional sailing ship design, is under a white cover.* (Joseph Novitski)

Computer work. François Faury and Gérard Boulenger record oil pressure readings from the sail control console in Wind Star's *pilothouse. The gauge readings could be correlated with sail positions and used to reset those positions, with or without the sailing computer.* (Joseph Novitski)

To market. Wind Star *arrived at the entrance to Miami harbor under power and sail on Saturday, November 1, 1986, to a long traditional maritime welcome. All staysails are fully unfurled in the 20-*

*knot breeze from astern, except the second from bow to stern, which was set thirty minutes earlier with three wraps of cloth still on its damaged roller furling stay. (*Paula Novitski*)*

Damage control. Gérard Boulenger reaches the pilothouse roof after a trip 160 feet into the air in the bosun's chair to inspect the roller furling stay of number 2 staysail, looking for sheared rivets after staysail number 1's furling stay had twisted in 30 knots of wind and sheared scores of its rivets. He found none, but one week later the number 2 furler rained broken rivets on deck on the night before the ship's arrival in Miami. (Joseph Novitski)

Faury under fire. The shipbuilder took advantage of a still blue-water calm south of Bermuda to send Boulenger aloft along the damaged number 1 furler. Seated in one place, waiting for reports from Boulenger, Faury made an easy target for those with complaints about unfinished details in his windship. (Joseph Novitski)

3

PART

THE RIG

9

CHAPTER

Masts

Mariage pluvieux, mariage heureux.

—Norman proverb

Through all the shaping and welding of *Wind Star*'s hull, past her launch and through the storms of the winter over her decoration and accommodations, the shipbuilders drew confidently on years of their own experience and were never at a loss. They knew what they were doing. Except for the luxury passenger cabins, they had done it all before. *Wind Star*'s hull was simple. Her basic outfitting, the steel frames and walls inside, the piping and wiring, was uncomplicated, compared to the cable layers and gas tankers they had built before. Dealing with a decorator whom they all thought crazy added some spice. At the yard, men called Held "decorator" because they knew he insisted that his title was "designer." But through that winter, *Wind Star* was not a sailing ship. She was, therefore, quite routine.

Alongside the concrete pier in Harfleur, the hull looked vaguely stylish but unremarkable. It even seemed slightly out of proportion. Three aluminum deckhouses, as they went on above the main deck, raised the ship and made her total height more than a seaman's eye expected. The principal curve in the ship's profile, the concave spring of the main deck line, started at the bow and dropped away slowly toward the water, then came level for the run to the stern. The pilot house, the discotheque, and the piano bar seemed to be piled on top of that curve, crushing it. At the end of her winter months, immobile and externally unchanged, the ship had become just another large metal shape in the industrial scenery at the uppermost corner of the harbor. She was not much taller than the warehouses behind her, not much different in shape from the fuel storage tanks on the flat foreshore beyond the warehouses.

From November through June, nothing but announcements and

newspaper stories made her a sailing ship. She had no masts. The masts, four metal columns listed as "approximately 48 meters" (157 feet, 6 inches) tall on the Wärtsila specifications, were the central engineering challenge and the backbone of the job. Every engineer, draftsman, and shipwright on the project had known it from the start. Even before the keel was laid, Fournier's mast simulator program had permitted the engineers to design mast after mast and to test those designs, singly or together, under every conceivable load.

The shipbuilders, trained to imagine forces in action while looking at static line drawings, were also sailors. The computer program designed by their president made what they were going to attempt very real. It sobered them, and that was exactly what Fournier had intended. In fact, just after they had signed the contract to build Andren's first ship, Fournier chartered the *Velsheda,* one of the huge sloop-rigged sailing yachts that once raced for the America's Cup. Those powerful, 135-foot-long sailboats had 165-foot-tall masts.

"I wanted them to see what they were up against," Fournier said. "I wanted them to feel for themselves the effect of wind on a mainsail over one hundred fifty feet tall on the luff."

His staff did not cruise. They were sent off to enter a race and they came back chastened. Winds of 20 knots, which might require a modern ocean racer to shorten sail, prevented *Velsheda* from hoisting her huge mainsail at all.

From that race onward, the shipyard engineers always thought about their windship's masts and rigging with respect. They pushed ideas around gingerly and tried all that survived their brainstorms on the computer and on two scale models in the artificial breezes of the wind tunnels at Morvane and Saint-Cyr.

"Trop fort," they told one another often, *"n'a jamais manqué."*

Andren and Heinan left them to their testing. Andren said, "They're engineers. They know what they're doing. They'll figure it out."

Still, in the first year of construction, until after *Wind Star* was launched and he had learned to trust the builders he had chosen, one of the three things about his ship that could wake Andren at night were the masts. Would they stand up at sea? he wondered. The other two worries, which stayed with him even longer, were: Will she sail? and Will the computer work?

Outwardly, the shipyard staff was all confidence on all three of Karl's worries, but they approached the building and testing of each of those unknown elements of their project very slowly, as if with hesitation or reluctance. They put off a start on the computer, the rigging, and the sails well beyond Faury's initial projected dates. The first wind-tunnel and tank tests, whose results were blended by computer calculation in the summer of 1985, showed a disappointing performance for the ship under sail. One afternoon Faury and Castetz politely avoided answering my questions on the details of the wind-tunnel tests. That evening, as we went through a doorway together, a younger engineer who had overheard the afternoon session said to me out of the corner of his mouth: "She's going to be a cow."

The engineers were never forthcoming about their sailing design, but it was clear that, after the first two tests in May and June of 1985, they again reworked the Wärtsila design in an attempt to get more speed under sail. The masts grew taller and the designers tried to find room for more sail area without changing the rig design. Faury even tested, and tried hard to incorporate, an extra ballooning jib, almost a spinnaker. The lead engineer himself directed all design work on the rigging.

"He does not delegate," one of the sailmakers who watched the design develop said of Faury. "He decides everything himself." But he was forced to decide in a void illuminated only by the performance of small scale models of the ship and by calculations. There was no performing example before him and there would be none until he built it. He moved as cautiously as the contract deadline would allow.

Wind Star's performance under sail and the competence of her sailing computer could not, in any event, be fully shown until her sea trials, which had been scheduled to take place on two days in September 1986, one week before the contracted delivery date. By then, if Andren's business plan worked, he would be almost wholly committed to taking the ship, like her or not. Potier's staff had to sell cruises in advance, which meant booking cruises before the cruise ship was finished and counting on timely delivery of a well-functioning ship. That set of facts sharpened the edge on Andren's three worries.

Of the three, the masts came to their trial first. By the end of 1985, Faury had decided on their length, their shape, and the thickness of metal each would need. He delegated the task of figuring out how to build them to Adam and Turquetille.

They are not hasty men by nature. After the rush of construction was over and *Wind Star* had been towed away to Harfleur, they became, mentally at least, mastbuilders. They thought about what they would need to do, imagining each major step and then thinking through all the steps in sequence. Between them, over the months, they built the masts in several ways in their imaginations before they committed themselves to a method they might use. Unlike the design engineers, who work on paper and with computer projections, Adam and Turquetille are not given to brainstorming. Neither one is very talkative and neither likes laying out any idea in public before it has had time to ripen.

Separately, the two men went about the daily business of building the second hull for Andren and managing 180 yard workers and their problems. As they walked about the shipyard and shops, as they drove to and from their homes, each thought the problem through from his own point of view. From time to time, something else might make them think of masts, and they tried out their ideas on each other in the shops, where the noise made it very difficult for anyone to eavesdrop. There were no mast-production meetings and no memos.

"You know, I've been thinking about our masts," Turquetille might say one day. "The more we can do with them laid out horizontally, the better off we'll be. You'd best be thinking about a method that will allow that. I don't think vertical welding is going to work at all in this case."

On paper at least, they knew what they would have to produce. The ship was to have four circular, hollow masts made of aluminum, each exactly 169 feet, 6 inches long. Each mast would need to taper as it rose, from a diameter of 30 inches at the base to 25 inches at the flat masthead. The original Finnish design had foreseen three sets of aft-facing spreaders, like long, cylindrical semaphore arms pointing out from the masts at a forty-five-degree angle that made them look streamlined. Often at sea, names follow functions; the spreaders were there to spread out the stainless-steel cables that would hold the masts aloft and keep them fixed in place. Spreaders do not carry sail, as yardarms did on square-rigged ships. Their effect is to open the angle of the rigging that supports the mast, thus making the shrouds behave as though their ends were fastened much more widely than the breadth of the ship permits.[1]

The nineteenth-century clipper ship *Cutty Sark* had aft-facing spreaders for the shrouds sustaining all her uppermost masts, but, when it first appeared at the beginning of the century, this technique of supporting tall masts on slim boats, using struts and thin wire rope, was dubbed "Marconi rigging," because it resembled the tall, thin antennas in webs of wires needed for Guglielmo Marconi's wireless radio. The technique has been the standard for sailboat masts for years.

"We're not inventing anything," said one of the mast designers. "We're just trying to make it bigger than ever before."

Andren had asked for steel masts that could double as funnels. He wanted no smoke on his sails and no smokestack showing above the decks of his sailing ship. Faury decided that steel masts would weigh too much for the ship. Steel was too heavy at that height and might make the ship unstable. They dreamed of space-age metal alloys or plastics strengthened by carbon fiber, but found themselves constrained. There was not enough experience in commercial shipping with such materials, they were expensive, and their reliability was unproven.

So, like almost all designers of modern sailing yachts, the French designers were left with aluminum, the standard mast material of this age. Aluminum is strong and light, but it has some drawbacks. It can be brittle, compared to steel of the same thickness, and it is very tricky to shape and weld. By midsummer in the first year of construction, the design calculations had forced out all other alternatives. All of the structures above *Wind Star*'s last full steel deck had to be built in aluminum; aluminum masts, a separate aluminum funnel, aluminum pilot house, and an aluminum discotheque and piano bar. Methodically, Adam set about creating an aluminum-working section within his shops. He had to call in new suppliers, and free advice on how to build sailing ships began to rain around him. Welding machinery salesmen, tool salesmen, the metallurgists at Europe's largest aluminum manufacturers, all seemed to want to have a part in building the windship.

"There were people who said the masts could only be done a certain way," Adam recalled. "It almost always happened that the welding machines they were selling worked best that way; or would only work that way."

"Then we got more general suggestions," he said. "Everyone knew just how to do it. One would say that with aluminum it was very important to get a good paint job inside and out, to avoid corrosion; the next would say that with aluminum we must, above all, not paint any surface, in order to avoid corrosion. There were those who said we had to seal the inside of each mast off from sea air, to prevent corrosion, and those who said we'd better be sure to have good ventilation inside the masts, for the same reason. All of these people were professionals, in the business."

"In the end, we will have made them each a little happy," said Adam when the building method had been settled. "We painted the outside of the masts, but not the inside. We sealed part of the masts but not their whole length."

That was as close as Alain Adam, in his unflamboyant way, came to saying that he built the masts his way. He sifted through his welders and sent twenty-four of the best, with two foremen, back to welding school for a two-week course in aluminum. He selected the most promising welding methods and tested the joints made by each by bending and stretching samples under pressure until the metal broke. Then he chose the new welding machinery and used it to make samples of the joints the yard would have to make in the masts. He tested again.

"In every case, the metal broke before the weld," he said. "And that, at least, was reassuring." The metal itself, they knew, had been tested by engineering laboratories that found it worthy for the loads they knew it would have to bear. The welds they were making had proved even stronger.

After one year on the job, the shipyard men had grown accustomed to thinking of themselves as sailing-ship builders. Occasionally, they saw themselves suddenly through the eyes of others, and were reminded that the windship was unusual. It was like that when they looked matter-of-factly for ready-made masts; like rounding a corner in a dark hall, and finding oneself suddenly under a light, in front of a mirror, and, for an instant, unrecognizable.

ACH first found that Pechiney, the largest French aluminum manufacturer and the sponsor of Jacques Cousteau's experimental aluminum windcraft, could not supply *Wind Star*'s masts. That French factory's equipment was incapable of pushing out shapes as long and as thick as the new ship would need. Then a salesman for a Swiss aluminum company raised the yard's hopes for a quick and simple solution. In the middle of the winter, Adam and Faury flew to Zurich and were driven to an aluminum extrusion plant called Alusingen across the border in Germany. Quite innocently, Faury and Adam said that, if Alusingen's aluminum were technically satisfactory, they were prepared to order four tapered tubes 169½ feet long, and had come to discuss techniques to reinforce the tubes internally and to make them taper gradually.

Their hosts choked, politely. The longest tube Alusingen, or anyone they knew of, could make by pressing hot aluminum alloy out of a form, was just under 100 feet long. Furthermore, they said, such an extrusion certainly could not be made 30 inches across. It would flatten under its own weight, and become oval as it pushed out over the factory floor. The two Frenchmen asked what Alusingen could make. The yard, they saw, would be obliged to make *Wind Star*'s masts out of what was already available on the market.

Back in Graville, a group of the youngest designers, engineers, and draftsmen in the second floor loft were delighted with the news. They were the yard's Young Turks, tigerish under their formal manners and coats with ties, and practically squirming with ambition to make something really exciting. It was a loose group that usually included Enault and his computer assistant, two naval engineers, and a sailing draftsman or two. At thirty, Antoine Castetz was their elder statesman, because he was a manager with an office of his own and because he had the readiest wit in a very quick-tongued crowd. The ringleader was Gérard Boulenger, a twenty-seven-year-old professional sailing skipper and army ski instructor, who had returned to a desk at Graville as a draftsman, his money-making trade, in order to design the windship's rigging.

Boulenger, a taut bundle of a man, had been drawing plans for masts and fittings since November. He built remote-controlled sailing models of *Wind Star* with which Faury demonstrated his rigging ideas to the owners in the muddy water of little ponds by the edge of a truck bypass from the harbor to the oil refineries up the Seine estuary. It was Boulenger, pausing to explain a setback on his hurried way out to Harfleur one day, who gave me what amounted to the motto for the group.

"We're a shipyard, right?" he said. "So other people's problems are our problems. And if it's our problem—no problem."

On the shop floor, Adam and Turquetille were not so cocksure. They rearranged their mental mockups to accommodate the biggest pieces they knew they could get from Alusingen, the largest aluminum factory the European Common Market had to offer. They started thinking again. In the dreary winter weather, Adam traveled to look at the ways others made long welds in aluminum, but he found no technique that he would send to sea with the ACH name on it. Between them, he and Turquetille invented a process and built an assembly line for masts in the North Shop.

Based on what Alusingen could make, the young designers had worked out a plan that would make each mast out of four aluminimum columns, each just under 40 feet long, stacked on top of one another. Each section would be a perfect cylinder of constant diameter, but to make the mast taper the diameters would diminish from section to section, going toward the top. To make the transition between aluminum cylinders of differing diameters, the group proposed three 2.5-foot steel cones that would also strengthen the mast where the spreaders thrust against it and a steel mast head. Faury approved, but experienced metalworkers at ACH told Adam that the design could not be reliably built.

"It's not what you call simple," Turquetille said. "But we can do it."

Adam had found a technique for joining steel and aluminum.[2] The two dissimilar metals, which cannot be reliably welded to each other, were blasted together by a rippling explosive charge and the dark steel stuck to the silvery aluminum like the patterned cuff of a knit sweater. The steel cuff could be welded to steel, so the aluminum cylinders would have one at each end. Turquetille settled on a way to make up the aluminum columns, welding together a cylinder from three curved extrusions 40 feet long. Each extrusion was a sort of long, shallow trough with ridges, for strength, down the length of its concave face. That was the best Alusingen could do, and the first pieces were a week late arriving.

Welding alloys is never easy. The sharp expansion and contraction around the point of heat applied by the welder's arc deforms metal. And, unlike steel, aluminum cannot be heated and hammered back into the designed form after welding has pulled the metal out of shape. The form of the tubes had to be true from the start and each tube had to stay true as it was joined to the others to make the mast.

"Unless we are very careful," Adam told the master shipwright, "the welds could twist as we go along and, instead of a mast, we'll get a giant corkscrew."

"Don't worry," Turquetille told him. "We'll do it right."

Five months to the day after they had first put their minds to the problem, Adam and Turquetille set the welding of the first cylindrical section in motion. Three welders worked at once, moving in the same direction along separate parts of the same seam, with a foreman and three assistants in constant attendance. When one had to stop, all stopped. They stood on a raised platform, with the mast section clamped down in front of them at an ideal working height. In their full suits of light gray leather, they looked like surgeons preparing to treat an immobilized monster. When the welding began, the resemblance ended.

The welding wire used on heavy-gauge aluminum burns with a fierce blue flame so bright with ultraviolet light that any close bystander can be badly sunburned, right through his clothes. A foreman who inadvertently glanced at the work went snowblind for two nights. The men at work seemed to be wading through fountains of light. Each welding arc sounded like a huge mechanical rattlesnake. The welders worked slowly and very carefully and each time all three struck an arc together, their machines lit the whole gloomy shed with a leaping blue glare.

When the first 40-foot tube was finished, Turquetille walked out onto the shop floor and watched as his foremen measured it with calipers and stainless-steel measuring tapes and searched it for distortion, using levels and plumb bobs. A little later Adam dropped by on his rounds, almost as though he had not been waiting for this particular report since November. He bent close to listen to Turquetille in the shop noisy with the dentist's-drill whine of air-driven grinders smoothing down the new welds. He walked off the floor and out the door, away from the noise.

"There is good news. It worked. No deformation," he said. And then, more quietly. "No deformation."

The Graville mast factory could weld up one tube each working day, and there were sixteen to make for *Wind Star*'s four masts. Each end of every cylindrical tube had to be machined to a circle with a perfectly flat face, and all the faces had to be perfectly parallel, so that each completed section would go into the column without the least bias, thereby making the finished masts absolutely straight.

With no breakdowns or setbacks, Adam and Turquetille slowly recovered the one-week delay provoked by late delivery and told Faury he could plan to step the masts beginning June 28. By mid-June, the Graville yard had started trucking each finished mast section up the harbor to Harfleur. There, Graville men set up two 180-foot-long cradles on the dock next to *Wind Star* and Graville men assembled the masts, starting from the bow and working aft. From forward aft, in the order they would go aboard, the four masts would once have been called foremast, mainmast, mizzenmast, and jigger. Such confusion had arisen between traditional terminology in French and English, now infrequently used, that the foremen in Graville had begged for one standard nomenclature for the masts. From forward aft, Graville had decreed that they would be known as Mast 1, Mast 2, Mast 3, and Mast 4.

Mast 1 and Mast 2 were the first to go together on the dock beside the ship: 40 feet of silver-colored tube as big as a tree trunk, then a red steel ring, like a knot, then 40 feet more of silver tube, and so on to the mast top.

The Harfleur staff was responsible for wiring the masts for electricity and installing lights, antennas, sensors, and rigging. Finally, Harfleur would paint them. All but the painting was painstaking work, best done with the masts firm and fixed in their head-high cradles on the dock. The building and the fitting yard both knew that.

Men trying to work in the air, on scaffolding or in crane cages, move much more slowly than the same men doing the same job with both feet on the dock or a deck. But prudence bred frustration, when the first two masts were nearly complete. The builders from Graville wanted to step those two upright on the ship. They were pining to see if all of their ideas would work. The fitters from Harfleur wanted the job done carefully and right. They knew that any mistakes in finishing and rigging the first two masts would be laid to them, so they would not be pushed. Rivalry surfaced between the two yards.

Adam and Turquetille had been pushing the mast project all winter, and did not let up when the masts moved to Harfleur. Top-quality work, delivered on time, is their mark on the world, the goal they set themselves and the standard by which other men judge them. It is the source of their professional pride. Overtime at Harfleur would have put the masts in the ship on schedule, but Lesage did not see why his yard should pay overtime to make up delays created at Graville.

"Monsieur Lesage was not easily convinced," Adam said. "It seems that I made myself a little unwelcome by my insistence."

If there is a table of organization in the ACH shipyards, where the staff is so pleased with its own adaptability, Faury ranks above Lesage on it, and the yard manager wanted the mast stepped fast. But he followed his own rules for teamwork, and did not move Lesage with a flat order. The tension between the two yards was resolved by indirection. Faury decided it would be a good idea to have the Graville assemblers work overtime, so the Harfleur fitters and painters did too. Lesage had scheduled the first mast stepping to begin on Saturday, July 12. Late in June, there were two weeks of warm, sunny weather, and he moved the maneuver ahead by one week. Adam and Turquetille did not make their June 28 delivery date. Lesage did not hold them off for an extra week, and the delay was exactly equal to the delay in delivery, a factor beyond the control of either yard.

"The weather helped," Lesage said, explaining the change in his plan. "Without sun, we couldn't have painted them and you know sunshine in Normandy. Can't count on it."

On the fifth of July 1986, one day after the school ships, sail trainers, and fine old yachts called "the tall ships" had paraded under sail past the rededicated Statue of Liberty in New York, the shipbuilders and the outfitters agreed to give *Wind Star* her first mast. If the operation was smooth, if nothing broke, if all the ideas worked and all the welds held, on that day she would become the tallest ship afloat. Her tallest mast was 169 feet, 6 inches long. Once in place on deck, it would rear 205 feet off the water and just pass under the Verrazano Narrows Bridge at the mouth of New York harbor; a man at the masthead might look into the eighteenth-story windows of a shoreside office building.

Stepping that first mast on deck, however, meant moments of a particular kind of terror for engineers, a professional echo of the human fear of formlessness, and the void. The hollow mast, weighing 11 tons, had to be lifted from the dock, swung upright, and gently lowered aboard. The Young Turks had a professional slang phrase for such a large-scale maneuver. They called it a manipulation, *une manip'*, for short.

The *manip'* on July 5 looked clear to the layman, but the engineers approached it as they might have walked toward a crumbling cliff edge. They probed and calculated and practiced the manipulation on scale models and still remained cautious, taut. During the righting maneuver, the mast would change its fundamental nature, as seen by engineers, and pass through a nonstate between two forms, where the engineers' vision dimmed and calculation was not enough to forecast what would happen.

Engineers are practical Platonists, and look at the man-made parts of the world as a series of structures composed of a few fundamental forms. There are blocks, wedges, cones, columns, pyramids, walls, beams, and cables in various materials. Blocks make buildings, dams are wedges, and beams, columns, and cables go together to make what the rest of us call bridges. The masts were made to be columns; to stand erect and bear all stresses downward, from the masthead to the hull. That was their nature, and Adam's trial welding sections, piled in a corner of the North Shop, betrayed it. They looked like tumbled portions of stone columns in the ruins of the Roman Forum.

Lying in twelve cradles on the dock, however, with three pairs of spreaders reaching upward for more than 20 feet and stainless-steel shrouds tightened into place at the ends of the spreaders, the first two masts were not columns to an engineer's eye. They looked more like suspension bridges, which are designed and built to stay horizontal.

The masts looked like bridges, but they had not been built to bear a bridge's load. Lifted horizontal, in the air parallel to the dock, each would be under stress it had not been prepared to carry. Welds might tear. The aluminum skin might crumple. The mast might bend, before it could be swung upright. This unnatural strain could be calculated, but the slow righting to the vertical could not. In those moments lay the change of state from beam to column and the incalculable risk.

"There are people who say our profession consists of taking risks." Faury said on July 5. "I do not agree. To be an engineer is to minimize the risks, to calculate carefully and determine the dimensions of the risk and to accept only those that are tolerable."

They calculated the risk to their first mast, then hired out the job of lifting it to professional riggers. At six on the morning of July 5, two long, squat, mobile cranes started up their 320-horsepower diesel engines and began telescoping out six-part hydraulic booms. Each could lift 200 tons 150 feet in the air, but that day one had been set up to lift as high as 220 feet and to swing a weight of 15.7 tons 60 feet away from its base. It would take the mast top; the second crane would lift the bottom.

First light comes at 5:30 in Normandy in the summer, but in the normal Norman summer one rarely sees the sun rise. Fog banks squeeze off the Channel and cling to the creeks and pastures. At six it was still hard to decide whether the wet, gray air was high fog or low cloud. It was Saturday, and only those involved in the *manip'* had come to work. The Young Turks were all there. A few large drops of rain fell and someone said that morning rain never stopped a pilgrim.

"Faury called me at home and asked me to check the weather forecast," Lesage said. "For me, those guys, forecasters, don't stand a chance around here. I get my forecast when I swing my legs out of bed in the morning and look out the window." The home forecast had been reassuring. Lesage wore a short-sleeved shirt, open at the collar, under a lightweight summer jacket.

Adam arrived before Faury or Lesage. He made one round of everyone there, shaking hands and wishing a good day to each. Seven of his own men, from Graville, wished him a good day and good luck. He thanked them and told them not to worry.

"If it breaks," he said, "we'll have two years to find new jobs."

Turquetille moved away from the Graville group to the edge of the dock, his shoulders hunched and his cigarette smoking in the mist. Only Deporte, his friend and understudy, walked with him.

A rigger wearing the green hard hat of the mobile crane company clambered up onto the mast and the operator dipped the crane hook gently down toward him. His hard hat, face, and a round slice of his blue overalls showed through the curve inside the huge hook. He slipped the bridling cables from a lifting brace at the topmost spreaders onto the hook and jumped down off the mast.

At a quarter to seven the idling crane engines snored softly with a deep and steady tone and the lift began. The mast moved so smoothly upward it seemed that both cranes were directed by a single, gentle intelligence. In two minutes Mast 1, the heaviest of all and the first to go aboard, hung clear of all twelve cradles, 6 feet off the dock. There it stopped. Adam had moved to a far corner of the dock, alone. Turquetille had not stirred. Faury and Lesage walked quickly along the full length of the suspended white column, measuring the distance between mast and cradles to test for flexion in the suspended tube.

"We gave the mast its shape with shroud tension while it lay on the cradles," Faury said. "We wanted, just now, to see if the shape was satisfactory."

It was. Walking away from Faury, the crane contractor shouted for his foreman.

"Hey, Manu," he called. "Take it up."

The foreman, a short man wearing a working man's suit of faded blue denim pants and jacket, had been unremarkable among the loose groupings of people on the dock that morning. Summoned, he raised himself slightly onto his toes where he stood and whistled once. It was not a particularly sharp whistle, nor long, but in the silence on the dock, it was commanding. Looking only at the mast, and not at either of the two crane operators in their glass cabins, he pointed his left hand, index finger outstretched, at *Wind Star*'s stern, and turned the erect index finger of his right hand in tight counterclockwise circles just above his hard hat.

The mast, slung near the base and top by the two cranes, rose and moved aft without a tremor. The foreman's was the single intelligence that moved both cranes. He was the master rigger. His crew called him the master of the lift and his name was Manuel Yglesias, but by the end of the morning, Adam had given the man a nickname that stuck. The chief of the orchestra, he called Yglesias, the conductor.

The foremast swung through its change of state from horizontal to vertical, from bridge to column, from ungainly assembly to mast, in fifteen steady minutes. The chief of the orchestra talked gently to himself, in a tone so low neither operator could hear. He used gestures to signal the operators and such was the power of his concentration that everyone on the dock watched him more often than they looked at the rising mast. It spent eleven minutes as a bridge, feeling out its own strength in an unfamiliar position, then fifteen minutes in silent transition. For all that time, Adam said later, he had been thinking "Can't they hurry? Can't they hurry?"

The master rigger halted the mast 60 feet from the ship, with its base only 18 inches off the dock. He blew a short sigh and smiled, a flash of white in a face tanned to mahogany. Behind him, the master shipwright unfolded his arms and nodded. Turquetille fished into his dungaree pocket and tried to light a cigarette in the fitful, wet wind. Like iron filings drawn into a clump on paper over a magnet, the men of Graville and Harfleur gathered around Faury, gazing up.

"Well," said Faury. "The anemometer is turning. That's a good sign."

The little cups at the masthead that spin on a shaft to measure wind force were turning in the breeze aloft.

"Hey! It's beautiful!" exclaimed Gérard Boulenger. The white mast gleamed in the high fog. The riggers clambering up to the platform at the first spreader, to release the secondary crane, had set the whole tall structure swaying very gently. To see its top, hanging from the trellised tip of a single crane, all of those around Faury were obliged to throw back their heads and hold onto the visors of their white hard hats.

"Impressive, isn't it?" said Kell Andersen, the Danish naval architect who supervised the shipyard work for Andren. "Beautiful job. That will sell the tickets, you'll see. Now she looks like a barge, but once that mast is on, she'll begin to be beautiful."

The crane men and their riggers took an hour to unfasten the bridles and dismount the bracing at the bottom spreader, where the second crane had hooked on to lift the lower part of the mast. It was no longer needed. Then the first crane most gently lifted Mast 1, like some huge trophy on display, and as gently swung it in over *Wind Star*'s deck. It was 8:40 and large, ragged scraps of dirty black cloud drove in from the sea under the solid gray overcast. The rain that had come and gone in little pattering promises since dawn fell on a wind-driven slant.

Boulenger, his blue denim pants and jacket dark with rain, grappled the base of the mast first as it came over the bulwark, 12 feet forward of the pilot-house windows. Four riggers, a foreman, and three Graville men joined him and clung as though they would wrestle the mast to its target by main force. The master rigger loped up the dockyard's steel ramp into the ship. His hair bounced in gray curls under his hat. He reappeared on deck, out of sight of the operator controlling the crane, but talking to him steadily through a handheld radio, and the mast moved again. With six men clinging to its base, it moved sideways like a levitating tree and settled toward its place on deck. Yglesias crouched by the butt of the mast.

"Two or three centimeters; let's go. Slowly, slowly, slowly," the master rigger said to his radio. One could hear his soft voice all around the circle of silent men on deck. "Stop. One. Stop."

There was no light visible between mast and deck. He looked up. "If we could have some wedges?" he said. "To align."

Kell Andersen, standing behind Faury, suddenly said: "You forgot the coin."

Turquetille and Deporte knelt at the base of the mast, slowly turning the whole tall tower with steel wedges they had levered by hand into alignment braces welded onto the deck.

"I did not know of that tradition," Faury said, over his shoulder.

"My guys, start rigging the temporary supporting cables," the chief rigger ordered.

Deporte looked up and said: "Aligned."

"Bring it in," the rigger told his radio. "Softly, softly."

"Well, in a ship with two or more masts, the coin went under the mainmast anyway," Andersen said.

"It's touched," said Deporte. Faury stepped to the mast.

"What coin?" asked Lesage. Andersen explained the sailing tradition of a silver coin laid, for luck, between the mast and its step. A welder, who had been waiting in his protective suit, helmet in hand, struck a blue arc in the rain and laid down a series of short, provisional passes to hold the mast in place. It was home, and the focus of attention widened. Slag from the welder's rod spat and sputtered in the rain.

"Mâtage pluvieux, mâtage heureux," said Antoine Castetz, speaking up for the first time. The French laughed and I asked why.

"In France one says: *'Mariage pluvieux, mariage heureux'*—a rainy wedding day means a happy marriage," Castetz explained. "So a rainy masting day should mean a happy masting."

Riggers called out to one another, tightening the temporary shrouds to hold the mast in place. They came back and carried the thick silver ends of the ship's permanent shrouds out to steel chain plates welded at the edges of the deck and the wings of the bridge. The yard engineers wondered out loud if the tradition of a coin under the mast were French. Boulenger, who had finally let go of his mast, straightened and said it was.

"We don't build sailing ships," Lesage said. "Haven't in a while, anyway. That's why we didn't know about the coin."

"We're going to get a yard flag up there," he announced to the group at large.

"ACH or SCG?" someone asked. *ACH* are the initials of Fournier's shipbuilding group, which got its start at the Harfleur dockyard. The initials *SCG* stood for the building yard at Graville.

"ACH," said Lesage. "Remember, you are all subcontractors here."

The flag flew from the foremast by midday. The rain stopped and Yvan Martin came back from Le Havre with an 1889 U.S. silver dollar, to put under Mast 2, the mainmast. He had found it at a numismatic shop before the city stores closed for the weekend. But Mast 2, the second on the dock, was a long time rising. The concentration and euphoria of the morning slipped away, through a long lunch hour and into a polite but lengthy disagreement between Faury and the master rigger over how to rig the mainmast for lifting. It was a draw until the mast bowed visibly as it took the first horizontal strain. Then Yglesias, the "chief of the orchestra," reset the tension in his bridles, as Faury had asked him to do.

When the mast rose again, after four, the rain returned, stiff and steady, and grew colder as the long summer twilight deepened. It was 9:30 P.M. before Faury agreed to halt the day's work, and Mast 2 was upright but stayed only temporarily. All the rigging work that Faury had scheduled for that afternoon was carried forward into Sunday.

"These engineers tend to be a bit optimistic," the master rigger said. "They don't know how much slower a man works, eighty or a hundred feet in the air."

The slip in their schedule struck the engineers as a reproach and Adam walked away from the ship that night with his shoulders hunched in a wringing wet summer raincoat.

"Well, at least she is properly dressed now," he said. "Good night. See you tomorrow."

The wind went north on Sunday and whipped the sky clear. The hired riggers managed one-half of their postponed worklist, swinging through the sky in a steel cage lifted by one crane and bobbing up and down both masts. Watching them work in the windy sunlight, one's eye adjusted quickly to *Wind Star*'s new proportions. We who had seen the ship's profile change gradually as the masts rose on Saturday were not often taken by surprise, although once I turned around on deck and, for an instant, thought that the pilothouse, previously so tall to my eye, had shrunk. The two new masts towered above it.

At dawn on Monday a new working week began and the daily flow of cars across the low bridge just upstream from the dockyard started. Then it stopped and backed up into a silent traffic jam. The change in the ship was so arresting that, one after another, people driving to work slowed and stopped to stare. Her true transformation had begun.

10

CHAPTER

Sails

I did not know the center of effort in her sails, except as it hit me in practice at sea, nor did I care a rope yarn about it. Mathematical calculations, however, are all right in a good boat, and the Spray *could have stood them.*

—Joshua Slocum, *Sailing Alone Around the World*

The change in *Wind Star* was at once a relief and a challenge. With two of her masts stepped, and her rigging going on, she had become a sailing ship to the watching eye, and all of the engineers' calculated feats of imagination for the masts had worked. Her builders felt they had done so much that the feeling itself reminded them there was almost too much left to do. The six rotating stays on which the six sails would furl had to be assembled, hoisted, rigged, and tested. The hydraulic motors that would drive them, and all their pumps and pipes and valves, had yet to be installed. The sails themselves were not aboard, nor the sailing computer, nor any of its programming.

Down below, the ship's generators and some of her pumps had been tested under load. The engine room looked like an engine room and even smelled like one. The odor of heated oil overpowered that of new paint there for the first time. The ship's galleys and pantries were being assembled like stainless-steel stage sets. Bulkheads and doors had risen on all the empty decks. The outlines of cabins had been filled in, for passengers and crew, and it took no effort of imagination to recognize the dining room or the lounge. After long months of no apparent progress while the electricians and pipefitters had worked, the ship now changed inside almost daily. One could stay away for a working week, come back aboard, and find changes on every deck.

"Now you can see it," Kell Andersen pointed out. "The ship is a whole now. She is coming together. Now the worries begin about whether it can all be finished on time. I have seen it before. It can seem you won't make it until three weeks before delivery, then everyone pulls hard and in three weeks they do two months' work."

Faury never sounded worried.

"There is a very ungrateful, unlovely stage in the building of any ship," he said, at the end of one late afternoon tour of *Wind Star*. "For months it seems that nothing happens, and one needs a very experienced eye to be able to judge whether sufficient progress is being made. Now, everyone can see that we will hold to our delivery date."

Early in June, Lesage had committed his outfitting plan to writing in a memo of eleven lines. Sea trials for the power plant and controls would take place the twenty-second and twenty-third of September; the trials at sea for sails and rigging would take place the twenty-fifth and twenty-sixth. Harfleur would deliver *Wind Star* to her owner on October 4, a Saturday. Fournier himself announced this timetable to Andren in June at the shipyard, and committed ACH to keeping it.

At that moment an old dream, which Andren had put aside during the delays of the winter, began to burn inside him again. From the beginning of the project, Karl had wanted to introduce his first ship to the world by sailing her across the Atlantic to New York on her maiden voyage. He wanted to see *Wind Star* sail under the Verrazano Narrows Bridge, just clearing the suspended roadway, and past the Statue of Liberty. He wanted fireboats trailing fountains of water alongside her towering sails and the whole Circle Line fleet out to meet his ship.

Potier, however, had committed the ship to a shakedown charter with paying passengers on November 15 in the Caribbean, and it was not clear in June whether she could make both ports in forty days, allowing for shakedown and crew training, maintenance work, provisioning, and fueling. If all parts of the shipyard schedule held true and she were delivered in perfect, functioning order, the double trip was just feasible.

The prototype sailing ship would have to work on her first try, then sail immediately in the autumn, when the winter gales have already begun to growl in the ocean beyond the mouth of the Channel. The ship would have to hold her contract speed across the North Atlantic against the wind, using sail and power. After visiting New York, she would need to turn south into the Caribbean at the end of the hurricane season. Early in July, with two masts stepped, the trip began to look just barely possible.

Of all the things *Wind Star* needed to make her a working sailing ship, the roller furling stays that would carry her sails went aboard first. The idea of furling sails by rolling them up on a long, round rod spun in and out by machinery had been around so long that the shipyard engineers had, to a certain extent, taken that part of their sailing rig for granted. Square-rigged topsails had been set, reefed, and furled in the nineteenth century from rolling yards turned from the deck.[1] Cruising sailboats in this century used sails that rolled up to furl and unrolled to set—sails that could be reefed in strong winds by rolling in a portion of their area.

There was existing technology, tried at sea, so the shipyard engineers did not need to invent by themselves a way to roll in and out the 158-foot-tall sails for their windship.[2] They contracted out the job of designing and building the ship's six furlers to a French company.

Faury had expected three of the five rolling stays to be promptly rigged on Sunday, July 6, and bolted into place on the two masts stepped the day before. So he asked the builder of the furlers to send a representative that weekend to Harfleur. The designer, the manufacturer, and the president all came in the person of one man, a retired professor of physics from the University of Lyon, who had the lean, fit look of a competitor in the sixty-to-sixty-five age division of a marathon. I was surprised, after Faury introduced René Bernard as the furler stay manufacturer, to learn that he was seventy-eight. I was even more surprised to hear his dry, direct speech in those polite, formal, indirect, and competitive surroundings.

"These camels," said Bernard, within minutes after I had met him over a sandwich in the Harfleur conference room, "never showed me their calculations for the distribution of the effort of the sails along the furler. They had them, but they made me go all the way through it on my own when they already knew what the distribution of effort would be. I only found out about theirs when we all went to a maritime inspectors meeting together and I showed my calculations. And there was Faury saying: 'Yes, that sounds pretty close to our results.' "

Faury, sitting on my right while Bernard spoke on my left, blinked rapidly, as he often does when he is refocusing his intellect. The yard's chief engineer was silent for a long moment, as if computing. One of the mariners on hand for much of the building of *Wind Star* described this mannerism as Faury's "gyrocompass mode." When shoved suddenly by a thrust from an unexpected direction, Faury's mind, like the gyroscope spinning in a modern seagoing compass, never toppled. It seemed to precess, tracing an orbit with its pole once or twice in silence and before coming back to the vertical.

"In effect," Faury said. Then: "Lots of people tell you they know everything about a subject. Then you find out that they don't know anything about it. One must cross-check. By cross-checking, one finds out about other people. And checks one's own figures."

"But I knew nothing about the distribution of effort curve at the beginning," said Bernard. "And I said so."

"Yes," Faury said. "Perhaps our engineer should have given you the calculations."

What worried Bernard, he explained later, was the potential trap in the scaling up of the roller furling design he had invented for use on cruising sailboats, and had sold around the world. He had used much the same design for *Wind Star.* But he knew that the relationship between stresses and resistances, balanced in tension, does not remain constant when a structure is made bigger. The rules of prudent engineering require that the whole structure be recalculated if it is made larger. At some point in upward scaling, the first engineering solution stops being a solution at all. The same engineering and the same materials will not support a Statue of Liberty as tall as the Empire State Building.

Bernard had recalculated his sailboat furlers for the sailing ship, without help from ACH, and the yard accepted his solutions. He had matched sailing stress and metal resistance in a furler that was a long, flexible tube of interlocking aluminum extrusions, glued and riveted together so that a sliced-out segment looked like an outsize horseshoe, with its open end covered by a rigid tongue of metal. There were two grooves at the corners of the horseshoe shape, and the ship's plans showed that the sails would rise in the roller stay with two full-length tabs of cloth, stiffened by flexible wire, called luff wires, slotted inside those two grooves. The furler profile had been clamped together in seven 23-foot-long sections over the fat, smooth stainless-steel cable of the stay itself. The profile was to spin around the wire cable, driven by a hydraulic motor at the bottom and supported by plastic bearings inside.

The officers of *Wind Star*'s crew-to-be watched closely and took pictures as the furlers were assembled on the dock at Harfleur.

"It's good to know how things are put together," said the first mate, a bear of a man named Alexander Maresca. "Then, if something goes wrong at sea, you know how to fix it."

Each completed assembly of furler and stay had to be rigged aloft as a whole, but that whole was long, and flexible only within limits. If it bent too far, the joints between furler sections might crack. So the riggers, with the engineers, had decided to hoist the assembly fixed to the underside of one of the long boxes of steel tubing that stack on top of one another to support standing cranes at skyscraper building sites.

The long box to hold each stay rigid as it was hoisted into place and bolted on at mast and deck looked like latticework and the riggers called it a trellis. On the Sunday after the rainy masting day, the first furler stay was bolted and tied off like a vine beneath the trellis, but the riggers were still busy with shrouds and spreaders. Bernard went home to Lyon, and Manuel Yglesias, the master rigger, set his own pace for the job. He said he would lift and place one furler stay per day and Faury acquiesced.

Yglesias had been accepted as a worthy colleague by the shipbuilding foremen during his first day on the *Wind Star* job when he lifted their first mast aboard so smoothly. They recognized him. Like them, he was the confident master of his craft. Like them, he did his job with evident pleasure and spoke of it warmly, not quite bragging. Gérard Boulenger, who also liked to work aloft, took to him immediately, called him by the diminutive 'Manu,' and watched him closely. Even Faury forgave Yglesias for his challenge to the engineer's authority. Faury and the master rigger had tested each other's competence repeatedly on Saturday, the first mast-stepping day. The following day, it appeared that each had passed the other's test. The two men spoke to each other as professional equals, masters of different spheres in a common craft. Yglesias even piqued Faury's interest.

All Sunday, as he spun in a steel cage dangling aloft to complete the rigging of Masts 1 and 2, the master rigger had thought about the ship beneath him. When he climbed out of the cage on the dock that afternoon he reported the end of the job to Faury, then wondered out loud if a question would be permitted.

"Of course," said Faury.

"The sails are computer-controlled, correct? What happens if you're entirely without power?" Yglesias asked. "No main propulsion; no generators; no way to rig stabilizers. Nothing at all. And a storm's coming. How do you get the sails in?"

"We've foreseen that case," Faury said briskly. A group of his own foremen and an engineer or two had come up around the two men. "In the computer program, reefing begins automatically when power is lost. The sails are furled completely, automatically, when anything goes utterly wrong."

"What do you use for power, if it's gone?" Yglesias asked. His tone was curious, reflective and not challenging.

"We have tanks filled with oil under pressure."

Yglesias smiled. "I see, you store energy."

"Yes," Faury said. He smiled too. "We use the stored energy for emergencies. The computer has an interlock. It will not allow any sail to be set if the reserve tank for that furler is not full."

"All that trouble to please people who can afford a thousand francs a day to sail on one of these. It's good, but it's crazy," Yglesias said. Faury blinked.

"No, you see. I ask myself about all this work and expense for what we call leisure," Yglesias added. He looked around at the gathered group. "Some guy works all week at what he calls his job, and he doesn't like any of it; so then he goes out and works all weekend on his leisure. If you like your work, the work is leisure, for me."

The men listening nodded, and their assent rippled around the ring in a murmur.

"I wonder what man's future is," Yglesias went on. "What do you think?"

"I don't know much about man's future, but of one thing I'm certain," Faury said. "He'll always have to work."

"Yup," said Yglesias. "That's for sure. Better to like your work, then." His voice rose and he looked for his men in the circle around him. "All right, let's finish it."

The finishing was not that simple. The master rigger, his cranes and crane men, and his riggers stayed through Wednesday to complete the jobs the engineers had laid out for them to do on the two-day weekend. The day they left, Adam and Turquetille sent over mast sections with Graville men, who began assembling the next two masts outside Lesage's office windows.

It turned hot, for Normandy, and the Young Turks in short sleeves loosened their neckties under their blue overalls and wrestled with the business of tuning the tall masts and their rigging on board. Using the permanent shrouds alone, the masts had to be trimmed exactly upright, then bent slightly aft like a fishing rod at the top of a back cast. The precise bend was checked by a laser generator leveled on deck. It shot lines of light up the forward edge of each mast until, one after another, five targets welded to the mast aloft aligned their bull's-eyes over the laser beam. Then the furlers, which had been left hanging slack like silver curves drawn in the sky, could be put under their designed tension. Jean-Eric Enault, the lead computer programmer and the numbers man among the Turks, had figured out a way to run the mast simulation program backward to tune the masts. Run that way, he said with pride, the program would give him the tuning adjustments for each shroud on a mast "to the tenth of a turn."

The turnbuckles that needed to be turned were 4 inches thick. To adjust those fastened to steel eyepads on deck, two men heaving in opposite directions on 4-foot chain wrenches got about one-tenth of a turn with each heave. But their feet were braced on deck. Aloft, the turnbuckles would not budge. In the air, suspended in a bosun's chair dangling at the end of a 170-foot halyard, a man heaving on a chair wrench just pulled himself close up to the wrench shaft. Nothing moved but the man in the air.

"Any rigger could have told them that," said the rigger the Young Turks sent up to try. He spoke to me after he came down, loudly enough for them to have to ignore him. They set their minds together to figuring out how to adjust the turnbuckles in the air and had three potential solutions by the next day at lunch.

The Young Turks lunched every day in the Graville cafeteria, occupying a table together during a lull they had timed by observation —a lull that fell between waves of yardworkers in overalls, who were sent to lunch in sections. They had recommended the food and the lull to me, and, when I was in Le Havre, I often found myself buying the cafeteria's "visitors' lunch" at the same time they arrived. They invited me to join them and together we kept up with progress on the ship's sailing computer program by sensing, at lunch each day, the degree of taciturnity in Jacques Bouché, Enault's neat and practically silent deputy.

Bouché lunched at Graville every day but worked on the sail-control program downtown, in the brick building housing the corporate and engineering division headquarters. There, he and his programming partner were close under Gilbert Fournier's eye. They had been working at it together for four months, and had only two months left to finish.

"I think the program is coming along," Boulenger told me one afternoon. "Monsieur Bouché talked at lunch today."

A few afternoons later Antoine Castetz and I visited Bouché and his sailing machine. He had agreed to demonstrate it at the end of his working day, which came near six, almost two hours after the shipyard quitting time.

The program had long since been designed, in the free-form way that prevailed at ACH. Through 1985, about ten people at the shipyard thought about the sail-control program while they did their daily jobs. They discussed their ideas whenever thoughts came to them. Faury kept a loose-leaf folder for the programming ideas and that was as binding a form as the program took until the close of the year.

The list of ideas was about two hundred propositions long, when, after *Wind Star* was launched, Faury and Fournier and Enault began to codify and simplify. They opted for artificial-intelligence architecture, which is to say that they decided to try to make a computer program that would act like a sailing watch stander. They wanted the computer to feel the wind on its electronic cheek, the way Elis Karlsson once did on the deck of the *Herzogin Cecilie,* and sense the ship's heel in its electronic inner ear, then to consult its own codified experience, written in by men, and decide the proper sail trim and issue orders. That definition of the program was made in January 1986, and it excited Enault and Bouché. It meant working out and writing the instructions for a limited replica of one portion of a trained human brain, and fitting that replica into a real ship, ready to work in what computer programmers call real time.

"The computer speed we selected will scan all its inputs and process instructions every half second," Enault said, tapping his pen on a desk one day. He was an able violinist and the tapping sounded metronomic. "The scanning speed is the beat for "La Marseillaise"; that's the easy way for me to remember."

However, the writing of computer instructions was first assigned away from Graville, to an ACH Engineering Division programmer named Jean-François Hutt. Bouché joined him in April, after supervising four wind-tunnel tests and compiling the data from these tests. The wind-tunnel data was set into the program to represent the real world of winds and squalls and swells at sea for the computer, until *Wind Star* had showed she could sail and the computer could learn her real ways. By mid-July, when we visited them, Hutt and Bouché working together had written almost five hundred thousand lines of computer code.

There was a smell of fatigue trapped in their workroom on the third floor of the ACH building, along with remnants of the heat of that windless day. The single window was open and the two young men in shirtsleeves were wrapping up their day's work when we came in. Bouché, a small man with smooth black hair cut short and a white face with features so composed he barely seems to blink, sat down to demonstrate.

The terminal screen filled with a four-color display including a plan view of the ship and her sails. With instructions to the computer, Bouché wrote in an artificial breeze of 15 knots, and set his artificial ship sailing, according to the readouts displayed on the screen. The speed showing on one line flickered up past 8 knots. He changed the display to show one sail at a time and trimmed each, as it showed on the screen, with computer commands. The screen display wavered. Lines developed an odd tic, and Bouché stopped the program to tinker with connections. Castetz started asking questions, and the younger man stopped work to answer. The screen display went on jumping behind him.

When we had come in, Bouché had had before him a handwritten list of things to do, steps to correct, and processes to rethink. The list in blue ink on graphed paper had ended at a neatly numbered item number 80. When we stood up to leave, the list had grown to eighty-eight items, and Castetz saw what his questions had done. At his request, Bouché was just then talking about the possibility of putting a flashing propeller on the screen to show when the ship's own propeller was turning.

"That will be for the fifth ship," Castetz said. All knew that Andren had not yet committed himself to building a fourth windship. They laughed. Bouché was still sitting.

"Are you going home tonight?" Hutt asked.

"For a change," Bouché said, and they all laughed again.

"You're not going to go on vacation?" Castetz asked while the younger man undid connections. The French vacation month of August was nearly at hand.

"No," Bouché said.

"We'll put an ultraviolet suntan lamp in here for you," Castetz said.

"You see how they keep us in mind?" Hutt asked his colleague. He used the familiar *tu.*

"It's nice to see that, after four months together, you still speak politely to one another," Castetz put in.

"That's only in the evening, when there are visitors," said Bouché.

"Ah, I see," said Castetz. "Now I understand the bloodstains on the floor by the door."

We left together, closing the door on the eight extra, unanswered questions, including the heaviest of all.

"Who's going to write the manual?" Castetz had asked. "They'll have to have a manual on board to run all this."

"I don't know," Bouché had said. "It's a huge job. I don't know that anyone has thought about it."

There were so many things to think about, for the ship, and the list requiring immediate attention got longer as the time grew shorter. The first of her six sails arrived in Le Havre by freight train late that July, bound to a wood pallet because the 3,767 square feet of doubled synthetic sailcloth weighed over 500 pounds. The heft of that single folded sail was such that the Graville engineers were spurred to check on the progress of their colleagues downtown, where ACH was manufacturing the hydraulic system that would handle all the ship's sails. The hydraulics were behind schedule. The sails, however, were coming in from their maker on time. From bow to stern they were the jib, a fair-weather sail, then four staysails, one before each mast to make the working sail area, and finally the boomed sail over the after-deck that all called the mizzen.

Wind Star's sails were built[3] in a high hall full of natural light in the south of France, where I found an easygoing tolerance for the Cartesian precision of the Graville engineers. The sailmaker, Bruno Navarre, knew the style. He had grown up in Le Havre, the son of a coffee importer who was also the son of a coffee importer. Bruno was captivated early by the sea, then by sailmaking, and he served his sailmaking apprenticeship working after high school each day, and started his business in that gray northern city, where, he said, "the same families are still doing the same things: seeing each other on Sundays and worrying about money."

Navarre left Le Havre by choice, taking his loft south to the sun where there are more sailboats, and more sailmakers. Several of his twelve competitors for the *Wind Star* job were his neighbors on the shore of the Mediterranean between Nice and Cannes. He found the competitive bidding for the job oddly structured. No one from the shipyard talked about his bid price until the last forty-eight hours of the competition, when there were four sail lofts left in the running. Until then, the talk was all technical, and not easy.

"We're sailors; we see things and we know what will work," Navarre said. "Ours is a trade in which you invent very few things indeed. It's too old. But they're all *polytechniciens.* They were hard to convince. If I couldn't prove it with figures, they wouldn't believe it. It was that simple."

Sometimes, Navarre could convince the engineers from Le Havre by demonstration as he did when he talked Faury out of a safety-release hook at each masthead for the top of each sail. The hook was Faury's final, failsafe, mechanical backup to all the computer's safety instructions. If the wind blew too hard, Faury had foreseen that the hook would open and the sail would blow over the side and be recovered by hand, by the crew.

"The captain was here, so I asked him how many people he'd have to haul the sail back in. He said twelve, including himself. The first sail was half unfolded on the floor, so I asked him to try picking it up. He tried and couldn't. I told them again: if it's blowing over thirty knots and you can't furl by machine, let the sail go. There's nothing else you can do. Twelve men could never haul a sail this big, this heavy out of the ocean by hand. That time, they believed me."

The hook was erased from the masthead plans, but Faury controlled all the rest of the sailmaking as he had the shipbuilding and computer programming: by making the design decisions himself, at the beginning, in the theoretical stage. Navarre did not design the ship's sails; aerodynamic technicians using computers at the French Center for Research and Assistance to the Naval Industry did. The Center, which had also calculated the distribution of effort for the roller furling stays, computed a theoretical sailing performance for the windship that was derived from ship-tank and wind-tunnel tests. The technicians there formed three possible sail shapes.

Those three shapes were tested at the Saint-Cyr wind tunnel in January 1986, and Faury chose a sail form that had a bellying sail's full curve already built into it, about one-third of the way from the leading to the trailing edge of the sail. The Center then generated computer instructions for a computer-controlled machine at a sail loft, not Navarre's, in Cannes. The machine used laser beams to slice 50-foot panels of heavy cloth and did the job three or four times faster than Navarre's sailmakers could have done it by hand. The Cannes sail loft sent the cut and numbered panels to Navarre's loft on a knoll above Antibes for assembly.

To a sailmaker like Navarre, Faury's choice revealed what his tests and calculations had showed him that the windship would be able to do best. The sails were made for free and following winds, breezes blowing easily over the ship's side, abeam, on one side or the other. They were not made for winds that blew from ahead or astern. Flat sails, sewn together without full bellies, are wanted for that work, and Wärtsila's first design had included flat sails.

Kai Levander, the sailing Finnish naval architect who first planned her, had set the windship's sails up on booms for ease of handling, but he had drawn the booms to swing along a concave path in the air, highest above the deck when they swung out and closest to it when they were near the center of the ship. Sheeted to the end of such booms, Levander foresaw that the sails would be kept to their flat shape against the wind, when the booms and sails were trimmed close to the ship's center line, but would grow full as the wind went aft and the boom shifted sideways and up. The clew, the corner of the sail rising with the boom, would free slack cloth into the sail and the wind would fill that slack, shaping a curve. Without changing the booms, Faury ordered the curve built into the sails.

Navarre saw that and predicted that *Wind Star* would slow badly when the wind blew on her bow. The sailmaker wished that she could have had more sail for more power. He would have made the sails longer in the foot, along the lower edge of their triangular shape. But there was no room for more sail between the masts, so a longer foot would have meant still more belly. Faury had extended each swinging boom to within 3 feet of the mast behind it. Navarre admired that, as the *polytechnicien*'s attempt to get the most speed under sail out of the design he had been given by contract.

"I think they contracted to build a cruise ship with sails on it as an added attraction," Navarre said. "Then they became convinced they were building a pure sailing ship."

Navarre was not quite caught up in that conviction. He built the sails in a warehouse painted white throughout that he rented from one of his unsuccessful competitors. The contract was a good piece of business, he said; sailmaker's work is hard to get in the winter. He laid the job out like factory work on the varnished plywood floor of the sail-loft warehouse. He redesigned sailmaking sewing machines and had three manufactured to hold up to the job of sewing through four thicknesses of Dacron woven so tight that every square yard of single thickness weighed 9.3 ounces. He put the sewing machines in pits level with the floor, so that his operators would not have to hoist the heavy cloth across their laps by hand. They would not have been able to. To carry the sail along the loft floor, he adapted clamping metal rollers and hung them on one wall, like a giant dry-cleaner's rack, to hold the sail as each seam fed through the sewing machines. Two men still had to haul at each fold, while another person sewed, each time the sailmakers stitched a seam.

Each sail was made by joining two mirror images of single cloth and stitching each seam four times over, so that the final sail was a double thickness of sail cloth. At the stress points, in the three corners of the sail, the thickness built up to twenty layers of cloth. A finished staysail, one of *Wind Star*'s four principal working sails, was longer than the 148-foot-long loft and so heavy it took at least four men to move it; so they made each in four pieces, finishing each piece as completely as possible before joining the four.

"Technically, it was not a very interesting job," Navarre's master sailmaker told me. "Once the problems were solved, intellectually, it became assembly-line production."

That did not mean he did not like the work. Sailmakers are an artistic and demanding lot. They are as proud of the free-standing shapes they make as sculptors and they love powerful sails that last. Navarre's loft was a pleasant place, broad and light and calm, where the sailmakers and apprentices moved quietly and smiled often. It was a place that fulfilled Faury's conditions for work on a passenger ship, a happy place with no psychological strains or tensions.

Wind Star's second pair of masts was completed three weeks after the first went aboard, and Manuel Yglesias returned to step them on July 31. There was no rain, but the wind blew from the southwest, the rainy quarter, and it blew too hard for Yglesias's liking.

"Look at that windvane," he said at dawn. The anemometer cups at the top of the first mast spun so fast one could barely distinguish them. "It's at a gallop."

Faury arrived at 7:40. The third mast already hung upright over the dock.

"It's routine now, I feel," the yard manager said. "It's almost as though I had nothing to do here."

The lift proceeded with the gentle caution that had given Faury confidence in Yglesias. Mast 3 went aboard and was stayed off. Mast 4 was ready, upright, and balanced like a pendulum at three P.M., ready to lift aboard. The wind had increased very slowly all day, but the local weather office told the shipyard it had peaked and would hold steady. Yglesias began to talk the last mast aboard, up first, then over the ship. He was standing at the forward end of the lifting crane when inside the operator's cabin first one alarm, then another, went off with high electronic squeals. The wind had increased, just as mast and crane swung broadside to it. Yglesias froze.

The crane operator ran his throttle up and shifted to the lowest, slowgst lifting range. It was the first time anyone at the yard had heard the quiet Mercedes diesel engine roar, and a sense of unease spread outward with the noise. No one moved. The crane and the dangling mast crept through the air and back over the dock, then down until the base of the mast stopped over land again with the crane tower pointed dead into the wind. The engine noise dropped to an idle and the operator jumped out.

"Manu!" he said. His face was gray under a four-day brown stubble of beard. His eyes were very large. "Manu, I can't take the mast out there! It's blowing thirty knots up top. One good gust and the whole thing will be one pile of scrap metal, crane and all."

They waited overnight, standing watch over the mast where it dangled from the crane. No yard engineer wanted to try passing the mast back through its change of state, from column back to bridge. The sense of routine had been stripped away.

The next morning at 5:30 the wind had died to nothing. In the gray first light Yglesias talked the last mast aboard *Wind Star*. It was so quiet that one could hear his murmured radio instructions whenever the crane engine idled. The sun showed like a low bulge of red, dead on the bow, as the mast slid home. For those standing behind Mast 4, the sun as it rose was exactly bisected by the ship's four masts in a line.

"Good," Faury said to Adam and Turquetille, once the final mast stood aboard. "I'm off on vacation. Work well. Monsieur Castetz has a list of points that need looking after. Monsieur Adam, I've left you a note." He paused. "And thank you all."

He shook hands and left immediately to join his family at a house on a canal near the Atlantic, where his sons played tennis and sailed their boards along the canal to a pond where they met their sailing friends. He could be gone only a week that year instead of the month of summer vacation that is a matter of course for the working French. When he had left, René L'Heryénat, the very quiet chief of the *Bureau d'Études* at Graville, came aft to stand looking at the masts against the sun and said, in his sidewise manner:

"Well, now she's a sailing ship, no matter what they say."

Below us, the day's work force had punched in and was coming across the dock in an irregular, broad, blue stream of men in hard hats, wearing coveralls faded by hard wear and hard washing. It was the first day of August, vacation month in France, and Andren's supervisor in residence at the yard as well as the Norwegian engineers and officers held their breath to see whether French workers could be made to keep up their effort when their families and mates were off and the city's neighborhoods seemed empty in the long summer evenings, with so many children gone.

Yvan Martin counted and classified the work force for me that day. There were 394 people working on *Wind Star*, representing both shipyards, almost all of the twenty-five subcontractors, and twelve separate trades.

"We'll do it," the Harfleur foreman said. "Impossible is not a French word."

Slowly, that month, the watching foreign supervisors began to think Martin might be right and, beyond them, the shipowner's eagerness pointed toward a decision. Karl Andren had been honored, early in July, by one of eighty-six New York City Liberty Awards to outstanding immigrants, and then thrilled by a sail in New York harbor on the Norwegian full-rigged training ship *Sorlandet*, which was in New York for the sail-past in July to mark the rededication of the Statue of Liberty.

"I think it was the first time I'd ever really been on a sailing ship, under sail," Andren said afterward. "You know, the sailing purists have been after me for months. They ask how fast *Wind Star* will sail. They think she will not be a real sailing ship. On *Sorlandet* the engine was running when the crew started setting sail. All the guests looked up, then went on talking. When the engine shut down and she began to move under sail alone, those same people got very excited. I looked over the side and we couldn't have been doing more than four knots at first. That made no difference to the way people felt. They were moving on a ship with no noise."

The following month he saw his own ship, masted, for the first time, and she filled his eye. *Wind Star* lay at a dock down harbor for dockside trials of her machinery. She had been given a first coat of white paint and she measured 100 feet longer than *Sorlandet*. Her masts stood 90 feet higher off the water than those of the Norwegian training ship.

"She is really impressive," Andren said. "She looks like the real thing and I think she will be the real thing."

He resolved, then, to reinstate the plan to sail *Wind Star* across the Atlantic to enter New York harbor on October 28, 1986, the true centennial anniversary of the Statue of Liberty. To make that gesture, a kind of genuflection of gratitude to the city where he had made his success, Andren was willing to push his shipowner's luck hard.

Andren's plan meant asking the ship to average 7½ knots for every hour at sea, which was asking a lot in the shifting autumn weather of the North Atlantic. The winds are normally contrary then along the track westbound from Europe to New York. *Wind Star* would twice cross the route that some hurricanes have taken along the Atlantic coast in past Octobers. Her captain wanted at least twenty-one full sailing days at sea and had to allow for refueling stops in the Azores and at Bermuda. Her builders promised they would deliver the ship on October 4, and even in August they recovered lost time. But there was no room for any slip in the schedule.

Faury said there would be none, and Andren believed him. He wanted to. The builder's driving optimism, with his pride in his team, met the owner's optimistic intuition that he would get his first ship, on her first voyage, to New York. The two emotions made a powerful match.

In the last week before the sea trials, the shipyard's flexibility, which had so long been a virtue in dealing with what its staff engineers did not know about passenger or sailing ships, with the changing opinions of the owners and their consultants, and with Marc Held and twenty-five subcontractors and the new captain's wishes and Kell Andersen's suggestions drawn from twenty years of passenger-ship building, became a vice in the eyes of others. Months of flexibility had committed the yard to finishing almost everything on the ship all at once in a monumental rush. The weather turned against the yard and the final consequences of all the accumulated delays showed at the same moment. There simply was not enough time left before delivery to finish the ship in every detail.

The officers waiting for their ship knew it; shipyard foremen and engineers knew it; but Faury was still sure he would deliver his ship on time. He went aboard every day, saw the same evidence everyone else saw, and drew an opposite conclusion. No one would tell him publicly that he might be wrong. His optimism was so powerful that it stopped the mouths of the men reporting to him and caused those reporting independently to Andren to pause. Two weeks before the trials, Captain L'Orange messaged Andren that the race to finish the ship would be "very close." The next week, when he was saying privately in Le Havre that he had decided the yard could not make it, he telexed Andren that it was "a very, very close race."

The only other naval architect there with previous experience in building passenger ships was Kell Andersen and Andersen said that he admired Faury's optimism.

"I think he has done miracles to catch up with all the owners' changes and all the delays," he said of Faury. "But I feel sorry for him. What he is saying is not right."

It was a point of pride for Faury to show that he could catch up no matter what delays had been imposed on the fitting-out schedule. He did not then speak of delays the yard had brought on itself, by delaying major orders to avoid committing funds until the last feasible minute. The yard staff was reminded of all the changes the owner had required when the ship's stability was tested afloat by loading weights on board, first on one side, then the other. The result of the tests yielded the ship's final floating weight and displacement. In their adjustments to the test weight, the Bureau d'Études tabulated 104 structural changes approved by the owners since 1984, with a total extra weight of 68 tons. No matter who might ultimately be held responsible, the shipyard faced immediate, heavy financial penalties for late delivery in the ACH contract with Andren.

However, each hesitation over an interior-design decision had meant an equal delay in the final installation of pipes and wiring, all of which had to be in place, checked and tested, before any of the final decor could be installed. The conduits and wires for every lamp, every spotlight, every light switch and dimmer and thermostat, had to be finally installed before the wallpaper and sockets and rugs and beds and signboards could be put into the ship. The ship had to be furnished and covered and painted, inside and out, before she could sail. All these steps take their own time and, under normal conditions, are not all done at once.

In that final week before the September sea trials, with a cold rain pushing the season, wiring and piping and painting and rug-laying and plastering and wallpapering and cabinetry and lighting installation all went on simultaneously on board. The engine compartments, the first that would be tested, were painted in coded colors and looked prepared for their purpose. Work in the rest of the ship appeared chaotic.

On Tuesday, September 16, there were five working days left before the first sea trials and a total of ten full working days before the delivery date announced by Fournier to the owners. That day there were fourteen men working inside *Wind Star*'s small pilothouse. Jacques Bouché, his lips pursed and the elastic waistband in the back of his blue overalls making him seem even more erect than usual, conjured over his computer keyboard. There was a tiny envelope of silence around him, imposed by his concentration. But the other men working there all talked at once, raising their voices to be heard. Cabinetmakers hung shelves and doors and cut and glued moldings. Two pipefitters were plumbing the bridge toilet. Electricians were still soldering skeins of wiring to the ship's instruments and two whistling mechanics tried to get the remote engine controls to work. Technicians, each bent in his own corner, each with his own open toolbox and book of plans, tested and adjusted telephones, two radars, a remote monitor of the engine room's computer, and the VHF radio.

Outside, the rain fell on deck, mixing sand and dirt and welding slag into a gritty muck. Piles of discarded packing had drifted against the bulwarks and into deckhouse corners with used paint pots, and the cut ends of tubes, pipes, and conduits. Power cables ran in haphazard braids over every deck. And everywhere men moved as fast as they were able, in the limited space on board. There were traffic jams on every one of the stairways, between the ship's decks.

"Pardon," the workmen said, easing past one another. *"Excusez-moi."*

Under the upswept aluminum roof of the discotheque, twenty-five men tried to weld, and to wire lights and fit ceiling panels and glaze the glass walls, all at the same time. An artist on a scaffold had begun brushing clouds onto the blue plaster dome in the entrance hall. The impression of chaos reached the intensity of a windstorm in the hall between the ship's main entrance and the passenger lounge.

Four teak doors, already stained, oiled, and polished, had been unhung and stacked in a corner where three used paint pots and a burst carton of floor tile had piled against them like storm wrack. A shipfitter, instructed to adjust the closing mechanism on the watertight steel doors that would close over the teak doors in severe weather at sea, ground at a hole in the door coaming, enlarging it. His grinder spat sparks into the compartment, where painters were at work. The painters stood on one scaffold, plasterers on another, and on a third, two sheetmetal workers tried to fit one corner of the false ceiling frame. Between them, two air-conditioning ducts were held in place by lengths of dirty rope.

Sometime after lunch, a cabinetmaker had seized some open space to set up a packing crate as a makeshift workbench. By midafternoon, that space had become the only open traffic route in the hall. The joiner started a mitred cut in a Formica panel once, and was jostled. He was jostled again, then rejostled. Each time, he restarted the cut.

"You've got to keep your sense of humor," he said, looking up. "It's always like this on ships."

One deck below that hall, I heard Pierre Gravé, the cabin subcontractor, climbing the stairs between the two passenger decks.

"Merde, merde, merde, merde," he said as he climbed, and the word clanged in time with his feet on the uncarpeted stairs. He reached the landing and saw me.

"Oh, hello, how are you?" he said. We shook hands and I turned to follow him into the corridor between cabins on the second deck.

"Five or six weeks, that's what we need to do it right," Gravé said immediately. "Four maybe, but this is impossible."

He insisted on showing me a finished cabin. We squeezed past yard workers on ladders, cementing the openings through which piping and wiring passed from the cabins to the passageway so that fire would not be able to lick through those holes. No ceiling panels had been placed. None could be, until all piping, ducting, and wiring had been completed and inspected.

"They gave us these two cabins today, piping approved. Finally. Now we can do the ceiling," the contractor said, waving right and left. "Now."

He stopped one of his supervisors.

"Where's a finished cabin? Don't forget to cover all the carpet we've laid," Gravé said to the supervisor. "Plastic. All over."

He opened one locked cabin with a passkey, then another. The second was completed. The noise in the corridor faded as we stepped inside. The lines in Gravé's face lifted.

"It's classic," he said, running his hand along the edges of the wood paneling. "Nice. I like the wood. I ought to. It cost me a packet to find the process. A bundle. See, here's the bathroom. And that's what we built instead of the trunk thing. Lights here. Nope. Not working. Ah, well."

He showed me out, locked the door, and caught sight of one of his employees on his knees in the cabin across the corridor, laying a stainless-steel molding.

"You put glue on the whole thing, you hear me?" he said, nearly shouting. The workman looked up, then down again at his work. His putty knife moved inside the curved steel molding, but he said nothing. "You get a good joint. And clean it afterward. Don't leave a trace."

Gravé walked on, a big man in khaki overalls, shouldering people aside, and calling for Denis, his foreman on board.

Marc Held came aboard that afternoon, cool and businesslike, fresh from Paris. He shunned the use of overalls on a ship that was two-thirds fresh paint inside, wore no hard hat, and walked about, trailed by foremen with clipboards, in a clean belted trenchcoat and new penny loafers.

"I've come to do quality control," he said when he saw me. Workmen rolled out two lengths of carpet in the wood-paneled dining room, while he was there, and set up a decorative screen and a table, so he could see all those forms and colors together.

"The light is good," Held said, leaning over to pass one hand through a spotlight beaming onto a table top. "The colors will work."

He looked up and said: "You know, I feel like a composer whose music is being played by another conductor. Well played, you understand. It is exciting to see this happen."

At the end of his visit, the designer gave his judgment to his shipyard liaison man, a designer from the *Bureau d'Études* who had been detailed to assist him since January. "Clearly, there is enthusiasm enough for the job at hand," Held said, speaking slowly and clearly as if dictating. "People are willing to work. The quality is good, except for the little things that we have noted. I cannot help asking myself, however, if the time that remains is enough."

He suggested that a team from each of the decorating contractors be sent on the sea trials, to work while the ship was away from her dock; then he left to catch a ride to the train station. The shipyard designer sighed and smiled.

Kell Andersen, who had also followed the Held tour, asked the yard designer in English why twenty-three out of seventy-five passenger cabins still had no wall coverings at all. The shipyard man seemed not to understand and looked to me. I translated the question. The designer's eyes showed pain.

"Do not ask me to tell you whether I think we will finish on time," he said rapidly to me in French. "I would have to say what I think. Do not ask me to do that."

11

CHAPTER

Sinew

Ships are all right.

—the cardinal article of a seaman's faith, according to Joseph Conrad

A sea trial was once as stark as its name: trial by sea. Before Descartes and Monge made modern engineering possible, before three generations of English shipwrights who used mathematics wrote down their formulae for successful ships in the seventeenth century, shipbuilders took their ships to sea for the first time fearfully, without knowing what their newest ships might do. Often enough, they came back to port under severely shortened sail, holding on and hoping that the lurching, tipping thing under their feet would not roll over before she could lean on the land again. After a sea trial like that, the shipbuilder might fasten another band of bent oak timbers around the hull just above the waterline, to make the tender new ship sail as though she had a broader hull. Broad hulls are more stable than narrow ones and it was common practice, when shipwrights first tried to develop fast, narrow hulls by trial and error, to add breadth after the hull had been built, wrapping more wood around it on the outside in those extra bands of timber, called wales.

The *Wasa,* a high wood warship built to lead the king of Sweden's fleet in 1628, had such external bands of wood fitted before she ever sailed but the wales did not save her. On her first sea trial, *Wasa* had just left her dockyard in Stockholm harbor when the wind struck her and she heeled too far. Water poured in through open gun ports. She filled and was gone.

In this age of Cartesian engineers and computer projections, sea trials no longer test the ship's ability to float upright. Any new motorship's stability is foretold by calculations, and trials at sea have become demonstrations. They are only tests in that the builders must show the owners and insurers that the ship will do what they said she would when they signed the building contract. She must be as fast as they said she would be and hold and handle as much cargo as they had promised. She must have the emergency equipment required by national laws and the international Convention on the Safety of Life at Sea. Very rarely does a well-built modern ship's first time at sea become a trial. Prototypes are an exception to that rule, and, high in one corner of the hall that runs past their offices, the French naval engineers building *Wind Star* had a line drawing of *Wasa* under full sail, as if to remind themselves of exceptions.

In *Wind Star*, ACH had built a hybrid that was at once a predictable motorship, although quite underpowered by modern standards, and a prototype sailing ship of unforeseeable performance. So the shipyard planned to test the new ship in two separate sessions at sea: the first to try out *Wind Star* as a motor-driven ship and the second to test her sails. With engineering precision, the shipyard engineers had planned to demonstrate the motorship on Monday and Tuesday and try the sailing ship on Thursday and Friday of the same week, the third week in September, the week of the autumnal equinox, which, by the stars, is the beginning of winter in the northern hemisphere and, by tradition, is the season in Europe of equinoctial gales that break the pattern of summer weather and open the way for winter.

By mid-September, the ship was ready for the first trial but not for the second. The engine rooms had been substantially completed. The hydraulic system that would control the sails had not. Only three of the six furlers worked well enough, under human control, to roll up the sails, and so only three sails had been hoisted into place before the first trial. The hydraulic housings and the booms along which the moving corner of each sail would run had all been left unpainted where the hydraulic technicians were still at work, and those unfinished places, covered with oil-stained red primer, showed like wounds against the ship's first full coat of white paint. Computer control, the most prideful risk the shipyard had taken, had not been installed at all. In fact, the sailing computer[1] was carried aboard *Wind Star* for the first time seven days before the first trial and immediately developed an unwillingness to talk to the closetful of sensors at the back of the pilothouse that would tell the program about the ship and her sails. Still, the shipyard managers asserted that completion on time was within their reach and ordered the motorship trial to start on schedule.

It is hard to say with clinical precision when a new ship's life begins. For the men and women who designed and erected her hull in Graville, *Wind Star* lived from the moment the hull floated. For the marine engineers putting her machinery together and making it work, the ship had been alive since the day her power plant was first tested under full load in Harfleur. But for the ship's people, the professional seamen who would take her across the Atlantic and sail her for the pleasure of her paying passengers, *Wind Star* was still a floating workshop. No ship comes alive for a seaman until he can feel her move underfoot, listen to her creak and mutter as she rolls in a seaway, and watch her nature unfold. If a ship is a kindred spirit, as all windworking sailors believed, that spirit does not come alive until she is at sea. Any ship grows cold quickly to the seaman's touch in port, at the end of a voyage. So, for a seaman, sea trials are still trials; they prove what sort of ship the new one will be.

When she left port for the first time on Sunday, September 21, 1986, *Wind Star* belonged to the shipyard and flew the French flag; therefore her captain had to be French. The yard invited Captain Jean-Marie Guillou, a friend of Potier's who had been his marine advisor for fourteen months and was the navigational planner for Andren's new cruise line, to take command. Guillou, short, solid, and smiling, was a great favorite with the shipyard. He did not fluster easily and he blustered not at all. He had commanded freighters, in his time, and tankers and, five years earlier, a French cruise liner.

Captain Guillou took *Wind Star* out at 2:08 that Sunday afternoon with a crew of three tugboat helmsmen, hired by the day, a young French merchant marine officer to assist him, and Yvan Martin, the Harfleur foreman, as his first mate, chief quartermaster, and bosun. The deckhands were shipyard workers in overalls and hard hats. The engine room was manned by shipyard mechanics. There were 148 people aboard and it seemed that more than half of them had tried to crowd into the 350 square feet inside *Wind Star*'s pilothouse to witness her first departure. The pilothouse is the enclosed section of the ship's command center, always called the bridge. *Wind Star*'s steering wheel, her engine-room controls, and the wide panel of sail controls were inside the pilothouse, with her radios and radars and, that Sunday, Harfleur mechanics, Graville engineers, chattering technicians, silent Norwegian officers with nothing to do, and the serious French inspectors of her safety and performance.

Faury and Lesage looked over Guillou's shoulder. Captain L'Orange stood behind them, watching his every move. I climbed onto the pilothouse roof to get out of the way and Guillou caught sight of me there, after he had backed the ship away from her quay. He stood at the edge of the ship, where the special overhang called the wing of the bridge allows a maneuvering captain to see both ends of his ship at once. His head was thrown back and he grinned.

"She's doing fine," he said. "She's a good ship."

Wind Star revealed her character first to the seamen aboard. Her builders had made arrangements for the sea trials that were prudent and formally necessary, but those arrangements hinted at mistrust. The ship got underway with two round black balls hoisted, one over the other, on the foremast to make the international signal for a vessel not under command, a ship that might not be able to turn or stop. The black balls were never hauled down. At night, two red lights at the masthead made the same unconfident signal wherever *Wind Star* went.

Captain Guillou, looking at charts of the Channel the day before, had planned to take the ship out into the shipping lanes past Cherbourg where she might smell the Atlantic and feel the lift of an ocean swell. He wanted to go looking for wind and try out the sails. But the shipyard gave him a chart with his navigational limits marked in two straight pencil lines like a fence that would keep the ship always within 25 nautical miles of the Le Havre harbor entrance. He asked why. Embarrassed, Faury explained that 25 miles was the limit for harbor tugs. If the ship broke down more than 25 miles from her harbor, the yard would have to pay oceangoing tug rates to get her home and those rates were higher than harbor tug fees.

The shipbuilders had been showing off *Wind Star* to friends and colleagues ashore for a week before the ship first sailed. On one afternoon Faury and his assistant Castetz led a tour for the Le Havre Lions Club; next day they showed the city's *polytechniciens* and their wives around. Fournier and his partners, the owners of the shipyard, brought visitors aboard. And when she slid through the lock that holds the water level in the port between the large Channel tides, the friends and families of many shipyard men lined up ashore to wave and watch her pass. There was public recognition for the builders as well. Tugs and small boats in the outer harbor gave the traditional salute to a new ship when *Wind Star* first appeared on the seaward side of the harbor lock, sounding three long blasts on their horns and whistles, and that noise attracted more onlookers to the edges of the harbor. When the harbor pilot left the ship at the seventh to seaward from the entrance he shook Faury's hand and said:

"Bravo. You have made a very beautiful ship."

Yet the builders were anxious and on edge when their ship first put to sea and professional seamen felt her inborn qualities first. The seamen on the bridge noticed that the electric motor and the single adjustable-pitch propeller shook the ship so little that they could not feel changes in power, the way they would in other ships, by the change in vibration underfoot. Inside the pilothouse, there was no vibration. As soon as the ship was clear of harbor traffic, Captain Guillou put her into a series of hard turns, swinging her through ninety degrees time after time in the calm waters of the Bay of the Seine in order to adjust her compasses. The wake boiled out astern and clumped, every thousand yards or so, into a dirty white clot of roiled water where the rudder had gone hard over to one side or the other. But the ship did not heel in those turns at 10 knots and the curve of the wake between them was smooth, tight, and therefore, very unusual.

Tom Heinan, on board alone as the owner, looked astern and said, "I don't think I've ever seen a ship turn so tight. She's one slick piece of steel."

Captain L'Orange stepped out of the pilothouse, where the crowd had hardly thinned. He watched three turns from the bridge wing, looking down at the dull water.

"She handles well," he said. "That is very important."

The seamen's confidence in the new ship spread only slowly to the shipyard men. So much else seemed wrong. The toilets, hooked to a constant vacuum that was meant to flush them in explosive inhalations of air and water, did not work. The public address system had died in a fizzling chain of short circuits, leaving all those aboard with no way to follow the progress of the ship's tests. Those with nothing to do, those in need of information, and those gripped by the emotion of seeing the ship they had built move under her own power at sea for the first time went to the pilothouse. Seen through its high, sloping windows with panels of lighted instruments beneath them, the crowd inside made the pilothouse look like an overfull aquarium tank.

In the last light of Sunday evening, I saw Fournier, the shipyard president, leave the pilothouse alone. He started up the ladder to its roof, wearing gray suit, white shirt, tie, and office shoes. There was no one else on that side of the bridge, for the moment. As I walked forward from the ill-lighted middle section of the ship I saw Fournier swing out from the ladder above the deck with one arm and a leg free, like a boy swinging from a swimming pool ladder on a summer day. He turned, caught sight of me, smiled, and did it again. Then he came down and went back inside.

While the compasses and bridge controls, the instruments and alarms, the radars and radios were checked and calibrated that first afternoon, some of Faury's stiff optimism was softened by the seamen's pleasure in his ship. He sounded relaxed and realistic at sundown.

"She is beautiful," he said. "We're in a race against the clock to finish by the delivery date. We will not have the time to finish the ship as we had wanted to. We have sound insulation problems; the passenger cabins are not finished; we have problems with the rig, but, all the same, she's an extraordinary ship."

By four the next morning, Captain Guillou had made up his mind. He had been on the bridge for twelve hours and, since midnight, had been running *Wind Star* along a tight racetrack pattern just offshore to let technicians record the distortions in her radio direction-finder. There were ships moving through both ends of the ellipse that the ship moved in, and ill-lit fishing boats working in between. An Indian summer of still, hazy weather had drifted into the Channel and fog rolled along the coast in banks of unpredictable thickness. The upper two-thirds of *Wind Star*'s masts disappeared when she drove into a fog bank, and only radar showed Guillou where the things he might run into were.

"It's striking how quickly one gets to know a ship," the captain said. He slapped the teak rail of the bridge, then rubbed it. "When you've had her under your hand for a day and a night, you know what sort of ship she'll be. She's straightforward. She has no vices. Of course, I'm talking about the motorship now; for the other, we'll have to wait and see."

After that seaman's judgment was made, the rest of *Wind Star*'s sea trials became anticlimactic. One comes to the first working test of any prototype bringing expectations of definition and drama. At her sea trials, a new kind of ship should show whether she will work or not. There had been no partial tests of the huge new windship, no half-scale working mockups, and no chances to correct any errors or misconceptions along the way. Therefore, the four sea trial days in September had been set as the time when she would prove to the world that she could work. But the ship was not wholly ready for her trial and there was no weather to test her. All that week, no wind blew.

There were some definitions at sea. The motorship *Wind Star* passed twenty-one of her twenty-six scheduled tests, her first time out. The fire alarms worked and so did the anchor windlass and trash incinerator, all the engine controls, and the ship's entire power plant, but the toilets and the fresh water plant did not. The ship's measured speed at half throttle proved one-half knot faster than the 10.2 knots the shipyard had contracted to provide. Her full speed under power proved to be 12.7 knots, but all those aboard had come to see her sail.

Everyone wanted to see the sailing ship *Wind Star*; not just her owners and her builders but every man and woman who had worked on the ship, some who had only heard of her, and much of the city around her, which had discovered with *Wind Star* that it yearned for its maritime past. Spiritually, Le Havre still lived in the time when by far the greatest number of long-haul passengers traveled by sea. For a hundred years passengers took ship in Le Havre for New York, Buenos Aires, and Rio, for Sierra Leone and Sydney. Even at the end of that maritime age, the weekend arrivals of the transatlantic liners S.S. *Normandie* and *France* were city-wide events that drew tourists from half the hinterland of France.

"We miss her," the *patronne* of a city café told me when I asked her why she kept a picture of the *Normandie* behind her cash register. In seventeen months of visits to Le Havre, I heard riggers and welders first, then farmers, shopkeepers, laundry men, and the amiably tough women who ran restaurants by the port say how marvelous it would be to see *Wind Star* leave the harbor under full sail.

When she came down the harbor in August, towed from her fitting-out berth in Harfleur to a quay near the coffee roasters, within sight of the city's center, the new ship superimposed herself on a long, collective memory of transatlantic sailings and brought back a special, nonindustrial pride. The rest of France believes that the natives of industrial Le Havre, a rebuilt city of oil refineries by a harbor too large for its diminished shipping, are a minority of uncaring bourgeois and a majority of Communist union men, barricaded behind a hostile faith in class warfare. But, as soon as *Wind Star* was tied up alongside a stone quay within sight of downtown Le Havre, the people of the city began to visit her.

Men came to the quay alone, after work each day, and stood alone in silence in any weather, gazing up at the lifting flare of her bow. Families came on fair-weather afternoons and children in their fathers' arms watched the late workers on deck. They could not go aboard, but people came to see the ship every day. She went into dry dock for new bottom paint just before the sea trials, and there was a traffic jam around that corner of the port on the warm Sunday of her only weekend in the 1,026-foot-long dry dock where *Normandie* and *France* had once rested for repairs.

Wind Star might have been a model where she lay at the bottom of that huge dock that looked and smelled like an upturned sea cavern. She was only 439 feet, 7 inches long from her stern to the point of her overhanging bowsprit and only 361 feet long at the waterline; just longer there than the big Cape Horn barks. But her masts soared over all of the flat and featureless dockyards and the weekend spectators had only to look up to find her in the port.

"They like her," Claude Lemoine told me. Lemoine was a native of

Le Havre, a shipyard-taught naval engineer who had directed all of the engine-room and machinery design for *Wind Star.* She was to be his last ship before retirement.

"It has something to do with nostalgia," he said. "This one looks like a ship."

As he spoke, an 800-foot-long container ship got underway from the other side of the warehouse next to the dry dock and stood down the harbor. Black hull and white superstructure, that slowly-moving freighter with her decks covered by stacks of 40-foot-long steel boxes was so blocky and angular that it seemed, when the ship first moved, as though a section of the building beyond us had begun to slide toward the sea. Lemoine looked at the *Wind Star,* at her low, curving deckhouses and wood decks; the white masts with four booms raking upward beneath them, and the narrow white hull. He smiled.

"This is the most beautiful ship we have ever built," Lemoine said, and the weekend crowd around the dry dock and the silent daily visitors on the quay appeared to agree. They may also have sensed that the final drama in the construction of the ship took place not at sea in her trials but alongside the quay where over five hundred people struggled simultaneously every day to finish her on time.

The motorship trials were cut short and the sailing trials postponed to make time in port to finish the ship. On board, there was very little of the panicky snappishness that often comes as impossible deadlines approach. Men and women worked steadily, day after day, at what they knew how to do. Many stayed late. The local and national newspapers that week reported events that signaled France's shipbuilding industry was dying. Two more shipyards closed and a marine repair works, just across the quay from *Wind Star,* declared itself bankrupt.

Then, on the morning before the postponed sailing trials, the whole computer program crashed. Jacques Bouché and his programming partner Jean-François Hutt, who had been working twelve hours daily on the program, promised each other they would not go home until they made the computer restart. At 1:30 the following morning, the program ran. They came back before eight, but still only two sails worked, and fitfully at that, under computer control.

Five of the six sails made for the ship had been hoisted into place and rolled up on their furling stays, but the sail closest to the bow, the jib, would not respond to emergency commands; the boomed sail furthest aft, the mizzen, did not have working hydraulics; and two of the four staysails in between suffered from constant control failures. Sometimes they worked, sometimes they didn't. The reasons were not wholly clear. The shipyard engineers, ashamed that such a glaring delay had been brought on by a division of their own company, would not discuss the details of their sailing troubles. At noon, I met the shipyard president leaving the pilothouse, where the sailing computer lived. Fournier smiled a tight and very sad smile.

"We will not be ready," he said. "We will have trials, someday, but not tonight."

He left to tell Faury and Heinan, who expected the new ship's owner to arrive that afternoon, ready to sail. The lunch hour had just begun and the ship was almost empty of workmen, but young men in street clothes came striding toward *Wind Star* in twos and threes. They hesitated, grouping briefly alongside the two flat, steel ramps that led aboard the ship, then the men lunged aboard. They spread out astern, and sliding rolls of cloth and short stakes from under their jackets, these men unfurled little red flags on the pool deck and stretched banners by the water-sports ramp, banners that proclaimed their demands for wage negotiations, full employment, retirement at fifty-five, and a thirty-five-hour work week. The men blocked both gangways and pasted small stick-on labels with the letters CGT in red onto their jacket lapels. The Communist shipyard union, believing she would sail that night, had occupied the ship.

Fournier returned in a keen, well-mannered fury. He had been negotiating with bureaucrats in Paris, pleading for government contracts to keep alive the shipyard in La Rochelle, where his men had built Cousteau's aluminum windcraft. Yet there were La Rochelle shop stewards among the men blockading *Wind Star.* Non-strikers recognized very few Graville men. He had been given no advance warning of that day's strike and Karl Andren, the shipowner to whom he was trying to sell a fourth windship, had just arrived to watch the sea trials of his first. Tight-lipped, with two bright patches of color at his cheekbones, the shipyard president walked directly at the men who had bunched together to block the ramp that led aboard and, not slowing, said: "Stand aside." They did, and the yard president disappeared on board, alone. An hour later a shop steward returned to the still-blocked forward ramp, struggled through his comrades, tested and adjusted a scratchy bullhorn, and announced: "The yard will not negotiate.

"The ship, which was to sail on its sea trials tonight, is occupied," he said. "It will not leave until they negotiate."

"This is profound stupidity," Fournier came back to tell the television news crew that had arrived just after the strikers. "They have chosen the very day the shipowner arrives to demonstrate their stupidity."

Along the quay the strikers milled through the crowd of workers returning from lunch and kept them off the ship. The CGT men roughhoused together like small boys under the stands at a football game. They shoved one another and shadow-boxed. They kicked out at one another's crotches, halting the blow at the last moment, and pummeled one another's shoulders. Slowly, through the afternoon, the crowd alongside the ship thinned. Workers went home, and so did many strikers. At dinnertime there was only a handful of pickets left on board, and at nine Fournier and Captain Guillou signed a police complaint and stood by while the Le Havre police, summoned unsuccessfully since four, made a small show of force, promised the union that the yard would negotiate, and persuaded the pickets to leave.

The next morning, there were police on the quay and dog-handling private guards at the ladders leading aboard as men arrived, whistling, to work. Above them Bouché and Hutt furled and unfurled the two working sails with their computer. One third of the sailing system was ready for trial, but there was no wind.

Long ago, in a U.S. Navy course on marine meteorology, I was taught to regard high pressure systems in the atmosphere as mountains of air. It is a fitting and useful metaphor for a sailor. If he is under a high pressure system at sea, the weight of dead air crushes the sea as flat as the base of a mountain might. No air moves and the swells are dull and oily. When the air mountain moves it sheds sharp, dry breezes from its sides. Where it stops, so do all the winds.

Such a mountain covered most of France and half of England, late that September, and Le Havre lay under its center. The equinoctial gales spinning eastward out of the Atlantic hit its base in the western approaches to the English Channel and flung themselves north around the high pressure mountain, through Scotland and on to Norway. The North Sea was a churning caldron. The Channel was a pond. Only low, tumbling clouds and slowly floating fog banks moved on it. One could hear a motorship coming for miles.

Into that calm the *Wind Star* finally moved on Sunday, September 28, to try her sails. Karl Andren was aboard, ill with a virus that had swollen his neck and thinned his voice. Faury, normally formal, came dressed in jeans, boat shoes, and a crew shirt from the J-boat *Velsheda,* the huge America's Cup sloop that Fournier had chartered for his engineers two years earlier.

Favored sailors had been invited along to see the largest modern sailing rig on its first trial. The attempt was hopeless. There was no wind.

The ship posed for pictures on the afternoon of that still Sunday, eventually filling five sails with the wind created by her forward movement under minimum power. She drifted all afternoon along the cliffs just north of Le Havre while a helicopter hired by Jean-Claude Potier buzzed alongside and overhead with publicity photographers aboard. Then she drifted home, to be alongside in time for more desperate work on Monday morning. The contracted delivery date was six days away. Faury had promised a meeting on Monday that would show Andren how his ship could be finished in one working week. Karl and Louise Andren slept on board the tied-up ship, forsaking their hotel room ashore. They were confident.

"She'll go to New York," Louise had said when the ship turned back to Le Havre through the haze. "It's written in the stars."

The next day, however, Faury and Andren learned where work on the ship stood from the only people who knew: the foremen from the shipyard and all its subcontractors. The meeting began in a crowded crew lounge on board with a chain of optimistic forecasts. One after another, lead artisans said their men could complete the work at hand by the following Saturday, with perhaps a few little things that might need to be polished off on the crossing to New York. They would send a few men along, they said. The owner, they knew, had already agreed to allow working passengers.

The ship's Norwegian officers and the owner's technical supervisors listened, then began to smile at one another. They knew where the work stood, had decided that it could not be finished, and, in the case of the ship's officers, preferred a working ship to any amount of free publicity that might come from sailing under the Verrazano Narrows Bridge on the true anniversary of the Statue of Liberty.

At midmorning Pierre Gravé's foreman stood to report on his part of the job, the passenger cabins. He said he could not speak for the other subcontractors but his men would never make it. He might, he said, finish thirty-five or forty-five of the seventy-five passenger cabins by Saturday; more likely thirty-five. And how, he asked the meeting, did the yard expect to finish the rest at sea? He did not know how the work they had not finished on a stock-still ship could be done while rolling around at sea.

The tone of the meeting changed. Coming after him, other foremen spoke as frankly as Gravé's man. Some who had been optimistic earlier changed their projections. Faury's unchanging forecast of on-time delivery died unmentioned. No one at the meeting could say with certainty how much time was needed to finish the ship. No one, it seemed, knew. There was no schedule to revise, no plan to update.

In the end, the owner and the yard resolved that day to declare Friday, the tenth of October, the last day of work aboard. No one said the ship would be finished in every respect; just that the tenth was the last day the yard had to work on her. The shipowner could decide then whether to take the ship, or apply the penalties for late delivery to the shipyard. Andren gave up his plan to send *Wind Star* to New York, and went back to bed ashore under a doctor's care. A day later he left for Paris and New York.

On the morning of October 10, Annick Faury awoke at six. It was still dark, but the wet, warm air told her that high pressure and the unusually long Indian summer had held for another day, the twentieth in a row without wind. She saw that her husband had not been to bed all night and heard a discreet splash in her bathroom. She found François Faury in the bathtub.

"What are you doing there?" she asked, knowing that he preferred to use the shower in the boys' bathroom upstairs. The fact that he was bathing before sunup did not surprise her; nothing about her husband's absorption in *Wind Star* did any longer.

"Bon jour," he said. "We just got home. Tom Heinan is upstairs, taking a shower."

Annick resolved to make breakfast for both men and had started when her husband joined her in the high-ceilinged kitchen. He opened the paper and began reading, waiting for Heinan. At 6:30, breakfast was ready. Together, they waited for Tom. Six forty-five came, then seven. Annick climbed the stairs to look for her guest from New York, who had been negotiating at his own pace through the whole night with her husband. She found him asleep, sprawled backward on her absent son's bed, one sock on and one sock off. He had fallen asleep while pulling on his socks.

On Tuesday, October 7, Heinan had assisted his wife in natural childbirth in New Jersey. The following morning he took the Concorde to Paris. At nine A.M. on Thursday, the ninth, Heinan was in Le Havre with the Circle Line lawyer, preparing to take title to *Wind Star*. It was four in the morning, New Jersey time.

"You wouldn't have believed it," he later told Karl Andren. "The first thing George and I did was start organizing the closing papers for the shipyard. They were in a mess. At two-thirty the following morning, they were still passing me extra items. So I sent everybody home. I told them: 'Head to head, just me and François; we'll work it out.' "

"Tom was running on New York time," Faury recalled. "Five-thirty in the morning was half past midnight for him—but not for me—and that is when we finished."

The two men drove before dawn to Faury's house at the foot of the chalk cliffs behind the center of Le Havre to bathe, change, and get ready for a full day of signing documents and moving to the lawyers' minuet.

Faury and Heinan stayed away from the ship that day, but Jean-Marie Guillou, still a solicitous husband[2] to *Wind Star* and nominally her master until title passed, knew when he went aboard in the morning that the yard would deliver the ship. He saw workmen changing the mooring lines as soon as work started.

"You know they're going to deliver a ship when the shipyard takes its hawsers back," he said. The worn wire cables and scuffed polypropylene ropes were hauled aboard, one by one, and new, shiny blue polypropylene mooring lines that would leave Le Havre with the ship went over the side to the quay in their place.

"You'll see," Guillou said. "This will happen in a purely French way: efficacy in disorganization. They'll deliver."

He sounded satisfied. And the shipyard took its announced "last day of work" seriously. Yardworkers who had spent months aboard went about dismantling, coiling, and packing up their presence on board and unloading all afternoon. Women in dark blue overalls moved among them, sweeping and cleaning in carpeted passageways and stair trunks that they had to dispute with workmen carrying toolchests ashore, and others making final attempts to finish. The women rubbed at scuffmarks on bulkheads, past which apprentices dragged shoulder-high coils of black extension cables.

On paper, and at least for the banks, *Wind Star* was complete. The mortgaged ship cost $34.2 million, about $5 million of that for masts, sails, rigging, and automated windship controls. The French government paid ACH $10 million, and Andren's holding company, a partnership with the Stolt-Nielsen family and a tiny slice for Tom Heinan, agreed that day to pay the balance due. Yard and owner, near the end of their effort, signed a list of jobs that the shipyard had still to do and Heinan in effect refused delivery of the untested sailing rig. The shipyard guarantee on masts, sails, and rigging would not begin October 10, and not until the owner agreed that they worked.

Captain L'Orange found his new ship ready enough that Friday. He trusted her. He sat in the pilothouse in the afternoon, putting away charts of the Channel, the Azores, the Atlantic, and the Bahamas. Andren had ordered him to sail in two days for Miami, calling for fuel at the Azores and at Freeport, on Grand Bahama Island. The captain knew he would need to take along the shipyard's computer programmers and sail specialists and François Faury, as well as some carpenters and technicians.

"All is not perfectly ready," L'Orange said. "But we can make it work. We do not strictly need the computer. The mates will just have to learn how to handle the sails with manual controls."

Wind Star had belonged to the shipyard that made her for nineteen months, and for weeks the yard had appeared reluctant to let her go. On the sea trials, the shipyard managers ran the ship their way, leaving the crew and the owners politely to one side and reassuring them, when pressed, that everything aboard would work in time for delivery. The ship's crew, the seamen who would take her away and work her, waited through the delays ashore and the incomplete sea trials with desultory impatience, not believing the yard's promises. Then in a day, it was done; the deal closed and title passed. One day Captain L'Orange and his officers were diffident guests aboard the ship and the next day she was theirs, in some respects unfinished and at least half untried. No one could find the ship's new Bahamian flag, but the psychological shift aboard was clear. The yard's men were no longer at home. Ready or not, the seamen were taking her away. They would find out if she could sail.

The following day, a warm and windless Saturday, I saw Michel Lesage, the engineer in charge of all the finish work on board, gazing up at the figured baize ceiling of the cruise ship's small casino. One day earlier I had heard him upbraid a subcontractor in the same place so loudly that people moved away. On Saturday, he seemed lost.

"The ship is delivered," he said in a flat voice. "But she is not finished."

Then his voice recovered its edge.

"Even if we'd had her until the fifteenth," he said, "she would not have been finished."

However, *Wind Star* had to sail on October 12. The distances across the Atlantic would not change to accommodate more work in Le Havre. The swift closing that stopped the shipyard's tumbling rush to finish her had become unavoidable. The owners could have applied penalties amounting to nearly $15,000 for every day's delay beyond the contracted delivery date, but they had announced plans to present *Wind Star* to U.S. travel agents in daily cruises from Miami for the first week in November. And they had sold passages for a shakedown charter sailing from Martinique on November 15.

So Karl Andren took delivery of his first ship and sent her straight to market untried. Allowing for a difference in scale, his decision was akin to buying a new car at the end of a factory assembly line and driving it directly to enter a desert road race.

"We had to take delivery to get clear title to the ship," the shipowner said later, looking back on that decision. And he felt he had to show her to the American travel agents to prove that his sailing cruise ship existed.

"Anybody can pay five hundred dollars to a painter for an 'artist's conception,' " Andren said. "And the world is full of people running around with trick full-color photographs of some cruise project and announcing that they're going to build this ship or that ship. It occurred to me that people who make bookings were going to think we were the same kind of fly-by-night outfit, unless they saw the ship, came aboard, felt her move, and saw the sails."

The leaders of the yard's effort to finish before the owner's sailing deadline left the ship reluctantly, with a lingering sadness, on that Saturday in Le Havre. A large Norman shipyard had closed two days earlier, and Gilbert Fournier, calculating quickly, estimated that ninety percent of France's installed shipbuilding capacity had shut down since *Wind Star*'s keel had been laid. The shipyard president walked the decks, often alone, looking here and stopping there until late in the evening.

Yvan Martin, the good-natured boss of all the outfitting foremen, found reason after reason to go back aboard the ship after quitting time. So did the Harfleur men who had worked hardest with him. It was after seven, and dark, when they gave up and gathered inside an empty freight container in the quayside warehouse. Their wives had come to the harbor with chilled champagne and glasses in the trunks of their clacking Citroëns and small, square Renaults. The men opened two bottles and poured. This was the moment Martin had described to me months before, when he had likened fitting out a ship to raising a child, then letting it go.

Martin had given up his keys and *Wind Star* was to sail the next day. In the warehouse lit by bare bulbs set in dirty, white enamel reflectors dangling from overhead wires, the foreman raised his glass to Jean-Marie Guillou and said: "Fair winds, Captain." None of the Norwegians from *Wind Star*'s crew were there.

On the ship, Antoine Castetz, Faury's principal engineering assistant, sat on the floor of the purser's office, dismantling a new safe that had locked itself open. He had taken off his jacket and his spectacle lenses glinted with reflections from the overhead fluorescent lights. *Wind Star*'s officers looked down on him at work through the office window as they left the ship for dinner. Castetz did not look up.

Sunday was another gentle, hazy day and the distance between the ship and her makers widened. The owners were in charge and they had invited people who fit their purposes to join them, with the shipbuilders, at a farewell reception on board. Self-assured journalists, full of the importance of their own mission, bustled through groups of travel agents and ignored equally the local notables and the yard foremen and their wives, dressed in clothes suited to a summer wedding in the country.

The yard men stayed aboard for an hour or two, with two hundred other guests, while along the dirty stone quay a crowd built slowly behind the shipyard's barriers, erected after the CGT occupation and guarded ever since, until people stood three and four deep at the edge of the basin, ahead and astern of *Wind Star*, and filled the long quay across from her, one-quarter mile away.

The balmy, hazy autumn weather still had no wind in it. It was perfect for a party and pleased all the ship's guests, but it was not well-suited to sailing. Jacob and Nadia Stolt-Nielsen, who had last been aboard *Wind Star* in August, came to see her off and looked at their part interest very closely. Mrs. Stolt-Nielsen, who had objected with fire to Held's trial cabin eleven months earlier, found that the completed decor was "classic, uncomplicated, and simple." Stolt-Nielsen said he liked the ship but distrusted the hasty delivery.

"We are taking too many things unfinished," he said. "I don't like it that we have never tested that sail-control system. If there was no wind here, they should have packed their bags and gone up into the North Sea to find it and see how these things would work. We needed two weeks of trials for something as new as this, and I told Karl so from the beginning."

He straightened his legs, stretching where he sat in the main entrance hall. "But this is Karl's first contract, and, you know, too many cooks . . . ," he said. "Only one can be in charge and he has been; from the beginning."

Karl Andren came aboard with his father, Captain Wikar Andren, and they walked through the ship's public spaces slowly together. Louise had stayed at home. Jean-Claude Potier was the ship's host, beaming and expansive. The two Andren men avoided interviews and photographers. The shipowner's double-breasted pinstripe suit hung about him, loose and ill-fitting. He had lost fourteen pounds in an antibiotic battle with the infection that had seized on his throat during the sea trials. One end of a bandage strip showed above his shirt collar, covering the incision that had lanced the infection. He was not buoyant, but pleased. Late in the afternoon reception, he stopped under the painted dome in the entrance hall and swept his right arm from forward aft, in a gesture that took in the whole ship.

"Yeah, I like this ship," he said. "I like her."

Then he walked forward into the dining room, where the tables were all perfectly set for photographs and off limits to guests. He asked for coffee. In their first serving day aboard, the staff recognized him and pulled out a chair.

"I sure hated to give up the New York trip," Andren said. "But we needed the time to finish. We most probably need still more and we could have used more trials, but we had charters. Somebody had to make the decision. And, if you play quarterback, you get used to waking up with arrows in your back."

Andren was one of the last to leave the ship. He kissed his father on the cheek and said: "Good-bye, Daddy." Wikar Andren stayed aboard, to sail on the maiden voyage. Karl started ashore, then turned just short of the gangway and added: "I wish I were going with you."

When the harbor pilot came aboard, delayed by the crowd around *Wind Star*'s berth, Karl Andren stood alone in the cleared space between crowd barriers on the quay.

"We are leaving," Captain L'Orange told the tardy pilot as soon as he arrived. At 5:22 that afternoon, the captain ordered the mooring lines brought aboard. The pilothouse, so crowded during her sea-trial departures that one could hardly walk from side to side, was clear and quiet. Standing on the starboard wing of the bridge, 30 feet above the quay, L'Orange slipped the ship sideways. She sounded three long blasts on her air horn and the silent crowd stirred on shore. A boy waving both arms shouted up: *"Au revoir, Commandant,"* and L'Orange lifted his officer's cap and waved it twice with broad sweeps of his right arm. Then he turned back to the business of maneuvering his ship for the first time.

He backed *Wind Star* cleanly into the big turning basin and swung her stern to the east, toward the Seine and Paris. Her bow steadied on a line through the harbor lock toward the open sea, and the drawbridge over the lock opened. Three pilot boats and two line-handling launches accelerated through the opening ahead of the ship, like dogs bounding through an opened garden gate. Out over the Channel, the sun hung twenty degrees above the horizon and in its haze-filtered red light the outer harbor was stiff with the masts of small boats circling. Two helicopters, loaded with cameramen, circled and swooped like swallows feeding in the dusk. Beyond them all, the lighthouses at the seaward tips of the two harbor breakwaters clicked and flashed palely.

On board *Wind Star*, we who had been on the sea trials knew that we could expect a group of the ship's friends, yardworkers' families, and subcontractors to line the city side of the lock. She glided into that narrow gate to the sea and people we had never seen stood six deep along both sides. Once the racket of the helicopters and high-powered launches faded ahead, to the far side of the lock, it seemed that the ship and the people so close on shore were slipping past each other in silence.

The sail-handling yard employees, under Faury's direction, had taken stations at each sail to unfurl the four that could be set, no matter what the remote hydraulic controls or the computer did, so that the photographers and television cameramen in the launches and helicopters would have sails to record on departure day. The yard manager had stepped to the ship's side, just forward of the bridge, when applause began in the crowd ashore.

Beneath us all, the applause grew and rippled forward, accompanying the ship on her way through the lock. Faury turned to look and unconsciously came to attention. He faced the clapping people on the cobblestones ashore and his face worked hard. There was no noise aboard but the remote hum of the ship's engines; no voices sounded but those of the pilot and captain, quietly guiding *Wind Star*'s whole length forward to the sea. And the applause followed her to the end of the lock, where Faury turned around, blinking, and began speaking his sail-handling orders into a gray walkie-talkie in his hand.

The sails unrolled slowly, starting at the bow as it emerged into the outer harbor. In the very light land breeze working out of the Seine valley in puffs, the yard men set the first staysail to one side, the next to the other, in the sail trim that English-speaking sailors call wing-and-wing. The harbor opened into view as the ship cleared the lock, and all its stone edges were lined with people. Beyond the harbormaster's two-story office, its roof terrace black with people, more Havrais had crowded onto the cross-channel ferry quays and the tug station ahead of them. Off the starboard bow, the northern seawall appeared to have been fitted with crenellated battlements overnight. Crowds stood along its full, broad length, and on the harborfront between breakwater and Yacht Club, and all along the terraces of the uniform, gray-brown waterfront apartment houses. On every visit to Le Havre, I had jogged that waterfront and knew its distances. There were 4 miles of people at ground level, standing three or four deep, from the basin onto the beaches beyond the harbor. Behind those people, traffic on the waterfront streets stood still as others jumped out of cars to run to the harbor and see the windship sail. There was room in that space for between twenty and fifty thousand people who had come unbidden to give *Wind Star* the farewell due a local champion.

The air horns of two stubby harbor tugs and their larger, oceangoing sister moored on duty beneath the harbormaster's office suddenly pealed together for three long blasts, and every horn in the harbor sounded and re-sounded; the tenor horns of the harbor launches, the braying compressed-air cylinders in open line-handlers' launches, and the high, hoarse foghorns of motorboats and yachts bobbing alongside, all of them pointed, like their long white sister, to the sea. *Wind Star* sounded her baritone air horn back and the clamor lasted six full minutes, until her bridge drew abreast of the seawall and she accelerated slowly seaward.

For another 3 miles, the sailing yachts using their engines and the powerboats kept pace with the departing ship. The sun set ahead, dissolving into the murk on the western horizon. On the starboard side a 30-foot cruising sailboat with four people in her cockpit steered toward the ship until she was almost under the wing of *Wind Star*'s bridge and the man at her helm bellowed "Faury!"

He pointed at a small figure wedged into a cockpit corner by the cabin, wearing a foul-weather jacket and a life preserver. Faury recognized his seven-year-old son, Pierre. The boy waved hard at his father then seized a handheld foghorn and blew blast after blast until the little boat turned away.

High above him his father, the shipbuilder, waved with both hands for as long as his son was alongside, then stood watching the boat fade astern until the figures in her cockpit grew indistinct.

The ship was a half hour out when Captain Wikar Andren left the top of the wheelhouse, from whence he had watched her get underway.

"It was very touching," he said. "I will not forget it."

He turned back to look at the high white cliffs that rise just north of Le Havre. The buildings ashore had blurred into an indistinct gray wall on the horizon, darker blots in the haze held down by the high pressure that still kept the wind at bay. A low mist rose from the ocean at the foot of the chalk cliffs and they too dimmed into the evening we had left behind. Above the haze and the vanished city, a lighthouse on the cliffs flashed.

"Farewell, France," Wikar said in a clear voice. "God bless the ship and all who go in her."

12

CHAPTER

Shakedown

No one can know the pleasure of sailing free over the great oceans save those who have had the experience.

—Joshua Slocum

As a boy in the Åland Islands, Wikar Andren had two competing ambitions. He wanted to become a priest in the Lutheran faith of those islands and he wanted to go to sea. His father's long and fatal illness during the Depression settled the choice; because there was no money left for seminary studies, Wikar went to sea. But when he was seventy-one years old the two vocations came together again and, like a wise pastor, Captain Andren watched over *Wind Star*'s maiden voyage and unobtrusively showed her people how to get along with the ship and with one another.

When *Wind Star* headed out to sea alone in the dusk, with one diesel generator driving her electric motor and her sails swinging in tall, tightly furled bundles from the masts, the fun ended. The ship had to be made to work in every particular by the end of the nineteen days allotted to cross the Atlantic to Miami.

Building had been fun for the owners, for Andren and Stolt-Nielsen, Heinan and Potier, and also for Held, and for François Faury and his excited crew at the ACH shipyard in Le Havre. Through the stress of business, the delays and hesitations, and the dragged-out completion date, they had all enjoyed making something that had never been made before. Andren loved the idea so much he had wanted to sail his accomplishment right up to the waterfront of his adopted city, to show New York what he had done. Faury bubbled over about his sailing ship on any occasion, before any audience. Gilbert Fournier, the elegant shipyard president, enjoyed himself so intensely furling and unfurling sails and trying out the sail-control computer during *Wind Star*'s inconclusive sea trial that a watching engineer compared him to a child with a favorite toy.

Jacob Stolt-Nielsen, Andren's silent Norwegian partner who was the most experienced of them all in the business of the sea, had described the fun that men find in shipping months before the windship was delivered.

"It's a very romantic business," he had said. He sat with his back to me, looking out through the wall-to-wall sweep of his office windows onto the flat, blue water of the cove on Long Island Sound where he had chosen to build his world headquarters. A brace of late ducks, winging hard, climbed at a high, hopeful angle to the north.

"You can have a lot of fun," Stolt-Nielsen said. "I once bought a fiberglass boatyard. It made speedboats. Pretty soon, no one in the group was working on anything else. Everyone around here was drawing speedboats. Each making his own dream.

"You would not ever see Karl and me on an ordinary cruise ship, sitting in deck chairs and waiting to see which would come first: death or lunch," he said. "We have been planning a cruise ship for young people; designing the ship, making itineraries, selecting beaches, and choosing sports gear."

He turned back from the window and said: "You're really playing with tin soldiers. You're planning a holiday but it's business. How much better could it be?"

The time for tin soldiers had passed in October. The sea cannot be counted on to be forgiving, and working seamen behave at sea as if the ocean were about to be unforgiving. That vigilance is not just a rule of life on a ship; it eventually becomes second nature in a seaman, and that second, professional nature rejects jobs that are sloppy or half-done, decisions that are left unmade, or wishful thinking put in the place of work. None of those will serve at sea for very long. Good working seamen were in charge of the new windship, beginning on the October Sunday afternoon when she left Le Havre behind. They were in their element, finally, and very glad of it, but they had brought some of the incompletion, the indecision, the confusion of the land along.

The shipyard was still aboard. There were yard mechanics in the engine room, and a party of two hydraulic engineers and two electronics technicians to make the sail controls work. There were a couple of carpenters each from the two decorating subcontractors and sound technicians riding along to try to finish the most incomplete part of the ship, the discotheque. Faury was aboard himself and he had brought along his two computer engineers, Bouché and Hutt, as well as Gérard Boulenger, the tough little Graville draftsman who had been a professional skipper of racing sailboats. Jean-Eric Enault, the chief computer engineer, who had built the ship in so many ways on a terminal screen and sailed her for two years on electronic seas, came along as far as the Cherbourg pilot station, where he left *Wind Star* at midnight on the pilot's launch.

There had been tension ashore for two years between the shipowner and the shipyard but it was the kind of tension that builds between competing teammates striving for the same success. Seamen and shipyard workers, however, are ancestral enemies. Builders and sailors have always been rival suitors, contenders for any new ship's soul. Shipbuilders, bright and brittle, know their ship. They made her. Seamen, shy and slow, court a new ship with displays of their competence and care, while waiting for the ship to reveal herself. When she is new, they expect her to be perfect.

For a shipyard hand, a ship is always a job, no matter how new and exciting she may be, and he treats her like a workshop. He carries his tools aboard, tracks oil on the bright teak decks, welds over paint, and crushes his cigarettes anywhere. For a seaman, a ship is life itself. Good sailors treat their ships with great care.

Even Yvan Martin, the Harfleur foreman who had been to sea for twenty years and understood that, turned over the keys to the ship tangled together in two boxes, some of them unlabeled. Slouching out of the Channel in a fog and a lumpy, leftover sea on her first night, the ship rolled loose the stores that shipyard men had put on board with no eye at all for seagoing storage. The tools for the engine-room workshop had been piled, in their cardboard boxes, on the shelves of two tall lockers where they slid from side to side and fetched up with a rackety thud. The first mate eventually found the sextants, the mirrored instruments with which to measure the altitudes of stars and planets, in a pile of spare engine parts on the steering flat, as far away from the navigation bridge as was possible on that ship. That sort of thing strikes a seaman as convincing evidence of a lack of character.

The shipyard men, sleeping two to a passenger cabin and eating passengers' food served by attentive waiters in the deep blue calm of the ship's main dining room, saw none of the signs that to seamen mean neglect. The ship's officers, standing four-hour watches twice each day and working in between to clean off the shipyard grime and make order aboard, saw it over and over again in the first night and day at sea. They stiffened, and the yard men wondered why.

Wikar Andren also saw the state of the ship. He remembered the animosity between yard workers and seamen from years of his own experience, and he knew the sea. He was the most experienced seaman on board, and only he had sailed in large, working sailing ships. But

Captain Andren did not tell anyone what to do. In the first two days at sea, he established a self-sufficient daily routine of early breakfast, morning exercise alone, a visit to some part of the ship by prior appointment with the officer in charge there, no lunch, an afternoon visit to the bridge for a short talk with the mates, dinner, and bed. He read a bit, from time to time, and waited for the ship's first trial.

Wind Star made her way out of the Channel and into the gray Bay of Biscay, too slowly for the ship's three mates. They were all high liners, modern sailors taken from the best vessels in their Norwegian company's fleet, the 900-foot-long, floating steel parking garages called RO-ROs, ships whose cargo rolls on and rolls off on articulated trucks roaring in and out of their gaping sterns over a steel drawbridge let down from the ship itself, and which make one trip around the world every four months. The RO-ROs steam at over 20 knots at sea, flattening the waves under broad, round bows that look like the lipless smile of a toad. Because they are fast, roll-on roll-off ships are the clippers of today, the top of the line. They steam at the head of the daily convoy out of the Bitter Lake in the Suez Canal, where the ships of all the world are ranked in the order of their speed by pilots. After his first watch on *Wind Star,* the second mate said:

"The buoys go by so slowly."

"Well, you don't have to worry about maneuvering to overtake anyone," said the first mate who had come to relieve him. I was with the chief mate, the burly, pensive Alexander Maresca, on the bridge at four A.M. because I had asked permission to stand the first of his two daily watches, from four to eight each morning, with him as a guest. The sun comes up on that watch and it has always been my favorite at sea.

Within a day, the watch officers hardly had to worry about maneuvering for other ships at all. *Wind Star* set out on the sailing-ship route across the Atlantic, following steady, favorable winds the way Columbus and all who came after him did. That way is very little used by motorships which drive directly where they are bound across open ocean. It begins beyond the western edge of the Iberian peninsula where the winds called the Portuguese trades can usually be counted on to lift a sailing ship along, southward and to the west. The Portuguese trade winds blow from the north and east, parallel to the westernmost edge of Europe, and carry off the gray of the Bay of Biscay. The sky clears and the water beyond the continental shelf becomes so rich a blue it seems purple.

Wind Star found that weather midway through her second full day at sea. Faury and his staff had fussed over the computer, the hydraulics, and all the electrical connections between the two for a day. They unfurled the four staysails, all of the ship's working sails, and the windship sailed for the first time. She steadied her deep rolls away from the swells sent down by gales going by to the northwest. One could feel the change in motion anywhere inside the hull. The ship stopped yielding like a log to the deep ocean waves and made her way over each with a swift, sure balance. She was no longer a pendulum, swinging blindly in a void, no longer a runner on an obstacle course, but a gymnast balanced on a beam and people climbed up to the bridge to find out why. They all asked, first, about her speed.

On that day and on every fair-wind day thereafter the single standard that everyone on board used to judge the practical value of the $5 million sailing rig was the speed it gave the ship. The Cape Horn barks, on a good voyage, averaged 7 or 7.5 knots, in every wind, around the world. That approaches 8 miles an hour, a stiff pace for a jogger. *Wind Star*'s electric motor, that day, had been pushing her along at 10 knots, a competitive speed for a long-distance runner. Setting four of her six sails added 2 knots to *Wind Star*'s motor-driven speed. If a man could hold that pace for just over two hours he would be within reach of the world record in the marathon. The yard men were elated. They left the motor driving and the computer in charge of the four working sails and stood back, arms folded, beaming like boyhood friends who have all learned how to ride their bicycles with no hands on the same day.

On that day the computer could handle routine sail tending for the four staysails, but the yard's Young Turks stood by, watching it closely. They did not trust the system as a whole. Like any system of machines put together to do the work that men once did, the shipyard's sail controls had been designed as an extended mechanical analogy to the human body. The computer replaced portions of a brain, and was linked to the world by electronic circuitry that stood for nerves. It learned wind speed and direction from anemometers on top of *Wind Star*'s first and third masts and sensed the ship's speed and direction through her log and compass. It spoke to the rest of the body along circuits that ran through man-high electrical control panels, which worked the valves and switches controlling the amplified muscular tension of hydraulic oil under pressure. Pressurized oil fed through pipes and hoses moved the sails on their limblike booms. The whole system worked in remarkable quiet, making only a kind of self-satisfied groan, the sustained grunt of a weightlifter, each time it adjusted the angle of the staysails to the wind. But the system's brain was still an apprentice on its first trip to sea.

The computer had been programmed to work either wholly on its own or with sail trim changes ordered into its circuits by a human with a joystick at the terminal on the bridge. It could also be bypassed entirely. The console next to the computer terminal allowed manual control of the four hydraulically driven adjustments to each sail: the sheet tension, which held the sail in the wind and controlled its shape; the boom angle, which set the sail's angle to the wind; the furler, which controlled the amount of sail unrolled; and the sheet carriage, which moved in and out in time with the rolling furler to produce the best curve in the sail.

The French set a watch on their system's first sailing day, and Faury taped a note in his own hand to the sailing console, warning all others away from the sail controls unless an ACH hand were present on the bridge. They relieved each other through the day because, although they did not say so, the system had not yet learned to respond to any large change in the wind. Faury, or one of the Young Turks, stood ready always to step in with direct orders to the sails, using manual controls. Their elation grew all day while they watched their sailing rig at work. At lunch and at dinner, the yard men talking and laughing at their separate table were the stars of the dining room. The wind held and a yard man kept watch with the mates into the night. And Wikar Andren walked the deck alone, after dinner, looking up at the tall, white sails.

"How do you like the help from the sails?" Faury asked the first mate, when he came to the bridge for his sailing watch at five A.M.

"Twelve point eight knots is a very good assistance," Faury said, speaking English to Maresca and not waiting for an answer. "Did you know the ship has done twelve point eight knots with the sails today?"

Maresca nodded and turned away to the chart-table side of the bridge. Faury settled on a chair before the sailing console. The ship drove on through the night at her new pace under motor and sails and when the captain came to the bridge at dawn Faury told him the shipyard was ready for the sea trial under sail alone.

The day came blue and clean, light blue above with a brisk wind and dark blue below with a long, high swell. As one stood on deck, facing forward, the wind came over the edge of one's right ear with an impatient litle mutter. The big waves hove up from ahead and to the right, so that one's right foot lifted first when the ship rode up one's face. Those waves were almost bridge-high, some 20 feet from trough to crest, and the wind blew across their faces at 19 or 20 knots when, at ten that morning, Faury and the captain declared themselves set for the trial.

L'Orange himself pulled the ship's throttle back to nothing and conversation in the pilothouse faded with the vanishing thrum in the funnel overhead. Under four staysails only, the ship's speed faded from 10.6 knots to 6.6 in less than ten minutes.

"You know what happens?" Faury said. His voice was loud. "The propeller is dragging us."

The engineers feathered the propeller blades, turning them to slip edgewise through the water, and still the ship slowed, rising to the seas ahead and occasionally stamping her long steel counter into the back of a receding swell with a shock that rang and trembled through the hull. Her speed steadied at 6 knots and Faury resolved to try turning *Wind Star* through the wind, the tacking maneuver that many working sailing ships could not always manage in a big sea on their bows. The ship was already sliding sideways in the water away from the wind, making leeway that left a trail of slick water on the windward side and piled up stiff little protesting wavelets under the side away from the wind. To tack, she would have to stop sliding and forge over the waves under sail alone. Faury said, "You may tack," and slowly, slowly, with her rudder full over, the ship brought her heaving bow into the swells and through them.

The tension of men urging her forward silently on the bridge slacked suddenly and I heard the sea foaming under her forefoot that rose slowly and fell back into the dark blue trough. Passing through the swells was the critical peak of the maneuver. The sails flapped then once with a dull, rolling sound like a wave breaking; the ship passed through the wind's eye; and Faury kept the boom of the foremost staysail well out over the side, where the wind would catch its back and push the bow around.[1] The ship had stopped dead in the water. She hung there while hydraulics brought the other three sails across the deck together, and those sails filled with the wind that came now from the left. The three sails pulled, the fourth staysail came across,and slowly the stationary foam and bubbles along the ship's side began to slide aft. Eleven minutes later she was sailing again at 6 knots. She had tacked alone at sea on her first attempt.

The shipyard men unfurled, then, the sail they called the mizzen, the fair-weather sail booming out behind the fourth mast, and jibed the 440-foot ship through the 20-foot swells, bringing her stern through the wind. Their excitement buzzed on the quiet bridge. She had done everything a sailboat one-tenth her size could do, in conditions at sea that might have stopped many of her purebred ancestors.

"You can restart the engine now, Captain," Faury said at noon. "We have seen enough. We must digest what we have done."

The shipyard manager stepped forward to the engine controls himself and Captain L'Orange yielded to him.

"Just push that button," Faury's chief mechanic said over his boss's shoulder, in French. "Did it all work?"

"Very well," said Faury, restarting a diesel generator from the pilot-house. The funnel behind the bridge hummed and a puff of black smoke blew away downwind. "Marvelously well. Better than the model ever worked."

The relief of all the shipbuilders showed in loud laughter from their table at lunch. Three of us who had sailed modern sailboats on ocean crossings, two Norwegians on board as sailing experts and I, were left quite startled that something as huge, for us, as *Wind Star* could do all that a nimble boat could do. But Wikar Andren reserved his judgment.

"I have looked at the sails for some time," he said. "I am afraid they are not well shaped for their job but we shall see."

The two-hour test did not relieve the pressure on the shipyard men. They had sailed on a shakedown cruise, literally in the same boat with all the breakdowns, the sudden malfunctions, and niggling uncertainties that pop up when any large and complex machine is first set to work. They caught cold in the cabins where the air conditioning worked at an unchangeable roar and could not sleep in those where it hardly worked at all. They listened to the reverse osmosis plant trying to make fresh water out of salt with a sound like that of ten demons trying to batter their way out of the engine room with iron flails.

Faury was pinned to his table after the celebratory luncheon that day by the ship's chief engineer, a determined woman named Grete Lil Gundersen, who wanted him to see the telex she was dispatching to his yard with a list of guarantee claims. A seawater pump had died, its electric motor flooded because the shaft between pump and motor had no packing. The reverse osmosis machine, the ship's only source of fresh water, had to be shut down. It was shaking itself to pieces. There were other items on her list.

Faury had other lists placed before him. Kell Andersen, the Danish naval architect who had followed the ship's construction for the owner, had come on the crossing too, because the passenger cabins, the ship's moneymaking core, had not been ready for final inspection until after she left Le Havre. On the day *Wind Star* first sailed without engines, Andersen gave Faury his second list of defects in the cabins, including 107 in the owner's stateroom alone.

"Monsieur Andersen amuses himself by making lists," Faury reported. His irritation mounted slowly behind a polite façade in the days following the sail trial. He said he had come along to make the sail-control system work, not to chase down carpenters and force them to repair screwdriver scars in wood paneling, or to see that they removed splashes of glue on the wallpaper or tacked down lifting corners in the cabin rugs. The reserved reaction to *Wind Star*'s first two hours of sailing without her motor annoyed him.

"The ship's officers are bumps on a log, except for the third mate who is taking a certain interest in the computer," Faury said on the bridge two days after the trial. His notice requiring shipyard supervision for any sail maneuver was still on the control console and three out of six hydraulic units for the sails were out of commission. The wind had dropped and gone aft. The ship moved toward the Azores under motor alone.

"If they had been French," he said, "they would have been pestering us with questions to learn the program, then telling us all about how they would use it in service and asking us for changes to suit them."

The Norwegian officers, whom I listened to at the end of the first mate's watch as the sun rose in pink layers of cloud astern, were waiting, as one of them put it, "for the French to stop playing with the sails and begin showing us a system that works." Captain L'Orange counseled patience.

"She is a good ship," he said. "She maneuvers very well and has a good motion. She is strong and very stable. A good ship."

On Saturday morning, six days out, *Wind Star* came to her first port of call, sailing with three staysails and motor to within sight of the long, high, stone breakwater at Ponta Delgada in a wind which poured down from the green tip of a dormant volcano that was rooted in the floor of the Atlantic and rose to form the island of São Miguel. The Portuguese pilot looked out over the breakwater, saw *Wind Star* coming, and called for a tug.

"With a sailing ship," he said once he was on her bridge, "I was not going to try to dock without a tug."

"Is this the first time the ship comes to the Azores, Mr. Captain?" he asked. He had never heard of her. The islanders, who live at the outer limit of the Portuguese trades in the summer, in the path of Atlantic gales in the winter, and beyond the edge of the Continental consciousness almost always, had never heard of her. Very few, except taxi drivers and postcard vendors, came beyond the town to look at her closely. The unspoken conviction of the French that they had built a ship known around the world trickled slowly away, leaving them edgy and slightly ill-tempered.

The computer programmers spent the day in port hunting bugs in their sailing program. The hydraulic engineers, with a reinforcement flown out from Le Havre, plunged into the steel closets full of pipes and hoses and stacks of valves. The decks in each of those hydraulic rooms glistened under a quarter-inch sheet of the transparent oil leaking from inside the tangle of tubes. The chief engineer occasionally looked into those rooms and shook her head. The captain called them "snake gardens."

François Faury spent the day as a foreman, checking off jobs done and listing jobs to do in all the passenger spaces. He left the ship late in the afternoon, for a brief visit to the steep hillsides beyond the town and the island churches of white stucco and black volcanic rock. He told the mate at the gangway he had had enough of the ship for a while.

The ship's officers were growing impatient with him as well. His good-natured insistence in Le Havre that everything would work by October 10 had offended their professional judgment. Once at sea, he had not relented. Among themselves, they called Faury "the optimist."

"Anyone could see the ship would not be ready," said Alexander Maresca, the first mate. "It was annoying to hear the yard say the opposite all the time."

Nonetheless, before *Wind Star* turned west again Faury demonstrated that Cartesian method could still work better than lists of complaints. He thought his way through the piping to and from the oil reservoir for one of the ship's two hydraulic stabilizer fins that had been shut down for lack of oil and deduced that it had never been completely filled. The chief engineer said flatly that the stabilizer leaked. She was wrong. Faury was right. *Wind Star* left the Azores with an uneasy truce on board.

"The Japanese would have been very good at finishing off the details of this ship," Maresca said on our first watch at sea again. "I took delivery of a ship in Japan once, a new RO-RO, and we left right away for Los Angeles. We had only two engine-room alarms the whole way across and that was it for problems. But I do not think I would have wanted them to design this sailing rig. The Japanese are good at set routines but they are not able to improvise. The French can improvise. Indeed."

Knut Helminson, the relief captain for *Wind Star* who had sailed on the maiden voyage to learn the ship, came to the bridge with coffee and a cigarette before sunrise as he did every morning. The ship had two sets of Norwegian deck officers: two captains and six mates contracted to serve four months aboard and two months ashore in rotation. Her radio officer, chief engineer, and chief electrician were also Norwegian. The chief engineer's assistants were Indian; the deck and engine-room hands, Filipino. There were twenty-two aboard, in all, to run the ship, and sixty-four men and women from several European countries training to serve her passengers. Captain L'Orange joined Helminson and, just before the sun broke the horizon the two captains began talking about their ship. They knew her now.

Wind Star had showed her character on her sea trials, but was slower to reveal her nature. The French shipping classification society, Bureau Veritas, an independent inspection agency (like Lloyd's of London) that had scrutinized every step in her construction and graded her sea trials, had temporized, not knowing how she would sail. She was not an M/V, a motor vessel, nor yet an S/V, a sailing vessel. Bureau Veritas classed the ship as WAP: wind-assisted propulsion.

Once at sea, the ship demonstrated what she was: a hybrid, like the first steamships, which kept their sails for decades; and the last sailing ships, which had tried fitting auxiliary engines to compete for cargoes. *Wind Star* had not enough power to spin in her own length inside a harbor turning basin, boiling the water under her stern while her propeller spun with massive applications of power. She had enough sail to move her well, under perfect conditions, but not enough to drive her as fast as the motor in every wind and sea. Yet the sails always added speed, when the wind was fair, and therefore pleased both captains and their officers. *Wind Star* was a motorsailer; less than a whole ship under sail alone but not at her best under power only.

She would never satisfy the purists, old or new. Measured against the human memory of sailing ships, her sails were too small for her hull. A retired Åland sea captain saw artists' renderings of *Wind Star*'s design in Mariehamn before she was built and said: "She is not a pure sailer. They will rely on the engines."

They did. But then her first crew on her first voyage also relied on her sails to add speed. And every modern sailor I knew asked first: "What'll she do under sail? Sail alone, I mean." Speed was what interested everyone who heard about the ship and her rig.

The ship's rig, as big and complex and quiet as it was, was too traditional for the theoreticians inventing new ways to draw the wind's power out of the air and into a hull. Early in 1985 Jean-Claude Potier saw Jacques Yves Cousteau among the passengers waiting with him to board a Concorde bound for Paris. Cousteau's experimental windcraft, the aluminum *Alcyone,* was then near completion and Potier introduced himself, identifying himself as a builder of windships too.

"I know your ship," Cousteau said. "It is old before it is born." And the great man turned away.

Late in 1986, Cousteau's ship with her two aspirated airfoils was on the Pacific leg of an around-the-world sales trip, looking for customers for the rig. The market did not appear ready yet for technical purity. At the same time *Wind Star* was motorsailing toward her market, with two-thirds of her available cabins already booked for the first eighteen months of operation. The ship had been designed and made to sell. And Karl Andren said: "This ship would never have been built if there were not a market for her."

On her bridge that Monday morning, one-third of the way across the Atlantic on her maiden voyage, Jacques Bouché, the quiet, concentrated computer programmer from Graville, began unfurling the motorsailer's staysails one after another in the rising sun. The breeze had moved away from the bow and looked just fit for sailing. Under sail, the ship's speed grew with the day from 10 knots to 13.8 on the log. The electric motor loafed along, helping. The sails stood tall, full, and steady against the morning sky. Captain L'Orange stepped out on deck and looked aloft at them, his head flung back and to one side, and his eyes narrowed, in a gesture many centuries old.

"I think it is more fun to sail thirteen knots with seven hundred fifty kilowatts of motor than to stop the motor and sail at six knots in this wind," L'Orange said. "I think the passengers will agree. The diesel generators must keep running anyway."

Wind Star settled into her motorsailing motion, the driving surge that the full sails lent to the long hull. The slope of the deck steadied at less than three degrees, a barely noticeable yielding to the wind in the high sails. The wind built all day from the south, pouring across the ship's heading from the left and pushing short, steep waves up against the hull with an occasional sharp slap that sent spray to the bridge. All the French engineers, except the sail-watcher, burrowed into the hydraulic rooms, squeezing and stretching to tighten each and every one of the screws that held each pipe joint.

Oceangoing routine, restored after two days in port, settled on the ship. That routine is comforting. The expectations of each day are precise and circumspect, except in storms, and the round of two four-hour watches, some off-watch work, and food and sleep at determined hours, makes a solid, established background for life at sea. For those used to steady noise ashore and to constant movement, the days at sea on a passage seem just less than dull, and sunsets, particularly on a westbound ship that sails into one every afternoon, become an event that stirs real excitement. The wind, near sunset on that day, had begun to hum in the sails and rigging. It poured past the ship at nearly 30 knots, a dry wind that would have tossed and shaken trees ashore.

In the last light and rising wind, Gérard Boulenger, standing watch for the shipyard, thought it best to shorten sail. He started to furl the foremost staysail and heard a muffled metallic snap. Standing sheltered from the rising sheets of spray, the sunset watchers at the other side of the bridge thought the ship had shouldered aside another wave, but Boulenger paled and sent Bouché running for Faury. He stood in the wind to look aloft at the partially furled sail and then brought it all the way in, breathing hard although the hydraulic winches did the work. The top of the aluminum furling stay faced away from the bottom, like a foot splayed sideways beneath a broken ankle. Somewhere under the wrapped layers of sailcloth, the rolling furler had twisted and something had snapped. The yard men brought in all the sails and the wind hummed in the empty rigging in the dark.

Faury had planned to throw a party for all on board at shipyard expense that night. He came aft from the broken furler to play host by the swimming pool bar in his jeans and sailing sweater, although he had been humbled. At the party, he privately and very formally thanked Captain L'Orange and his officers for their patience with the unfinished state of the ship. He told them that *Wind Star* should have stayed two more weeks in Le Havre. Then he came to a corner table to make an account to Wikar Andren of the damage to one roller furling stay.

Wikar listened briefly, then interrupted.

"Twenty-seven knots is not much wind," he said, looking up at the naval engineer.

"Oh yes, it is very strong," said Faury. "It is quite close to the limit of wind speed for our sails, close to the point where they must begin furling."

"Yes?" said Wikar Andren. In his face, only his eyebrows moved, lifting. The yard manager was animated, nervous. He seemed to say that 30 knots of wind was the limit for sailing *Wind Star.* Wikar said nothing more and Faury excused himself. Then the retired captain spoke, his voice shaking with anger.

"If these sails can only stand twenty-seven knots of wind, then they are just play toys," he said. "This is not what we expected."

After that evening, Wikar Andren's conversations with the ship's officers filled with purpose. He did not take a hand. He merely pointed. I was never a party to those conversations, but I heard Captain Andren's ideas about his son's ship from him. Then, each day, I heard echoes of those ideas as they spread and were applied. The day after the loud bang inside the furler, I heard two officers say that if the sails had to come in at 25 knots, *Wind Star* was not a sailing ship at all; after all, the old sailing ships only started really sailing in 30 knots of wind, the speed that had damaged the furler. Captain Andren said so. Then they noticed that the shipyard's own computer program allowed sailing in up to 50 knots of wind.

"He sees things with very clear eyes," the first mate said of Captain Andren. "He tells a very good story."

Wikar Andren told stories of his own days under sail in a calm, almost gentle voice and never again spoke in anger on that voyage. There were lessons in the straightforward stories, but he did not emphasize the morals of his tales, although sometimes they were almost parables. He recounted on board the troubled *Wind Star* the sinking of the worn-out clipper ship *Shakespeare,* the second ship he sailed in and the second that sank under him. He told of her grounding and the rescue directly and without any narrative tricks. Even the ship's cat had been saved in the ship's boats and lifeboats from a Gulf of Bothnia pilot station on an island nearby.

"And do you know, years later, I don't know where," Wikar said, "I met a pilot from that island who told me that all the cats on the island eventually looked like *Shakespeare*'s cat."

The moral, never spoken, was that there could be real disasters at sea, yet life went on after them. In some of Captain Andren's stories there were more practical points.

Within days of that damaging afternoon wind, I heard mates who had never sailed discuss the proper shapes for sails. They had been talking to Wikar, the former sailmaker on the four-masted Cape Horn bark *Lawhill.* When the shipyard men next unrolled the three undamaged staysails, very tentatively indeed, they left one roll or two of the cloth wrapped around each furler stay. The sailcloth, they said, would take the strain off the groove in which the sail rose up inside the flexible aluminum tube. I traced that idea back through a junior mate to Wikar Andren. With the failure of the reverse osmosis machine, storing enough fresh water on board for Americans cruising on vacation in the Caribbean had begun to worry Captain L'Orange. He had been forced to limit showers and shut down the icemakers by the passenger cabins. One day Captain Andren asked Captain Helminson, the relief skipper, if he might look at the ship's plans. Together, they found unused tank storage that could, if needed, hold almost 200 tons of fresh water, enough for a week of cruising.

Wikar Andren never interfered in the ship's work. He watched from one wing of the bridge when the damaged furler was unwrapped in a calm, three days after it had twisted. A number of the hollow rivets that held it together had sheared in two as if snapped by a chisel blow. Others had popped up from the aluminum surface, and seemed ready to fall. We—Faury, the two quiet Norwegian sailing experts, and I—hoisted Gérard Boulenger aloft in a canvas chair to survey it. We were the experienced sailors on board and each of us told the others how the hoisting should best be done. Wikar, who had climbed masts twice as tall as any we had worked on, said nothing.

"I thought there were perhaps too many chiefs and not enough Indians," he remarked to me later. "But you got the job done."

In those days between the Azores and America, the ship's seamen stopped waiting for the yard engineers to finish the sailing rig and found seamen's solutions for each problem they saw. L'Orange and Helminson decided that *Wind Star* should ignore the computer and sail the way sailing ships always had, adjusting her course to the wind rather than straining the hydraulics to constantly adjust the sails to varying winds on a steady course. Steer the course that suits the wind, they thought. "There's nothing wrong with computers," said Captain Helminson. "It's what you put in them."

And on the day Faury again tried sailing without power—this time with only three staysails in working order—Helminson leaned over the wing of the bridge and watched a band of stiff little waves pile up against the ship's side. The abrupt ripples on the south side, with the wind from the north, signaled that the ship was sliding sideways through the water and away from the wind.

"Four knots forward and three knots sideways," Helminson said. "Faury says we're not making any leeway, but if we keep this up we'll be across the equator in the week."

They did not keep it up. Faury called a halt to the test. And one week after the rigging failure, his attention drawn constantly to imperfections in her finish and malfunctions in the ship's equipment by the chief engineer, the hotel staff, the owner's representatives on board, and the captain, Faury very briefly wished he were someone else. First the others, then the shipbuilder had forgotten that shakedown cruises are made to find and fix problems.

"I envy the freedom of authors and poets, screenwriters, artists, and film directors to declare their work is finished and release it to the public, once and for all," the shipbuilder said two days from Freeport. "I wish shipowners would allow shipbuilders the same freedom."

Faury, the precise engineer, the thoughtful Cartesian, the optimist, very briefly became a diminished man, battered by technical events that had turned against him and abraded by evidence of the jobs left unfinished by his shipyard. The ship's officers relented. The service managers softened their complaints.

"I feel sorry for him," Alexander Maresca said, in the dark of our watch before the dawn one day away from port. "He has taken too much on himself."

The sea, south of Bermuda and east of the Georgia coast, had turned deep ocean blue that day, the blue that sailors mean when they speak of "blue-water sailing." So solid, so physically deep is that color that sunlight disappears inside it and white foam looks painted onto the ocean surface. The ship motored out of wind and into a calm that morning. She plowed through water as smooth as the glaze on an upturned ceramic bowl and it crinkled and broke at her bow. Flying fish lunging into the air from under the bow and the passing ship made the only marks on that burnished blue surface. There were not even the wandering puffs of wind called cat's-paws. Faury decided to remove the staysail that was still wrapped like a bandage around the damaged furler. Young Gérard Boulenger went up to the masthead again, and the sail-handling French, the two Norwegians, and I unfurled and lowered the sail in fifteen minutes. We flaked it in a net on one side of the foredeck like a sloughed skin, stiff and purposeless.

The shipyard manager looked up through binoculars for a long time at the silver roller, swinging in the sun with rows of black rivet caps standing out like stubble from its surface. The ship's triumphant first arrival in the United States, a sail-by off the beaches at Miami, under television helicopters, with the press on board, was three days ahead on *Wind Star*'s schedule and Faury knew he would have to repair that tube in the air somehow, in those three days. There were no cranes in Freeport to take it down; there was no time to build it anew.

"The profile may be very hard to repair in place," he said. His voice was so soft it sounded bruised. "The rivet holes, you see, slide with respect to one another."

Then Boulenger came down from the mast with a succinct, confident list of ideas for the repair. René Bernard, who had designed and built the furler, telexed the ship to say that he would meet her the following day in Freeport and make that furler work. The shipbuilder smiled without animation.

"We must think," he said to Boulenger. "We must reflect."

At lunch, Wikar Andren joined Faury and me at a table for four.

"Well, I see there are no gray hairs yet," he said as he pulled out his chair and sat down. Faury looked up.

"No," he said. "But perhaps soon."

"Yes, if you were going to get gray hair it would have happened in these last days," Andren said. He unfolded his napkin and added: "That was a joke, you know."

"Yes, I know," said Faury. He sliced at his salad. Wikar did not draw him out further. It was a hard subject at a bad time. He talked about himself instead.

"The one thing I regret when I look back at my life," he said, "is not having had as much time as I wanted with my family. After the war, we seamen had to stay at sea to keep a job. My dear wife, and the boys, they came on board, sometimes, but it was not the same thing."

"Men who are always working, who think of nothing but their work, leave their families aside," Wikar said. "That is not good."

Faury had straightened in his chair. He looked at Wikar with the intense focus that was his normal way. It was as if his drifting intellect had returned and was engaged again, weighing words and their implications and watching the directions in which their meanings might stretch away from that moment.

"I knew someone, that is I know of someone who had a very original way of dealing with that," he said, and his voice had recovered its strength and edge. Speaking English, he told Wikar of a French admiral, a commander of the country's navy, who had made a practice of transferring officers just as soon as they had managed to have their families join them near their duty stations.

"He found it effective," Faury said. "It seems like a good idea."

Perhaps Faury, whose family was a large and prideful part of his life, thought that the big, blunt-looking man across the table had been delicately offering him comfort; perhaps the harshness of his response was a trick played by the internal translation of his idea from French to English; perhaps he was preoccupied. Just then, he was summoned to the telephone on the bridge. The shipyard was calling to report the results of its furler load calculations and to make recommendations for repair. Faury walked out erect, taut and alert, his peculiar internal gyroscope spinning with an almost audible hum. He had been restored.

Wikar Andren smiled. That afternoon he sewed up the last of the loose-ended lines he had found in and around the ship's lifeboats, wrapping each rope end with waxed twine to keep the strands from unraveling. He had brought his sailmaker's tools on the voyage: broad-bellied, triangular needles in a glass tube with a bit of oiled rag and the partial leather gloves called sailmaker's palms. Very privately, while others were at lunch, Captain Andren had sewn end wrappings on all the ropes in *Wind Star's* four lifeboats. The mates first showed me the work, turns of twine so tight and even that the sisal fibers at the rope end stood stiffer than a deck brush, and so skillfully laid that the points where the whipping began and ended were invisible. That work was unmistakable: such wrappings are called sailmaker's whippings, and I asked Wikar how he had remembered a skill that he had not used for fifty years.

"It is only forty-nine years since I was a sailmaker," he said, looking up. His hands did not stop working. Then he relented and said: "No, you see, it is just in me."

Wind Star completed her first Atlantic crossing on the next afternoon, boiling up the Northwest Providence Channel under four sails and the motor to Freeport, with another helicopter for photographers and cameramen clattering overhead, alongside, and under the advancing bow like a rackety dragonfly. She was seventeen days out of Le Havre and ten from the Azores. The crew went ashore that evening, each in his or her own way. And the next day real life began.

Strangers came aboard. There were seamstresses in the lounge, adjusting the fit on white crew uniforms, and tanned young men and women in shorts carrying potted palm trees to decorate corners down below. An urgent man waylaid an Italian cabin stewardess to explain that he needed "towels, paper towels, lots of them, and a bucket and a bottle of Windex or cleaner or something."

"I've got to clean the lifeboats," he said, with dignity. It turned out that he was cleaning a patch at each bow of the motor lifeboats in order to apply Jean-Claude Potier's company logo, the corporate coat of arms for Andren's cruise line. A secretary from Potier's office staff in Miami came aboard wearing a *Wind Star* T-shirt and exclaimed: "Oh, what a really cute boat!"

Landsmen have taken to speaking of a sea change when they mean a gradual shift, a subtle realigning of known elements over a long time. But for seamen, change comes with a port. It boards suddenly, from the shore. Any sea voyage is an emotional whole, with a beginning, a middle, and an end. At the middle there is a solid center of self-sufficient life at sea, into which everyone on the ships I have known settles comfortably; so comfortably, at times, that poses drop and psychological armor slips. It is hard to keep up every affectation on an ocean.

"It is reassuring to be at sea," the first mate said on one of our first morning watches. "There are not the complications that people have ashore, like what the boss thinks or what the neighbors say. There is a routine at sea, a routine for living. To a degree for thinking, also. When you must make a decision you must almost always make it right away. There is no extra time to think and think."

The change on a sea voyage is subtle, and so gradual that the loyalty to a ship that grows while she is at sea and makes everyone aboard into "the ship's company," only shows when it is strained and broken by the abrupt shore change. The attachment to a ship grows steadily, unnoticed, and it breaks hard. The saddest sea chanty I know is one about paying off in port at the end of a voyage. The chorus is: "Leave her, Johnny, leave her."

The men and women who had been aboard across the Atlantic felt invaded on Thursday, when the purposeful transformation of the ship began. *Wind Star* had to be prepared to meet her market. Her stop in Freeport was the culmination of two years of work that Jean-Claude Potier, the president of the new sailing cruise line, had called "positioning the product." That was a euphemism with a feel of solidity and an almost mechanical sound, like the slow slide of a rifle bolt worked by hand. But the process it described seemed as airy and delicate as summoning a spirit. While the ship grew slowly in France, and well before she was tested at sea, Potier and his staff had discreetly taught her potential passengers what to expect.

"You create an identity by choosing one single major concept, one image, one way of talking, and then sticking with it in everything you do," Potier had said five months earlier when the cruise line of which he was president had no working ship at all. For managers, marketers, sales people, and staff at Windstar Sail Cruises, Ltd., he hired only people who he thought looked right and could think and act as though caught in a reflection of his image. He told them: "Windstar is cleansing your mind from what a cruise is like to think of what a cruise might be."

Karl Andren's initial intuition that there was an untapped market, a pool of people waiting to buy tickets on this ship, was the sole reason she had been built. Potier said that what he called product development and positioning meant ensuring that his market got exactly what it had expected, without ever being aware that it had expected a sailing ship from a French shipyard with slightly unusual French-designed cabins and subdued public rooms where what was not blue was gray and what was neither was a blend of both. Andren had felt that there were bits and pieces of individual dreams, dreams about the sea, and about sailing in comfort, floating free in a wealthy America and that these dreams would settle on a new sailing cruise ship if she were built. Potier had agreed, the first time he heard Andren's idea, and Potier stitched the pieces of Andren's dream together and took the whole cloth to market.

We who had been aboard for her shakedown cruise and had grown into a crew with a common loyalty to our ship had seen her every hesitation as a drama and rejoiced in all her triumphs, feeling for the ship and the ship alone. But she had been built for a purpose and she lay alongside a clean concrete pier in Freeport, gleaming, on time and ready to serve that purpose. Her shakedown setbacks were insignificant, compared to that accomplishment. The first large passenger steamship ever built, the *Great Eastern,* took four years to complete. She killed four men on her launch day in 1858 and ruined her builder and his backers. She took to the sea, a hybrid with auxiliary sails on masts too short for her bulk, and was never a commercial success. She ended her days laying communications cables on the ocean floor. By comparison, *Wind Star*'s building had been smooth and her maiden voyage a honeymoon.

"I think we will look back and remember a very pleasant crossing of the Atlantic," said Captain Andren, on the last day at sea. In Freeport that crossing ended. Wikar Andren left. Marc Held, the designer, the father of the interiors, arrived, and the grooming of the ship began.

René Bernard, who had designed and built the ship's roller furling stays, also came, flying twenty-two hours from Lyon to Freeport with a small suitcase and a brown paper package containing 33 pounds of parts to put the damaged furler back together. Wearing the same black shirt and faded, pressed jeans that he had worn to her sea trials, the seventy-eight-year-old designer rode up *Wind Star*'s forward furler in a two-man basket and came down nonplussed. What he saw had not been foreshadowed in any of his calculations. The synthetic glue in the long joints between the curved and flat parts of the horseshoe-shaped tube had let go. The aluminum pieces, fitted as tight as scissor blades, had moved and, like scissor blades, had cut the hollow rivets in two. The solution he had carried across the Atlantic in pieces consisted of solid, stainless-steel screws to replace each rivet that had snapped on the 160-foot-long furler. Hundreds were broken or missing.

"I was betrayed by the glue," Bernard said when he came down. "But it's too late for any of that. Got to do the job here and now."

He paused long enough to buy a cap with a visor, then rode up the furling stay in the subtropical sun with Gérard Boulenger. The two worked that afternoon and through the next day, drilling out the scissored rivets, tapping each hole with threads, lining up the holes, and driving in screws one by one by hand. When they returned to the deck for meals, Bernard climbed out of the working box as stiffly as though his feet had gone to sleep.

Faury had called for a French engineer from Martinique as an expert witness for the shipyard, signaling a willingness to sue Bernard. The dry old man described his design process to the expert, then went aloft again to work. The expert came on deck with some afterthoughts and squinted up at Bernard and Boulenger in the box aloft. His shaven head and sharply hooked nose made the yard's expert witness look like a vulture.

"But you're going to kill him like this," he said, turning to Faury. The protest sounded genuine.

"No," the shipyard manager answered. "I have the impression that he lives for this."

Bernard and Boulenger, then Boulenger working alone, replaced the rivets with screws. At dusk on Friday, three hours before the ship was due to sail for Miami, we hoisted the staysail back into place and rolled it onto the furler. Boulenger came down the mast in the dark, riding in the one-man chair driven by an electric winch that was the ship's own way of getting a man aloft into the rigging. Just before he reached the deck, the computer programmers testing the undamaged staysail behind us unfurled that sail all the way. Snapped rivets cascaded onto the deck with a metallic rattle. That furling stay too had torn itself internally. It was crippled yet the ship had to leave that night and set her sails the next morning off Miami and enter that port under sail on the busiest day of the week for Caribbean cruise liners. Sail was part of the script.

Bernard had left the ship to fly ahead to Miami. Faury's face turned gray in the floodlights on deck. Boulenger, the bouncy sailor, suddenly looked very tired. The rest of us gathered severed rivets from the deck, without speaking.

Wind Star motored across the Gulf Stream to the resort coast of Florida that night with no sails set. The first mate maneuvered in circles off the Hillsborough Inlet lighthouse until 5:00 A.M., then set her bow to the south for a rendezvous at 6:30 with yet another picture-taking helicopter. The wind blew onshore, warm and wet in the dark and gusting to 20 knots, a strength in which Faury no longer trusted the roller furling stays that held the sails. At 6:00 Captain L'Orange began telephoning Faury in his cabin, to request that the shipbuilder set some sails in time for the helicopter. There was no answer. Boulenger and Bouché, on the bridge, did not know where their boss was. He arrived at 6:24, gray-faced still and barely speaking.

"They will be very disappointed if they come in the helicopter and see no sails at all," L'Orange remarked to the shipbuilder. Faury said nothing. He stared ahead. At 6:28 he ordered Boulenger to set the first staysail. As it started unrolling from the furling stay repaired in Freeport, the helicopter flashed over the bow. Faury ordered the third and fourth staysails set, without knowing whether their furlers too might suddenly fail. He left the second staysail wrapped on its wounded furling stay, and *Wind Star* continued south under power and three staysails, with a blank between her masts.

Three hours later, in the sun and gusting breeze, she neared the Miami sea buoy. Faury came up to Boulenger and Bouché where they stood watching the curtain of concrete buildings along the shore and sportfishing boats, throwing spray to their outriggers, powering out into the wind and over the short, sharp seas to look closely at the new windship.

"What do we do?" the yard manager asked. "Do we set it or don't we?"

No one spoke, then Boulenger said: "I'm pretty confident."

"We have sinned by optimism at every turn until now," Faury said immediately. "This morning, again. We set two staysails without inspecting their furlers."

"They're certainly pressing us hard enough," Boulenger said. Bouché nodded hard.

"If we set it and keep three wraps on the furler, we won't be risking anything," Faury said tentatively. He turned away and went back into the pilothouse. The Miami harbor pilot boarded then from a heaving launch, and as the ship came abreast the first buoy marking her entrance channel we could all see boats hovering at the harbor mouth, in the shelter of Miami's two low breakwaters, twin lines of rock laid perpendicular to the beach.

"Yes," Faury said to Boulenger, at the sail-control panel. "Set it. And leave three turns on the stay."

So, with all four working staysails set and drawing and her propeller slowly turning, *Wind Star* turned in from the sea. There were fifty small boats, sail and power, inside the sheltering arms of the breakwater. Their horns brayed when the windship, with the wind dead astern, crossed the harbor threshold where the water turned a sandy green. There were crowds in a park on shore, waving. Faury, wholly restored, popped into the pilothouse, talking as he came and heading for the engine controls.

"Captain," he said. "We should try now reducing the engine and sailing in, sails alone."

L'Orange took two steps forward, effectively blocking Faury.

"Now?" he said, in a loud voice. "Not now!"

"Yes," said Faury. "Why not?"

The American pilot put a hand on Faury's arm. The wind was blowing hard, he explained in a quiet voice, and dead against a strong, outflowing tide.

"Let's get inside first," he said. "I don't want to scratch the paint."

Faury stepped back out on deck, where the ship's company waved at the spectator boats surging along at each side, ahead and astern. Helicopters racketed overhead. Jean-Claude Potier stood beaming in the noise and cheering. His eyes brimmed with tears.

Wind Star was still under all available sail, sweeping down the dead-straight channel dredged like a road cut through the coral rock to the sea. Her bow was pointed downtown and cars on the causeway to Miami Beach built alongside the channel stopped to see her pass so close. It was Saturday, November 1, and the long front of the cruise-line terminal at the other side of the channel was lined with the cream of the Caribbean cruise ship fleet, loading passengers and supplies to sail at sunset. Her officers, her builders, and their guests stood together on her deck as the windship sailed up to the first of her motor-driven sisters. Inside the pilothouse, there was no one but the helmsman, the pilot, and me.

The pilot stepped forward to the engine controls and tugged the throttle back gently. He unslung the portable radio transmitter at his belt. Looking down at the instruments where the ship's power and speed were displayed, he called one of the two tugs forging ahead of *Wind Star*, their bridge-top fire nozzles spraying streams of water high into the air.

"*Mary Belcher*," the pilot said. "This is *Wind Star*."

"This is the *Mary Belcher*. Go ahead, *Wind Star*."

The tug skipper's voice rang from a radio speaker at the back of the silent pilothouse. The Miami pilot spoke quietly into his own radio microphone.

"Would you believe we're doing eight knots under sail alone?"

"Roger, *Wind Star*. It's a great day."

Then the first motorship sounded three long, deep whistle blasts to welcome a new sister, and, one after another, the moored cruise ships saluted the sailing ship.

Epilogue

Wind Star took her place immediately in Miami among the working ships. Beginning the day she docked, the ship left the port twice each day for luncheon and dinner cruises designed to show invited travel agents, and some prospective passengers, that the world's tallest ship could really sail. For seven days the hotel staff made and served cocktails, lunch, and dinner for three hundred people; for seven days the deck and engine crew docked and undocked, motored out the channel to the sea, set the sails, turned around the sea buoy, and sailed back in, twice each day. The passengers never noticed the locally hired riggers who were hoisted up the furler stays every morning and clung aloft, drilling out the rivets and replacing them with screws until fifteen minutes before each luncheon cruise. On the eighth day she sailed for the island of Martinique, the base for her Caribbean cruises, and on November 15 *Wind Star* left Martinique on schedule with her first cruising passengers.

She became a happy ship, as François Faury had always hoped she would be while he built her. The asperities that arose on her maiden voyage over nonworking machines, unpredictable wiring, and the flawed rigging had obscured how deeply comfortable the ship had been, especially under sail. With those irritating difficulties fixed, the comfort remained. The only passengers who complained hard in the first sailing season were a group of single people from California. They found *Wind Star* too calm.

If one believes in signs, *Wind Star* was destined to be a ship of serene character and good fortune. I saw her sail through a rainbow at dawn on the last full day of her Atlantic crossing. Both ends of that rainbow, drifting with the light rain that trailed beneath a squall, touched under her bridge while the two captains, the first mate, and I watched. The rainbow made a perfect ring around the ship, from the waterline on one side, over the masts to the waterline on the other side. None of us had ever seen such a thing; none of us had ever been at the end of a rainbow.

Wind Star became a stylish ship, too, although most of the seamen who watched her being built, including me, had abiding aesthetic reservations about the shape of her hull. Judging her by the last commercial sailing ships, we all found that the new ship's hull rose too high above her waterline and was too broad too far aft. But she was much more beautiful than almost any modern ship, and an arbiter of modern taste, writing about *Wind Star*'s second cruise, called her "possibly the prettiest ship afloat."[1]

Slowly, *Wind Star* also became a reliable sailing ship. Riggers spent several weeks after the ship left Miami repairing the segmented roller furling stays between cruises, one after another, and the shipyard programmers spent months chasing down and killing the bugs in the sailing computer. Her people learned her ways and by April 1987 Karl Andren reported that the ship spent three-quarters of her time at sea under sail. She once sustained 10.8 knots under sail alone, with no assist from her electric motor.

The ship was not a cow under sail, as a doubting shipyard engineer had once foreseen. She was underrigged. "Horribly underrigged," Gilbert Fournier had said frankly, sipping coffee before dawn on her abortive sea trials. There was not enough sail area for her hull, to a sailor's eye. Yet she sailed comfortably and well and maneuvered under sail. After the rolling furler stays were reinforced, she stood up to stiffer winds than the Atlantic blow that crippled her first furler.

On balance, Andren was pleased. "I told Tom Heinan that we didn't do too badly at all, for our first ship," he said. With *Wind Star*, Karl became a famous shipowner, invited to sit on the board of directors of Bureau Veritas, the French shipping classification society, to lead a capital fund drive for his college, and to accept a French decoration. He was made a *chevalier* of the Legion d'Honneur.

At the end of *Wind Star*'s first winter season in the Caribbean, the Ålander immigrant's dream of showing his ship to his adopted city came true. *Wind Song*, the first sister ship, sailed into New York harbor on the morning of May 20, 1987, her furlers redesigned, her sails under perfect and unfailing computer control. The second ship sailed up the Hudson River, past the downtown office towers at the peak of the morning rush to work in finance and in services, and past the signs of America's abandoned maritime heritage at the water's edge beneath the office-filled skyscrapers. Her four working staysails sheeted flat in a wet and fitful northeast wind, she sailed past the disintegrating piers of the city and four huge, laid-up containerships of the bankrupt U.S. Line, and docked alongside Andren's own pier at the west end of Forty-second Street.

A band played and an invited crowd cheered. The shipbuilders, Gilbert Fournier and François Faury, stood on the dock grinning with pride. They had received no further orders, for sailing ships or any other ships, but the profound depression of their industry, the possible closing of their shipyard, and the almost certain fading of the ancient art of shipbuilding in France did not weigh on them that day. A new ship is always a brave beginning. Faury, however, sounded momentarily wistful, as if he longed for the high uncertainty, the decisions made at speed, and the engagement of his whole soul in *Wind Star*.

"It has not been the same," he said. "In this ship, we were able to incorporate most of what we learned building *Wind Star*, but it has become routine. There is none of the thrill of being first. That happens only once."

Chapter Notes

Chapter 1

The epigraph, freely translated, reads: "Sailing is truly necessary; any fool can live."

1. Two native shipwrights looked for deck beams in that year for a 45-foot trading schooner built on that coast, which I then owned.

2. Kåhre, Georg, *The Last Tall Ships* (London: Conway Maritime Press, 1978), p. 34. Kåhre is the principal maritime historian of Åland.

3. The Gripsholm stone.

4. The long agony of *Herzogin Cecilie* is described at chapter length in Derby, W. L. A., *The Tall Ships Pass* (London: Jonathan Cape, 1937), an excellent book.

5. Kåhre, op. cit., p.37.

6. Oral history of Skunholm gathered and preserved by the Ålands Sjöfartsmuseum, under its present curator, Göte Sundberg.

Chapter 2

The epigraph reads: "Sailing is profitable."

1. Kåhre, op. cit.; p.132. Kåhre's brother Hilding, an economist, was Erikson's administrative chief and the historian had access to the shipowner's correspondence—all of it, from his days as a young skipper forward, saved in laced binders.

2. Derby, op. cit.

3. A knot is a unit of speed. One knot equals one 2,025-yard-long nautical mile per hour. To convert to miles per hour, multiply knots by 1.13.

4. The steel barks, when they sailed for profit, had masts at least 20 and as much as 60 feet higher off the water than any of the sailing ships we now admire under the title of tall ships. *Preussen*'s masts were 223 feet from keel to truck, and *Thomas W. Lawson*'s were 195 feet long in all, making them 180 to 185 feet off the water, depending on the ship's load. The sailing four-masted freighters in Erikson's fleet and in the more famous Flying P Line, belonging to Ferdinand Laeisz in Hamburg, had working mast heights of between 170 and 180 feet. For comparison, the U.S. Coast Guard's training bark *Eagle* lists a maximum mast height of only 147 feet, 3 inches. The Russian ship *Kruzenshtern*, which came to New York's Bicentennial Parade in 1976, is the only one of the original four-masted steel barks still sailing. She was launched for Ferdinand Laeisz in 1926 bearing the name *Padua*, the last large engineless cargo ship ever built. Her rig has apparently been shortened and simplified and steamer-style houses have been built on deck.

5. Karlsson, Elis, *Mother Sea* (London: Oxford University Press, 1964), p.84.

6. Karlsson, ibid., p. 230.

7. Karlsson, ibid., pp.195–196.

8. Karlsson, ibid., introduction.

Chapter 4

1. Lubbock, Basil, *The Blackwall Frigates* (Glasgow: James Brown and Son, 1922), pp. 266 ff.

2. History compiled by the National Maritime Museum, Greenwich, England.

3. At the beginning of this century Hamburg became a center for research in wind propulsion for ships, perhaps because of centuries of maritime trading and perhaps because the last true sailing freight line, the Flying P Line of Ferdinand Laeisz, had its home there. The Laeisz square-riggers, all of them bearing names that began with the letter P, made three scheduled trips every twenty-four months around Cape Horn to the west coast of South America until the mid-1930s, which is probably the pinnacle of achievement in all the centuries of commercial sail.

The first Hamburg pioneer was Anton Flettner, a schoolmaster from Frankfurt who became a military inventor just out of normal school, just in time for World War I. Flettner's windship idea, tested and developed in Hamburg, was a true innovation. He had sailed to Australia as a boy, to cure a respiratory ailment, and he refused to give up on the power of the wind when steam was driving sail from the seas. Lazing one summer afternoon in the lee of a North Sea sand dune, Flettner dreamed of putting spinning, upright cylinders on the deck of a ship to drive the hull. The idea worked and a converted ship powered by two Flettner Rotors crossed the Atlantic to New York in 1926.

The idea had been skipping through the centuries like a flat stone on a lake. The Prussian government in 1794 announced a cash prize for a usable explanation of why cannon balls curved in flight. In 1853, Gustav Magnus, a professor of physics at the University of Berlin, developed the explanation, using brass cylinders, spinning in an artificial breeze and free to move at their bases. With a hop-skip-and-jump of serendipity, the idea came to rest in Flettner's machine-age windship.

Once it has been done by others, the explanation is fairly easy to see in one's own mind. Imagine a fat smokestack, standing in a fair breeze. Now set the smokestack spinning in your mind. The breeze keeps blowing, but on one side of the stack it blows faster, helped along by the smokestack's spin. On the other side, the wind is slowed down. The stack is spinning against it. Air piles up against obstacles, just as water in a river does when it comes to a boulder on the bottom, and where air piles up it pushes harder. So moving air is pushing harder on the side where the smokestack spins against the breeze. On the opposite side, the air slips past the stack quickly, hardly pushing at all. The result is that the smokestack tries to move away from the side the air pushes against toward the side where the air hardly stops. If the spinning smokestack is fixed to the deck of a boat, the boat will move, pulled along by the difference in the pressure of the wind on opposite sides of its fat, spinning smokestack.

The results of the difference in pressure on two sides of something spinning in an airstream is still called the Magnus Effect, but I have not been able to discover with certainty whether Professor Magnus collected the prize money. The rifling in gun barrels put a stop to erratically curving cannon balls, by spinning them like drill bits through the wind, not against it.

Between Flettner and the present, the most extensive work on wind propulsion for ships was done by Wilhelm Prölss, a German sail enthusiast who was a businessman in Hamburg. He tested his own modern square-rigger designs in the wind tunnel and testing tank at the Hamburg Institut für Schiffbau beginning about 1957. He called that design, a six-masted, 600-foot version of the huge Laeisz full-rigger *Preussen*, a Dynaship. Immediately after the oil embargo, almost all windship advocates used Prölss's data to develop, and his methods of evaluation to test, their own projections. He was, in that sense, the father of modern windship design.

4. The little ship's "sails" were so much like an airplane's wing that they were made at Ueda Ironworks, Ltd., not by a sailmaker.

5. The Japanese auxiliary sails were designed by Nippon Kokan K.K., under contract to the Japanese Machinery Development Association, which shared in taxes on motorboat racing to finance that research and development.

6. Herbert, C. C., *Proceedings of the Symposium on Wind Propulsion of Commercial Ships* (London: Royal Institution of Naval Architects, 1980), p. 199.

7. Herbert, ibid., p. 185.

8. Levander may have brushed past some history in his presentation to the board. The *Nina* was rerigged to put square sails on two of her three masts in the Canary Islands on her way out from Spain.

9. Herbert, op. cit., p. 199.

10. *See* Schenzle, P., "Wind Assistance for Motorships," lecture delivered for Hamburg Ship Model Tank at UNESCAP Conference, Tokyo, 1984.

Chapter 5

The epigraph reads: "Too strong is never too much, for strong enough has oftimes failed."

1. Schenzle, P., "New Sailing Ships for Indonesia," *Jahrbuch der Schiffbautechnischen Gesellschaft* (Hamburg), 1983, p. 135.

2. A shipyard in La Rochelle, which also belonged to Fournier's group, won the contract to build Cousteau's aluminum hull.

Chapter 6

The epigraph reads: "Too strong is never too much, for strong enough has sometimes failed."

1. Abell, Westcott, *The Shipwright's Trade* (London: Conway Maritime Press, 1981), p. 54.

2. *See* Villiers, Alan and Picard, Henri, *The Bounty Ships of France* (New York: Scribners, 1972).

3. To carry a curve in an overall pocket from the mold loft to the shop floor, lofters once used two thin leaves of hardwood joined by a piano hinge. The tool was called a "missal," because it looked like a pocket prayer book. With the hinge open at the center of a curve, the two wood flaps fell at points of tangency, which were marked. A protractor measured the angle made by the hinge. Using measured offsets, the lofter could redraw the curve wherever he wanted it. Resetting the measured angle at the hinge turned the wood flaps into a gauge to check a curved plate while it was being shaped. Gérard Jouan, who had seen "missals" used by older men when he started as a lofter, said they did not know much geometry or trigonometry. Yet the effect of the missal was to erect an equilateral triangle whose sides were tangent to a segment of a circle and a measurable portion of whose base formed the chord of that segment.

To transfer a measurement from a flat pattern to the curved shape that had been formed from that pattern, Jouan said the lofters who taught him the tricks of the trade used lengths of elastic for a stretchy ruler that experience taught one how to use.

Chapter 7

1. The initial decoration budget allowed just over $2 million for the passenger spaces on the $34 million ship. It was later increased to almost $3 million.

2. Builders and owners have probably been telling each other "I told you so" about unsuccessful ships since the trading boats of pre-Christian Egypt were built. The Dutch builder of the Swedish warship *Wasa*, whose sinking on her first trial in 1628 might be the most exhaustively investigated new ship loss in European building history, successfully absolved himself of any responsibility by showing a contemporary in-

quiry that the royal owner himself, Gustavus Adolphus II, had approved the ship's dimensions. For successful ships, owners and builders vie for credit. Sir Francis Chichester spent much of the first two chapters of his book *Gypsy Moth Circles the World* complaining in detail about the builders and designers of his yacht, when every reader already knew he had safely sailed her, singlehanded, around the world. Joshua Slocum, the first singlehanded circumnavigator, avoided the controversy. He rebuilt his *Spray* himself, as he had built the sailboat that carried his shipwrecked family home from Brazil in 1888.

Chapter 8

The epigraph reads: "I think, therefore I am."

1. *Monograph No. 4,* The Casemate Museum (Fort Monroe, Virginia), undated.

Chapter 9

The epigraph reads: "Rainy wedding, happy marriage."

1. Sometimes, maritime names do not follow function. Shrouds, aboard sailing ships, run from the masts to the deck at the ships' sides. Stays descend from mast to deck along the center line.

2. It was developed in the workshops of Nitro Nobel, the first company founded by the Swedish explosive magnate Alfred Nobel, who endowed the prizes that bear his family name.

Chapter 10

1. The square sail roller-furling device was patented in the 1860s in England by Collings and Pinckney, according to the National Maritime Museum, Greenwich.

2. *Wind Star*'s four staysails measured 157.78 feet on the luff, 55.77 feet on the foot, and 137.79 feet in the leech. The boomed mizzen was made 135.17 feet on the luff, 42.65 feet on the foot, and 141.07 feet in the leech. The outer jib was a staysail cut high in the foot.

3. In sailor's English, sails are built, not made, although those who "build" them are called sailmakers. I have found no explanation.

Chapter 11

1. The ship's sailing computer was a Hewlett-Packard 9000, Model 320. Gilbert Fournier, the shipyard president, called it "my gift to the owner," because he thought it was oversized for the application, or he did until the program had been written.

2. When individuals owned ships in ad hoc partnerships, one of the partners managed the ship's affairs for the others, paid the annual bills, signed charters, and kept the partnership accounts. The manager, usually a retired sea captain, was known as the "ship's husband."

Chapter 12

1. François Faury, the shipyard's chief engineer and a sailor, once described this maneuver, holding a staysail to weather to push the bow around when tacking, as "a discovery" he had made while using the sailing model on a pond in Harfleur. But not much, except design, is new in sailing. The Down East coasting schooners working the New England coast into the early twentieth century always tacked this way, according to their chronicler, John F. Leavitt, in *The Wake of the Coasters* (Middletown, Conn.: Wesleyan University Press, 1970); and square riggers, when they could tack, brought their courses across from aft forward, leaving the foresail, or the foretopsail, backed to the wind to help the bow around.

Epilogue

1. Dominick Dunne in *Vanity Fair,* vol. 50, no. 3, March 1987, p. 101.

Index